INDEX

ON CENSORSHIP

INDEX ON CENSORSHIP

WEBSITE NEWS UPDATED WEEKLY

www.indexoncensorship.org
contact@indexoncensorship.org
tel: 020 7278 2313
fax: 020 7278 1878

Volume 30 No 3 July 2001 Issue 200

Editor in chief
Ursula Owen
Editor
Judith Vidal-Hall
Web Managing Editor
Rohan Jayasekera
Associate Editor
Michael Griffin
Eastern Europe Editor
Irena Maryniak
Editorial Production Manager
Natasha Schmidt

Publisher
Henderson Mullin
Development Manager
Hugo Grieve
Subscriptions Manager
Tony Callaghan
Project Manager
Aron Rollin
Director of Administration
Kim Lassemillanté

Volunteer Assistants
Ben Carrdus
Chuffi
Claire Fauset
Paul Hoffman
Paul Isaacs
James Badcock
Andrew Kendle
Barbara Langley
Anna Lloyd
Andrew Mingay
Daniel Mitchell
Gill Newsham
Gbenga Oduntan
Tola Owodunni
Ruairi Patterson
Shifa Rahman
Polly Rossdale
Neil Sammonds
Victoria Sams
Fabio Scarpello
Katy Sheppard

Cover design
Vella Design
Layout and production
Jane Havell Associates
Printed by
Thanet Press, UK
Previous page
Credit: Jonathon Hexner

Index on Censorship (ISSN 0306-4220) is published four times a year by a non-profit-making company: Writers & Scholars International Ltd, Lancaster House, 33 Islington High Street, London N1 9LH. *Index on Censorship* is associated with Writers & Scholars Educational Trust, registered charity number 325003 *Periodicals postage*: (US subscribers only) paid at Newark, New Jersey. Postmaster: send US address changes to *Index on Censorship* c/o Mercury Airfreight International Ltd Inc., 365 Blair Road, Avenel, NJ 07001, USA
© This selection Writers & Scholars International Ltd, London 1999
© Contributors to this issue, except where otherwise indicated

Subscriptions (4 issues per annum)
Individuals: Britain £32, US $48, rest of world £42
Institutions: Britain £48, US $80, rest of world £52
Speak to Tony Callaghan on 020 7278 2313
or email tony@indexoncensorship.org

Index has made every effort to discover copyright owners of material in this issue. Any errors or omissions are inadvertent.

Issue 2/01, Identikit Europe
- We regret having inadvertently omitted the name of **Maria Margaronis**, guest editor of our file on Greece (pp124–64).
- *Erratum:* 'In Chechnya' (pp16–17): **Anna Politkovskaia** wishes to make it clear that her accreditation was not withdrawn by the military, as we stated. This misinformation was supplied from Russia; we apologise to Anna and our readers.

EDITORIAL

No change

This is the 200th issue of *Index* – a minor achievement, at least, given that the world turned and there were many who thought our job was done. Overnight, it seemed, the Soviet Empire exploded into a myriad new states, leaving Russia a flailing giant prey to all the ills of neo-democracy and primitive capitalism. The world would henceforth be a more transparent place, they told us. 'Go home,' they said, thanking us for our contribution to 'the defeat of censorship and the victory of the free world'.

But it was never thus: *Index* was far from a Cold War weapon. True, it started in response to the show trials of writers in 1960s Moscow but, from its earliest issues, its contents chart the map of silence as it spread from Greece, Spain and Portugal, all under military regimes in 1972, to the arrival of the South American *juntas* in the mid-70s, and on into China, Africa and Asia. Nor did it ever spare matters closer to home.

Moreover, the most cursory glance at the 600-odd column inches that fill each issue of 'Index Index' shows clearly that good old-fashioned censorship is still all too common in most parts of the world; on both sides of that same East–West divide. The varieties of censorship may have changed and proliferated in the new anarchy that has replaced the certainties of the Cold War, but our role, we think, is as necessary now as it ever was.

So, coming to this issue, why the death penalty? Why race and intolerance? Why the concern with language, democracy and war, and with the voices of prisoners in jail in Peru or the US? The world of rights and freedoms in 2001 is more nuanced, more complex, less obviously at risk than 30 years ago. The exponential growth of the human rights industry, and the lip service paid by governments to this now fashionable cause, has done little to bring into the debate the voices of people excluded from the 'peace dividend' or the joys of 'globalisation'.

Along with our enduring concern with the more conventional forms of censorship, the debate for *Index* is about wars that pass in silence – Chechnya, Algeria, Israel/Palestine – because governments control the rights of passage into those places. About prisoners gagged as well as behind bars; about the exclusion of voices that politicians everywhere fail to hear.

The right to be heard is not the privilege of the educated and articulate, nor an end in itself. Free expression is the barometer of all those other rights and freedoms that we value. ❑

contents

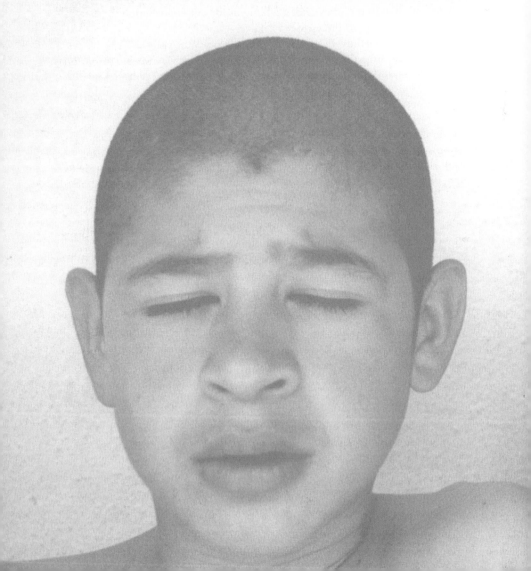

What makes a Nazi? p32

Chain gangs are back in style p126

Martin Rowson's 'Strip Search' p62

Background picture: Ivan and Jorge Nuñez (see Photostory, p176). Credit: Jonathon Hexner

MARIE GILLESPIE

Trouble in happy valley

A new kind of wizard haunts the de-industrialised valleys of South Wales, and he's finding plenty of willing apprentices

South Wales is one of Britain's top three most dangerous areas for ethnic minorities. The risk of racial attacks is almost ten times higher in rural areas than in inner-city areas, according to a recent poll for the London *Observer*.

In the South Wales valleys, unlike the urban areas of Cardiff, Newport and Swansea, ethnic minorities are geographically isolated and often economically prosperous. Bengali is Wales's third largest language and more books in Chinese are borrowed from Cardiff libraries than books in Welsh, even though only 1.5% of the population has a minority background. In the last census, people from minority backgrounds in Wales were four times more likely than white people to be in full-time education or training; and a relatively high percentage of their men (74% compared with 83% of white men) were economically active.

The reported number of racist incidents has more than doubled in the last few years, and some believe it is this relative educational and economic superiority of minorities in the valleys that is fuelling the high rates of racially motivated incidents. The police, on the other hand, see the figures as encouraging. Inspector Ian Bellshaw, who heads the Minority Support Unit of South Wales Police, said they reflect the shift to a perception-based definition of racist crme – if an act is believed to be racist, then it is treated as such – improved methods of reporting and increased confidence in reporting racist crimes in the aftermath of the Macpherson report.

But for minority families in the valleys, the reality is different: families may endure verbal and physical harassment, aggression and

Roath, South Wales, May 2001: graffiti wars. Credit: Marie Gillespie

violence for years. They are powerless to challenge their aggressors or speak out for fear of reprisals, for fear of losing everything they have worked for – a fact of life that race statistics cannot even begin to capture. There have been at least three racially motivated murders in South Wales in the last three years.

The isolated restaurants of the valleys, with names like 'Happy Valley' or 'Sweet Mountain', regularly have their windows smashed, graffiti daubed, their staff subjected to racial abuse. This is especially true as the pubs spill out on Friday and Saturday nights, but not only then. In certain areas, white skinheads harass restaurant workers, demanding free curries at knifepoint. The confessed aim is to drive them out of town.

'We want our country back and we'll fight hard until we get it back. We'll do anything to "Keep Wales White".' Thus spoke a group of three lads from Tonypandy, an area plagued by racist incidents, graffiti and heroin in recent years, who have little understanding of the ideology they purport to espouse. According to local newspapers, several doctors have been physically attacked by self-proclaimed supporters of the Ku Klux Klan (KKK), and are now retiring early – in fear.

The recent recruitment of Filipina nurses into the area is seen by a small and dangerous minority as a further sign of 'foreigners taking our jobs'. 'They get put at the top of the list and they get houses quicker. They get twice the amount of income support we get and brand new homes. They lead lives of luxury over here.' Such views are commonly expressed in local schools where they are challenged by Andrew Jones in race-awareness sessions. He works for the Valleys Race Equality Unit and claims that the mentality of valleys people is insular and fearful of outsiders.

'These used to be very close-knit, cohesive, working-class communities centred on coal and steel manufacturing. All that's gone,' he says. 'The problem of racism in the valleys should not be exaggerated. It remains a small group of people who spearhead the action. We work hard to educate the children. That is the only way to eradicate it.'

Valleys people had little or no experience of inward migration until recently, unlike Cardiff, which has a black community dating back to the middle of the nineteenth century. Valleys people perceive themselves as quite different from their urban fellow-nationals. 'There used to be a pride in being from the valleys,' said a man from the Rhondda, 'a distinctive identity associated with the mines, but that's gone. There has always been conflict too. Growing up in the valleys is like your people sitting on one side of the mountain looking out and hating those on the other side. Those feelings can easily be turned against outsiders.'

Most valleys people I spoke to argue that racism is no worse than elsewhere; that organised violence is the work of a handful of extremists. Indeed, hostility to a 1999 BBC Wales documentary, *A Welcome in the Hillside?*, that portrayed racism as endemic and rising, is still vociferous. Locals allege that BBC reporters bought a crew of local youths cigarettes, alcohol and a new Union Jack, encouraging not just the *Sieg Heils* that punctuated their sentences, but also their expressions of racial hatred.

Despite defensive local reactions, it would seem that the valleys – like other rural and semi-rural areas of low migration – have to take the threat of racism seriously. There is little doubt that poverty and racism go hand in hand, but valleys racism is by no means an inevitable expression of xenophobic rural communities. However, a loose alliance of diverse, more-or-less organised far-right groups espousing racist ideologies has progressively made inroads into Wales's most deprived areas. Their numbers may be small, but racism, for some, is a way of life.

Boredom is a big factor. Young men, uneducated and with no hope of jobs, easily find solace in the slogans promoted by the likes of the British National Party (BNP). 'Keep Wales Welsh and White' is fairly typical. Nick Griffin, the virulently anti-Semitic leader of the BNP, chose rural mid-Wales as his home precisely because it is a predominantly white area, 'untainted by ethnic minorities'. The BNP put a general election candidate forward in Newport for this year's general election, but were thwarted in Swansea by the vigorous response to their attempt to hold a public meeting in the Unitarian church. Griffin attempted to raise the asylum debate but local anti-racist activism is strong in Swansea, and alliances have long since been forged between journalists, local groups and academics in anticipation of such provocation.

Wales is also home to Allan Beshella, a Ku Klux Klan (KKK) 'wizard' from the US who recruits disaffected youth from the valleys' post-industrial wastelands where not only poverty, but heroin, is taking its toll. Evidence of his success is perhaps most apparent in the racial tensions that exist in Parc prison. Parc is one of three prisons in the UK currently under investigation by the Commission for Racial Equality, and is notorious for racist bullying and drug-taking. Last year, the KKK allegedly took control of a prison wing after it linked up with the Rhondda Valley Skins, a small local group whose initiation rites include head-shaving, tattooing 'RVS' on their arms and daubing graffiti on minority-owned houses, shops and businesses.

Other groups, such as the White Wolves, National Front and Combat 18 are also visible in local graffiti, but the number of people who openly acknowledge allegiance to racist groups is small. Given the legal strictures on openly voicing racist sentiment, a more subtle racism bubbles in the dark underbelly of these communities. The strength of feeling is difficult to assess, unpredictable but potentially explosive – as was seen in Oldham (see following article, p10).

Drive round any street in the South Wales valleys and you see graffiti expressing the fears of young men who have been bitterly failed by the government's social and economic policies. Along with fans that stretch throughout Europe, they listen to white power bands like Celtic Warrior and Broadsword (see p54). And they find hope in Nick Griffin's plan to revive the most reviled party in Britain. ❑

Marie Gillespie is a lecturer in sociology and anthropology at the University of Wales in Swansea. She is currently researching Welsh racism and working on diaspora cultures for www.transcomm.ox.ac.uk

STEVE SILVER

Myths, lies and urban warfare

When is a no-go area not a no-go area? According to television and newspaper reports, walking through the Oldham districts of Glodwick, Coppice and Westwood should be a very dangerous business indeed. Lurking on street corners, Asian gangs wait to attack white people. So they say

It is a hot day just a few days after the National Front (NF) was in town and football hooligans rampaged, attacking cars with Asians in them on 5 May. It could have been worse, and worse may yet be in store, but make no mistake, Oldham, a small, decaying industrial town in the UK's north-west, bore witness to the spirit of the pogrom that Saturday.

Anti-racist citizens of Oldham recognise that this is one defeat in a long battle. But they want to know why the media portrayed them in such a bad light. Why the police treated them so unfairly. Why the council let them down so badly. Why were the racists not kept out of Asian areas? Why was it that, in spite of a Home Office ban, an NF demonstration took place – and one for which there have as yet been no prosecutions?

The existence of no-go areas started as an urban myth, was perpetuated by the *Oldham Chronicle* and seemingly confirmed by the head of the Oldham Police, chief superintendent Eric Hewitt, when he gave out statistics showing that most reported 'racist' incidents were Asian or black on white. It reached its zenith on 21 April after 76-year-old Walter Chamberlain was attacked on his way home by a group of Asian youths. The police described the attack as racist; the press ran a photo of the hapless pensioner, who suffered severe facial injuries; and the racists had a field day. Here was absolute proof of the no-go myth. Or was it?

Chamberlain was attacked in Arkwright Street, which is not residential, either Asian or white. Neither he nor his family believe that the attack was racist. Three weeks before, an Asian taxi driver was beaten up in nearby Chadderton Way, yet that was not deemed to be racist. And there are other factors showing the spurious nature of the no-go-area myth. Oldham's most modern supermarket is in the predominantly Asian district of Westwood, but white people come and go all day. In all the so-called no-go areas there are pubs where white people go in the evening.

To understand the situation you have to put aside any illusions of a multicultural Britain. Through housing policies that put Asians into virtual ghettos, and work practices that meant the night shift in the cotton mills was known as the 'Paki shift', much of the community has been ghettoised. Of Oldham's 219,000 residents, 24,600 are Asian. Since the collapse of the textile industry, unemployment has been high and the community greatly impoverished.

Of course, there are groups of Asian youths, as there are white youths, who will see off whoever they see as outsiders. Whether there is a racial motive or not, it will always appear that way to those who want it to appear that way. When Asians are attacked, people feel aggrieved. An innocent person, especially a white youth, might be caught up in the reaction. It might not be the correct reaction, but it is understandable.

Both communities also include young men who get themselves into violent confrontations with others, often over girlfriends or drugs. They are no more representative of their community than their white equivalents. Similar conflicts take place in every town in Britain, but in Oldham there is a guaranteed racial factor because the part of town you are from is likely to denote the colour of your skin.

The media referred to no-go areas only in terms of places where white people supposedly could not go. Asian people to whom I spoke said that not only are there numerous attacks on Asians in areas where they live, but it has always been dangerous to go anywhere in Oldham at night if your skin is the wrong colour.

A large proportion of racist attacks are not reported at all because the Asian community has no confidence in the police. In March, a mass meeting of Bangladeshis called for Chief Superintendent Hewitt to resign over remarks he had made about attacks by Asian teenage gangs on 'lone white males'. Many of the youths at the 400-strong meeting felt they had been made scapegoats for what was already a deteriorating race relations situation in Oldham.

It is young people who feel the heat of the injustice. One youth, arrested on the day the NF came to town, told me how people stayed in the area that day to defend their communities. As word spread that police were failing to stop hooligans attacking Asians and pelting them with bricks, the young men mobilised to drive them out. It was during this conflict that one of the whites was stabbed. Many of his friends were beaten and sworn at by police; they compared bruised arms and legs, battle scars from the day. Because it all happened in a residential area on a hot day when people were outside, children, mothers and wives witnessed the events. In many ways, the greatest problem in Oldham is not the racists themselves, but the apathy of white people who could make a stand against them. Much blame needs to be laid at the door of the authorities. On the Saturday before the proposed NF march, Mike Luft, one of the leaders of Oldham United Against Racism, was telephoned and told that hooligans from Stoke were rampaging through Westwood. In spite of requests to police that they should be diverted away, they were allowed to march near enough for their abuse to be heard a second time, further inflaming tempers.

Credit: Steve Silver

Without consultation, the police launched a baton charge on the very people who had been protecting their homes. After the demonstration was dispersed, Luft made his way home past a police van from which officers shouted 'Paki lover' and 'nigger lover' at him. ❏

Steve Silver *is an editor at* Searchlight, *the anti-racist magazine, in which a longer version of this article appears*

SIMON DAVIES

The new battleground

The mass collection of DNA is the latest in a litany of incursions into personal privacy and the United Kingdom has become the guinea pig for the burgeoning DNA industry. The UK Criminal Justice and Police Act 2001 overrides earlier safeguards by mandating the indefinite storage of samples, notably those provided 'voluntarily', and extending access to these beyond police and other law enforcement agencies

The political mood throughout Europe – and particularly in the United Kingdom – appears to be increasingly hostile to the right of privacy. European countries have moved in the space of a decade to incorporating surveillance into their national infrastructure. New forms of communication and computing embrace surveillance as a core design component. Legislation not only mandates the covert collection of personal information, but requires it. Data systems, once functionally separate, are now linked, creating 'cradle to grave' monitoring of the citizen. Increasingly, Europeans are persuaded to surrender their information to satisfy the 'public interest'.

The mass collection of DNA is the latest in a litany of incursions. Police forces across the world are moving to embrace DNA identification as a replacement for the conventional fingerprinting system. For most law enforcement authorities, the technology offers possibilities that the old identity card systems could never deliver – not the least of which (unsurprisingly perhaps) is the creation of a global database of known or potential criminals.

National DNA databases are being established in a growing number of countries, including Sweden, the United States, Australia and Canada.

Access to this sensitive information is currently restricted primarily to law enforcement, but if previous trends in other areas of data protection prevail, there may soon be overwhelming pressure to extend access to other areas of government – the health sector and the insurance industry, to name only two.

Access to DNA data will soon be available across national borders under the provisions of a wide range of conventions requiring mutual international assistance in law enforcement.

The United Kingdom has become the guinea pig for the burgeoning DNA industry. There, DNA samples are compulsorily taken from anyone arrested for any recordable offence – including shoplifting, public order offences and traffic violations. The government estimates that the national DNA database will contain four million samples – nearly one-twelfth of the adult population – within five years.

DNA testing goes to the heart of the privacy issue (See Davies, *Index* 3/00). Traditionally, invasion of privacy has been justified on the basis of effective social management. Police have always argued that privacy and anonymity are bad news for law enforcement. Authority has always sought to create perfect identification of citizens. And DNA is the perfect identifier. DNA collection and analysis provides perceived solutions to a range of ancient and complex social management issues – not just the prevention and detection of crime, but also questions relating to paternity, health insurance liability, predisposition to ill health and disease, and racial origin.

In the face of such potential risks to privacy, the role of national legislation is crucial. Most countries have taken steps to restrict the use of DNA data, and to limit the period in which it may be stored. The UK has proved the notable exception to this effort. While the UK Data Protection Act requires that sensitive information be kept for the minimum reasonable period, the Criminal Justice and Police Act 2001 overrides these provisions by mandating the indefinite storage of samples, notably those provided 'voluntarily'.

The permanent storage of samples obtained through non-compulsory methods is crucial to any assessment of potential threats from the technology. Given the public's overall anxiety to 'do the right thing', there is a virtually limitless number of conditions in which DNA samples can be requested. A desire to broadcast one's innocence, or an anxiety to be eliminated from investigation, may well override people's instinct to protect their rights. The idea that 'consent' provides a guarantee of proper use is absurd. In most areas of life – banking, health or insurance for example – consent is frequently little more than a convenient device to pacify concerns about compulsion. Consent can be achieved in many unsavoury and unprincipled ways.

These issues are emerging in spite of the privacy protections within the European Convention on Human Rights. Despite Britain's new-found commitment to incorporate the Convention into its legal infrastructure, reform has been patchy and faltering. It has been fashionable to hold successive Home Office ministers responsible for this situation. Michael Howard, Jack Straw and, most recently, David Blunkett have aggressively pursued an agenda of law and order, frequently testing civil rights to the democratic limit. The right of privacy, more than other rights, falls victim to this aggression.

But while these ministers provide a convenient target for blame, two far more significant factors underpin Europe's litany of incursions on rights. It is becoming clear that policy convergence is creating a global push for seamless surveillance. A spectrum of conventions, treaties and agreements offer both threats and inducements to governments to pass laws and to promote technologies hostile to privacy.

But it is the prevailing attitude of the public that creates the greatest threat to privacy. A growing, yet undefined, belief in the amorphous idea of 'rights and responsibilities' together with the popular view that only those with something to hide should be fearful of government snooping, has provided the political foundation for greater powers of intrusion and surveillance. In this sense, the UK government is spearheading a trend throughout the democratic world.

During its average working week, the London-based watchdog NGO Privacy International deals with around 50 technologies that are hostile to personal privacy. They range from high-tech identity cards and spy satellites, through to Internet-snooping software, closed circuit television cameras and telephone interception systems. Many of these innovations have the capacity to cause grave damage to privacy and other civil rights, and yet none comes even close to achieving the absolute threat posed by genetic technology. The organisation predicts that within a decade, genetics will be 'the only game in town'.

Writing in the London *Guardian* on 14 May 2001, the chair of the UK Human Genetics Commission, Baroness Helena Kennedy, warned:

Human rights of victims are also hijacked to justify the abandonment of clear principle. There is little discussion about the way in which this body of rights is the mortar which a citizen in his or her relationship with the state.

When each civil liberty is thrown over, we subtly alter that relationship. The subsequent corrosion of trust will ultimately mean a huge cost to good governance.

The development of genetic science offers some tantalising rewards, but the field is without doubt the future battleground for privacy. The threat it represents is magnified by the promise it offers: the creation of a safer, healthier and more equitable society. A genuine and unstinting regard for privacy is the only means to ensure that future generations are protected from the threat of a hostile government, the encroachment of a greedy private sector, or, ironically, the well intended but thoughtless zeal of fellow citizens. ❏

Simon Davies *is the director of Privacy International and a visiting fellow in the department of information systems at the London School of Economics*

CLAIRE FAUSET

List to the right

Viewed in conjunction with the Regulation of Investigatory Powers Act 2000 and the Criminal Justice and Police Act 2001, the new Terrorism Act 2000 is further evidence of the government's indifference to fundamental freedoms

The UK Prevention of Terrorism Act of 1973 (PTA) was renowned among activists and lawyers as one of the most rights-abusive pieces of legislation on the statute book. It was strongly criticised by UN Special Rapporteur Abid Hussein for its chilling effect on freedom of expression, and was in clear contravention of the European Convention for the Protection of Human Rights and Fundamental Freedoms, incorporated into UK law in 1998.

Former Home Secretary Jack Straw claims that his new Terrorism Act, which came into force on 19 February 2001, is a 'human rights success' because it enables the UK finally to comply with European Convention rulings on the length of time a suspect can lawfully be detained without appearing before a judge. But the Act's definition of terrorism, and its extension to acts that take place outside this country, pose serious threats to freedom of expression, freedom of association and the right of asylum.

The Act's definition of terrorism fails to distinguish between violent and non-violent offences. It is so broad in scope that it includes any form of protest on ideological, political or religious grounds that aims to influence the government, or a section of the public, and which causes damage to property, or threatens the health and safety of any section of the public. Such a definition, if enforced, would include the construction of tunnels and fortifications in protests against road building; the destruction of crops by GM activists; and acts of vandalism by anti-capitalist demonstrators.

In effect, all direct action protest is threatened since the legislation creates a sense of uncertainty as to when a criminal offence is actually being committed and under what circumstances the police will actually make use of its powers. Inclusion within the new definition of terrorism brings activist groups one step closer to proscription. It has been suggested in the House of Lords that certain animal rights groups could be banned under the Act.

Moreover, not only is it illegal to be, or profess to be, a member of a proscribed organisation, but also to support it verbally, financially or in other ways. To wear clothing that declares your support is a criminal offence. To organise a meeting of more than three people that will be addressed by a member of such an organisation – on whatever subject – also comes under the Act.

The list of proscribed organisations, moreover, was based on information from the security services that parliament was allowed neither to review nor query. In the parliamentary review process, ministers were unable to discuss the merit of each listed organisation, but were obliged to vote for or against the list in its entirety.

Straw is reported to have considered what specific threat an organisation poses to national security and UK nationals overseas; the extent of its presence in the country; the nature and scale of its operations; and his political obligation to 'support other members of the international community in the global fight against terrorism'. Many of the listed organisations, however, have never targeted the UK, have no significant representation here or are currently observing cease-fires.

The extension of the list to include 21 groups based outside the country, notably Kashmiri and Palestinian parties, the Kurdish Workers Party (PKK), Tamil Tigers (LTTE) and the Iranian Mujihadin e Khalq, has provoked concerns about the targeting of refugee and minority communities. Membership of the Mujihadin, according to Home Office policy, is grounds for asylum in the UK. Its proscription means that individuals granted asylum are also be liable to criminal charges for membership. Lawyer Louise Christian reports that many of her Kurdish clients have been refused asylum on the grounds that they were not members of a banned party such as the PKK.

Immigrant communities that support such banned movements are effectively criminalised by the Act without playing any part in violent action. The Home Office has recently announced that immigration officials will be granted power to target specific ethnic groups, including Tamils and Kurds. Lawyer Gareth Peirce has compared the way that Irish

London 2000: Kurdish (PKK) demonstrators protesting against the new Terrorism Act.
Credit: Caroline Austin

communities were harassed under the PTA to the way refugee communities are likely to be affected by the new Act. A Muslim barrister active in human rights said: 'This Act has the potential to turn every British Muslim into an Islamic terrorist. We are the new IRA.' MEP Jean Lambert argues that the Act's blanket condemnation of any armed struggle against human rights violations in complex political circumstances is unacceptable.

The civil liberties organisation Liberty has raised strong objections, maintaining that the Act produces a two-tier criminal justice system in which those who commit, or are suspected of having committed, crimes on political grounds are treated more severely, while police are given enhanced powers of arrest, interrogation and detention.

'Banning organisations and criminalising membership is a serious attack on basic rights of free speech and free assembly,' said Liberty's John Wadham. 'This law is draconian, supported by a government that professes a commitment to human rights and passed by a parliament that is supposed to protect us from draconian laws.' ❏

Claire Fauset *is a volunteer at* Index

JULIAN PETLEY

A case of mistaken identity

What went wrong between the UK media and a report on 'multi-ethnic' Britain?

I've just visited an organisation which was so afraid of physical attack it dared not put its name at the entrance of its office building. It had recently published a report, distorted and inflammatory press coverage of which had put the organisation under siege and made its employees the recipients of hundreds of abusive and threatening phone calls, e-mails and letters. Along with the death threats came sentiments such as these: 'To show you what I think of your report, I'm going out of my house right now, and I'm going to slit the throat of the first Paki I meet.'

The organisation was the Runnymede Trust, the report its *The Future of Multi-Ethnic Britain* and the newspaper responsible in the first instance the *Daily Telegraph*.

The trouble began on 10 October 2000, when the *Telegraph* ran a front-page article by its home affairs editor, Philip Johnston, headed 'Straw wants to rewrite our history' with the strap line '"British" is a racist word, says report.' The article opens with the words: 'Britain should be formally recognised as a multi-cultural society whose history needs to be "revised, rethought or jettisoned", says a report that has been welcomed by ministers,' and continues: 'The inquiry was set up three years ago by the Runnymede Trust, a race equality think tank, and launched by Jack Straw, Home Secretary. Its report, to be published tomorrow, defines the UK as "a community of communities" rather than a nation. It says the description of its inhabitants as British "will never do on its own", largely because the term has "racist connotations".'

These few lines contain no fewer than five errors, but they were to determine the way in which not only the *Telegraph* but other papers were to cover the report over subsequent days. Apparently the decision to highlight the report was a last-minute one, taken by the editor Charles Moore himself, which may account, in part, for some of the errors. However, the tone of its reporting can have nothing to do with the pressure of imminent deadlines.

First, and most serious: the report nowhere says the term 'British' has 'racist connotations'. What it does say is: 'Britishness, as much as Englishness, has systematic, largely unspoken, racial connotations. Whiteness nowhere features as an explicit condition of being British, but it is widely understood that Englishness, and therefore Britishness, is racially coded.' It notes that for Asians, African-Caribbeans and Africans, 'Britishness is a reminder of colonisation and empire, and to that extent is not attractive'; but adds that although 'Britishness is not ideal . . . at least it appears acceptable, particularly when suitably qualified – Black British, Indian British, British Muslim and so on.' Since the *Telegraph* repeatedly substitutes the word 'racist' for 'racial' one can only assume that the editor takes them to mean the same thing, in which case he would also be bound to agree that the statement of fact 'The *Telegraph* is a national newspaper' is the same as the value judgement 'The *Telegraph* is a nationalist newspaper'.

Second: the report does not define the UK as a community of communities rather than a nation but simply uses the phrase as a means of picturing how Britain could, and in its opinion should, develop. Its purpose is to displace a different picture: Britain as one large homogenous majority plus various small minorities. Nowhere does it suggest renaming Britain. This is what it says: 'It would be consistent with the dictionary definition [of community] to envisage Britain as a community whose three principal constituent parts are England, Scotland and Wales, and to envisage each of the constituent parts as a community, as also each separate region, city, town or borough. Any one individual belongs to several different communities.'

Third: the *Telegraph* makes the elementary mistake of conflating the United Kingdom and the British Isles. What the report says is: 'many acknowledge that ideally there needs to be a way of referring to the larger whole of which Scotland, Wales and England are constituent parts. But the nation state to which they belong is the United Kingdom not Britain . . . The Good Friday Agreement of 1999 implies that there should be a sense of affiliation to the supranational identity known as

ENTRANCE STRICTLY ENFORCED

"these islands" [ie, including the Republic of Ireland]. Perhaps one day there will be an adjective to refer to this entity, similar in power perhaps to the unifying word "Nordic" in Denmark, Finland, Norway and Sweden. But for the present no such adjective is in sight. It is entirely plain, however, that the word "British" will never do on its own.' This is self-evidently true as applied to the British Isles, as Philip Johnston would no doubt discover were he to pop into a bar in, say, a nationalist part of Derry and tell the assembled company that they were all British. Applied to the United Kingdom, however, it becomes quite a different proposition, and one which the report never puts forward.

Fourth: to state that the report argues that British history needs to be rewritten, revised, rethought or jettisoned, is selective to the point of distortion. The passage to which this charge refers merely argues that if Britain is to acquire 'a broad framework of common belonging' in which 'cultural diversity is cherished and celebrated' then 'one critical prerequisite is to examine Britain's understanding of itself. How are the histories of England, Scotland and Wales understood by their people? What do the separate countries stand for, and what does Britain stand for? Of what may citizens be justly proud? How has the imagined nation stood the test of time? What should be preserved, what jettisoned, what revised or reworked? How can everyone have a recognised place within the larger picture?' What the *Telegraph* presents as a bald statement is actually a serious of questions for discussion. The report's remarks about pride in and preservation of aspects of British history are conveniently ignored.

Last: the role the paper allots to Jack Straw in the publication of the report – 'Straw wants to rewrite our history' says the headline – is unequivocally wrong. Nor is there anything in the article that remotely substantiates such a wild accusation. Straw's role in the report was limited to launching it when Labour first came to power. However, it is clear, and becomes ever more so as the controversy develops, that it is Straw in particular and Labour in general that are the *Telegraph*'s real target. Thus the article states that: 'although the Government finds some of the report's recommendations unwelcome, particularly on asylum and immigration policy, it apparently accepts the thrust of its conclusions,' and Home Office minister Mike O'Brien is quoted to the effect that: 'This is a timely report which adds much to the current debate on multi-ethnic Britain. The Government is profoundly committed to racial equality and the celebration of diversity. We are a multi-cultural society.' Similarly the editorial. Headed 'The British race', it begins: 'It is astonishing that ministers should have welcomed the sub-Marxist gibberish' contained in the report, and concludes that: 'Under the guise of "multi-culturalism", they are advancing their old Marxist dislike of *any* national culture. It is shameful that the Government should have been cowed into going along with this rubbish.'

It is worth pointing out that the passages of the report which so enraged the *Telegraph* occupy just over three pages of its total of 417. Nonetheless, the effect of its reporting on much of the rest of the press was galvanic. The next day, for example, the *Mail* ditched the front-page article it had intended to run and replaced it with one headed 'Racism slur on the word "British"'; the inside pages were also changed to include an extremely unflattering rundown of members of the commission which produced the report, a lengthy editorial ('What an insult to our history and intelligence'), an essay by Paul Johnson and a hostile commentary by Raj Chandran of the Commission for Racial Equality ('An insult to all our countrymen').

The same day's *Sun* ran a lengthy piece by its political editor, Trevor Kavanagh, headed 'Ministers welcome report which says "British" is a racist word'; an indignant editorial urging Straw to 'stick this report in the bin'; and a comment piece ('It's ridiculous') by the athlete Daley

Thompson. Such was the rat-pack mentality of most of the press on this issue that even the supposedly liberal *Guardian* joined the fray. The headline of its main article on 11 October reads: 'British tag is "coded racism"', although the term 'coded racism' appears neither in the report nor in the article itself. The paper also ran a broadly welcoming editorial entitled 'Prescription for harmony'. However, this also carries the strap 'But race report is spoilt by bad idea' – this appears to be 'dropping Britain', which is nowhere recommended by the report. The paper does, however, redeem itself to some extent with an article by Gary Younge which opens with the most pertinent words written during the whole of this furore: 'if you really want to take the racial temperature in Britain, you would be better off examining the reactions to the report on multi-ethnic Britain than the report itself.' The *Mirror, Star, Times* and *Evening Standard* also took the 'racist' bait. Only the *Independent* and *Express* avoided this line entirely and succeeded in dealing with the report wholly in its own, as opposed to the *Telegraph*'s, terms.

Over the next few days, the commissioners were to find themselves described as 'worthy idiots' and 'purblind, self-indulgent and insensitive' in *The Times*; 'middle-class twits' in the *Star*; 'crack-brained' and 'a bunch of cranks and losers' in the *Telegraph*; 'left-wing wafflers' in the *Evening Standard*; and a 'second-rate unrepresentative clique' composed of 'disconnected, whining liberals' in the *Mail*. The report itself was condemned variously as 'gibberish, 'balderdash', 'ridiculous', 'burblings' and 'rhubarb' in the *Telegraph*; 'right-on trendy trash' and a 'pile of cack' in the *Star*; and 'tendentious rubbish' in the *Mail*. According to the *Sun*, if the report's recommendations were implemented, 'children will be told lies about their history and encouraged to feel ashamed of their country'. Meanwhile, the *Telegraph* gave over its letters pages to correspondence, much of which would not have been out of place in the official publications of the British National Party or the National Front, in which rage and bile were relieved only by heavy-handed attempts at 'humour'.

The immediate purpose of all this fury and vituperation was, quite clearly, to force Jack Straw to distance himself from the report. It is equally difficult to wade through this endless editorialising without coming to the conclusion that the report was little more than a pretext to attack everything about the Labour government that the right detests, proof of which was provided by the *Telegraph* on 12 October. In a column by Boris Johnson, whom the paper coyly insisted on billing as the editor of the *Spectator* rather than as the Tory MP-in-waiting for Henley-on-Thames, in which he opines that 'this is a war over culture, which our side could lose'.

One of the major points at issue in this war is, of course, the Macpherson report into the death of Stephen Lawrence, which earned Straw the undying hatred of papers such as the *Telegraph*. And, sure enough, this hoves into view in its editorial 'Don't diss Britannia' (a headline which must have mystified most of its readers). This argues that: 'Mr Straw is unconvincing when he dons the mantle of John Bull. He has pulled a similar stunt before – making much of rowing back from some of the wilder shores of the Macpherson report on "institutionalised racism" in the Metropolitan Police.' Of that report, the editorial alleges that 'Mr Straw was able to smuggle it past the public by playing the role of common-sense watchdog. So it is with this commission. Mr Straw and Number 10 have distanced themselves from the report's most offensive comments, but they have not distanced themselves from its substantive proposals.' The editorial concludes that: 'the Conservatives

DEATH OF JACK STRAW

now have an excellent chance to make good their past silence on Macpherson. They must expose the Government's collusion in this attempt to destroy a thousand years of British history'. The *Sun* followed suit the same day.

The overtly party-political thrust of the *Telegraph*'s campaign was further emphasised on 13 October when it ran a lengthy piece by William Hague entitled 'Why I am sick of the anti-British disease' in which the report is lumped together with 'Cool Britannia', devolution, 'Europe' and every other hate object in Tory demonology to show that we have a government 'led by a Prime Minister embarrassed about the country he lives in and the people who elected him'.

And just in case anybody was still unsure of the message, the paper also carried an editorial again explicitly linking the Runnymede document with the Macpherson report, of which it states that 'no more disgracefully unfair document has ever been produced by a judge in modern British history'. However, 'its bigoted conclusions were accepted with only a whimper of protest by the institutions it criticised. The bullying of the "anti-racists" had won. At last, though, something is changing. To the obvious shock of the comfortable peers, millionaires' wives and public sector grandeees who lent their names to the report, people are starting to say that they will not take any more. The report's suggestion that the word "British" is racist has finally frightened even those ministers who thought that they could never go wrong by appeasing such doctrines. Jack Straw and Tony Blair have suddenly changed from their usual approval, and have reached instead for a Union flag in which to wrap themselves. It doesn't fit very well, but it is interesting that it has happened at all.'

What the *Telegraph* is referring to here are, of course, the official responses by the Home Office and No. 10 to the actual publication of the report on 11 October. However, even the press reports of these are spun to the point of distortion. What Tony Blair's official spokesman, Alistair Campbell, actually said was: 'Britishness to us is about issues as varied as how you manage the economy, the approach you take to issues like unemployment, your vision of society. Britishness is served not by ethnic nationalism, nor by the status quo plan adopted by our Conservative opponents – it's about how you develop and promote your values in a wider world.' This was interpreted by a *Mail* headline on 12 October as: 'Downing Street hits back over attack on our past', but that was as nothing compared with an article in the same day's *Sun*, headed 'Labour scorn for Brit pride', which managed to interpret Campbell's words thus: 'Tony Blair's official spokesman put the boot into Britain yesterday – and laid bare New Labour's vision of our nation.'

Most of the press accounts of Jack Straw's speech at the report's launch bear little relation to what was said. Most of Straw's lengthy speech is actually taken up with fulsome praise for Runnymede's work over the years. Given the amount of criticism directed at the report by the press, Straw was left with no option but to respond to it, which he did by rewriting at least parts of the speech he had intended to deliver, and delaying publication of the Home Office's official 40-page response. Key journalists were briefed by the Home Office to accentuate the more critical aspects of the speech, and much of the resulting coverage shows just how readily they accepted the officially spun line.

However, the positive parts of his speech (which also repeatedly praises the Lawrence report) massively outnumber the negative comments. The latter could be only be taken as its main point by papers with an axe to grind or by journalists who believe all they are told by spin doctors. Straw's criticisms are pretty mild stuff and come near the end of his speech where he says he feels 'the Commission were a little grudging in recognising what's been achieved already'; and 'I frankly don't agree with the Commission' over its views on Britishness (which he explicitly contrasted with what the *Telegraph* alleged its views were); and, via a reference to George Orwell's famous remark that 'almost any English intellectual would feel more ashamed of standing to attention during God Save the King than of stealing from the poor box', that the task of moulding Britishness into a 'single shared identity was always going to be a challenge, but it was in my judgement made more difficult by those on the left who turned their backs on concepts of patriotism and who left the field to those on the far right.'

Straw's strongest criticisms were reserved for the *Telegraph* itself; the *Independent* (but no other paper) quoted him as being 'astonished' at its 'extraordinary intervention', but his remark that it '*has had* [emphasis added] a record of separating its news coverage which, on the whole, has broadly subscribed to the facts, from its opinion which is its business', went unreported. Nor did any paper see fit to print the unqualified praise for the report voiced on the same day by Baroness Amos, a government Whip in the Lords. In this respect, funeral orations

MEDIA TRUTH OR LIES

such as those in *The Times* on 12 October – 'the sheer force with which Jack Straw, the Home Secretary, distanced himself from the most controversial aspects of the *Future of Multi-Ethnic Britain* report yesterday shows that this document will not influence official thinking in the future' – come across not only as premature but as decidedly wishful thinking.

This story tells us a good deal about the nature of the British press, not least its political bias, the rat-pack nature of its journalism and its susceptibility to spin – in the double sense that newspapers are both adept at spinning stories themselves and are all too easily led by the nose. Furthermore, the predominance of right-wing, and specifically English Nationalist, views in the press, and the virulence with which they are expressed, makes them appear much more widespread and predominant than they really are outside the bile ducts which pass for newspapers in the UK. These people are swimming against the tide of history and, deep down, they probably know it. Most of what in *The Future of Multi-Ethnic Britain* gave Boris Johnson, Charles Moore, Paul Dacre, Trevor Kavanagh et al a blue fit would appear as entirely commonsensical to any first-year student of history, politics, sociology or cultural studies, and is part of a long debate encompassing works as diverse as Benedict Anderson's *Imagined Communities*, the essays *The Invention of Tradition* edited by Eric Hobsbawm and Terence Ranger, Linda Colley's *Britons*, Raphael Samuel's *Island Stories* and *Theatres of Memory*, Robert Hewison's *The Heritage Industry*, Patrick Wright's *On Living in an Old Country*, Jeremy Paxman's *The English*, Norman Davies' *The Isles*, Andrew Marr's *The Day Britain Died* and Mark Leonard's *Britain™*, to name but a few. As Hugo Young put it in the *Guardian* of 12 October, the hysteria with which the report has been greeted 'throws a revealing light on these frightened spokesmen for the old canons of Britishness. They can barely contain their rage at the notion of the national identity, along with its hierarchy of historic icons, perhaps needing to be updated.'

However, given their prevalence in the press in particular, these spokesmen are doing a great deal to make discussion of the much-needed modernisation of Britain as difficult as possible. One has only to look at how they have entirely prevented a debate of any kind at all about Britain's future role in the EU to see the success of their endless hectoring and bullying. It is clearly extremely difficult for any government to live with this daily diatribe which is liable at any time, as in the case of the Runnymede report, to blow up into a full-blown assault in which truth is the first casualty, and right-minded liberals who read only the *Guardian* or *Independent* can have little idea of the sheer amount of raging reaction that daily erupts from many other newspapers. However, discussion of the future direction of Britain is far too important for its terms to be dictated by unelected, unrepresentative and unaccountable newspaper editors, nor do sermons about patriotism sit well in foreign-owned newspapers such as the Canadian Hollinger International's *Telegraph* and the mongrel Murdoch-owned *Sun*. Nor can such discussion be simply avoided as too awkward. As Stuart Hall, one of the members of the Commission, puts it: 'Britain always was and really is now a nation of nations. It cannot continue to conflate "Englishness" with "Britishness". Some commentators really do suppose that Britain will obliterate all trace of its imperial history, devolve government, integrate with the global economy, play an active role in Europe, treat all minority peoples as equal citizens – and retain its self-understanding intact since Magna Carta! This is not serious analysis, it is cloud cuckoo land. The question of Britishness is a time-bomb which is ticking away at the centre of this society and it is either faced and confronted or it will explode in our face in ways which we do not wish.' ❏

Julian Petley is currently writing a book on media censorship in Britain, to be published by Routledge next year
The Future of Multi-Ethnic Britain: The Parekh Report
(Profile Books UK 2000; £10.99 p/b). The commission's website at www.runnymedetrust.org/meb gives the text of Straw's speech
Illustrations by Alina Gavrielatos

UK election 2001: the British National Party candidate in Oldham parades in a gag after all
the parties were banned from addressing the crowd following the announcement of the results.
The atmosphere remained tense after riots in the town (see p14). Credit: Phil Noble / PA

Race matters

The extreme right is on the rise across Europe, on the street as well as in democratically elected parliaments. Index asks what we have to fear and concludes banning is not the answer

NICHOLAS FRASER

The voice of modern hate

The best argument in favour of the tolerance of hatred is that it allows us to see the outline of what threatens us and inoculates us against believing in the fiction of an atrocity-free world

Hatred of others is everywhere around us, but also ultimately unfathomable. It makes a poor field of study for those whose purpose in life is the provision of orderly systems. It torments political scientists and liberals alike, stinging the latter into secular sermons in which they fall waywardly prey to excess simplicity. So we have Umberto Eco in these pages only a few years ago, stating without qualification that 'nothing distinguishes' today's skinheads from their Nazi antecedents. More recently, speaking at Oxford University, Gitta Sereny linked such contemporary occurrences as the Macpherson report and the ordeal of the Lawrences to her own lifetime spent badgering the likes of Albert Speer to come clean. She concluded that there remains a 'racist' within each of us – an observation as unexceptionable as it is unilluminating.

Hating (and I hate to say this, so obvious does it seem) remains a banal, sad and unproductive activity. Perhaps the proximity of hatred is in some indefinable way bad for one's health. I spent about two years of my life consorting with those one must still, I suppose, call 'fascists'. I am certain that I won't do it again. But I can offer a concise consumer's guide to the emotion. The more I became acquainted with hatred, the faster it appeared to change character. I found many types of organisation – some serious, some less so – dedicated to what the novelist Albert Cohen called 'the pleasure afforded to good people (*braves gens*) of hating together'. But I learned, too, that so much variety in the expression of hostility was often delusory. Study hatred – as I did, not systematically but in the spirit of a reluctant connoisseur – and you might find yourself flipped around what appeared to be a giant, brightly coloured pinball machine filled with runic inscriptions, badges and weird totems from the half-forgotten European past. Nonetheless, you would end up helpless, in the same uncomfortably dark place at the bottom of the board.

One aspect of contemporary Europe in the past decade has been the growth of what is variously described as the far right, the new right or the extreme right. Ten years ago, the movement was restricted to France, now it is flourishing in Belgium, Italy, Austria, Romania, Poland – even in Scandinavian welfare states like Sweden, Norway and Denmark. At the most superficial level, the movement would appear to encompass differing views, styles of expression, or even uniforms. It is tempting to make comparisons, but not always easy. Does anyone really think that Jörg Haider has anything in common with a Leipzig skinhead, or a bourgeois language rights activist (and bigot) of the Flemish Vlaams Blok? The initial reaction is no, none at all; but closer acquaintance leads to a qualified yes. There are family resemblances among the ragged armies of hatred. They do think alike (perhaps the verb isn't quite right) though they may act in different political styles. However, some aspects of the new right are genuinely unfamiliar. It would be a mistake – and many have made it – not to see that the movement reflects grievances that are distinctively of our age. Hatred in our time faces forwards and backwards. Sometimes the forms of expression are modern, sometimes the objects of hatred are new. More usually, European hatred is a distinctive mixture of the old and new.

European anti-semitism would appear to be some sort of ineradicable cultural stain. Jew-baiting, with its long pedigree and its sulphurous texts, is the badge of identity among the rar right. It has survived decades of bannings and, more recently, rhetorical assaults of the correct. But raw hostility towards Jews is also the surest way of getting oneself excluded from anything like a bourgeois life in Europe. This explains how polemical anti-semitism has shrunk in scope, becoming the property of the fringe groupuscules out of which the neo-Nazi movement is formed. True, one may find it on the Internet with the greatest of ease; but that is where it tends to stay. It may be embarrassing for well-to-do Swedes to find their teenage offspring speaking the accents of Aryan Power; and for Germans, the revival of neo-Nazism tells a sad story of the inadequacy of 50 years of indoctrination. But these ragged fringe assemblies are not, properly speaking, threats to democracy. They may cause grief and injury (indeed they do, although the statistics proclaiming the year-on-year increase in 'racist' violence are not always wholly convincing), but even here they are only a small portion of the problem.

In Europe, the spectre of the dreadlocked, evil-smelling Jew that so exercised the teenage Adolf Hitler in 1900s Vienna has been replaced by the 'foreigner' – represented most virulently by the 'asylum seeker', to whom the word 'bogus' (I am not sure how it translates in different European tongues) is indissolubly and as a matter of routine affixed. Arabs most easily exercise the not very latent European sense of outrage (in France, prohibition of non-secular 'fundamentalism', or indeed most other forms of Muslim identity is strictly forbidden, and only the most French Arab will pass muster) but Kurds or Romanies will do. Only in the noxious rhetoric of Haider's Austria can one still find linked, and complementing each other, the Jew-as-foreigner and the Muslim Other. Austria has been the laboratory of Europe in the past, it is true, but it is nonetheless hard to believe in the export potential of lederhosen hatred. Haider's support in the recent Viennese municipal elections slipped somewhat. Can we expect another epidemic of ungenteel anti-semitism in Europe? I don't think so.

Political scientists allude to the 'new populism' of Europe, but it would be more accurate to call their adherents half-democrats, or neo-chauvinists, or simply frightened people who, not coincidentally, are neither rich nor powerful. The editorial views of the *Daily Mail* find a ready equivalent in the speeches of Pia Kjaerstgaard, formerly a nurse in a home for the aged, now head of the highly successful Danish People's Party. Both assert that there are people throughout the world eager to take advantage of the highly evolved generosity implied by the existence of welfare benefits. And that they should be stopped.

Prospective or actual loss of identity is the core anxiety agitating the new lost tribes of Europe. These so-called populists are not always electorally successful, but they have secured between 10% and 30% of the vote in Belgium, France, Italy, Denmark and Austria. They have become important for those whose disillusionment with politicians, and indeed with democracy itself, is intense. Among the betrayed and angry is to be found an aversion towards the European Union, which is seen as an agent of international capitalism, flattening boundaries in order to

'Free Padania', 1998: members of Umberto Bossi's Northern League. Credit: BBC

abolish nationality and facilitate the re-export of so many greedy aliens. One can argue that the EU does, in fact, serve as a fence against 'globalism', keeping out the poor of the world, often by giving them money in order to induce them to stay at home; but such observations cut no ice. A signal achievement of the EU – perhaps its greatest one – has been the creation of a shifting definition of 'foreignness' within Europe. But this has been acquired at the cost of a generalised mistrust of cosmopolitanism and of the EU itself.

So-called 'classical' fascism secured its support from the timid and confused, of whom there were many in Depression-era Europe. One might imagine that nowadays Europeans are among the most cosseted and protected people on the planet. But this is not how *Daily Mail* readers see the world each troubled morning. Nor is it what Jean-Marie Le Pen tells his followers. These lost souls are asked to believe that everywhere people are out to take things from them. Far from being a thin crust of tolerance under which fires of hatred lurk, civilisation appears to them as a brightly lit supermarket where they don't have the money to buy the goods and in which, behind every crowded aisle, dark-skinned footpads lurk. Scrounging is done not out of necessity, but because thievery is perceived as a birthright. And who can blame these wounded, last-ditch patriots? But this is an ageing, timid view of the world, one that disguises a pervasive fear of the future behind the robust evocation of so-called 'moral' standards. The success of the *Daily Mail* in imposing its views of asylum seekers on a government allegedly proud of its youthfulness and fresh-mindedness is an indication that these ideas are here to stay. How potent will Little Europeanism become? Every survey indicates that millions of fresh hands will be required to replace the ageing European population. There is no good speculating whether Haiders or Le Pens will arise to meet this perceived threat. In Europe, they are already present.

Of course, much is made among those whose role it is to sound reassuring about the return of nastiness of our 'democratic values.' But post-war European democracy has always depended for its existence on a successful consumer capitalism. The democratic roots of Europe are not as deep as we might like to believe. It was a fear of the recurrence of past catastrophe, and not a sudden interest in transnational institutions or brotherhood, that caused Europeans to throw down the borders separating them from each other. The evolution of Europe from a collection of weak nation states to a frontierless mélange of nationalities and jostling ethnic groups is probably irreversible. But we should also expect wrenching pains in its wake. Perhaps we shouldn't wish to avoid them. Why should we, the rich Europeans, the fortunate ones, be exempted from the pains of change?

After 1945, the European elite regarded with misgiving the large minorities in their midst ideologically attached to the recent and horrible past. What was to be done about the remnants of the past age – those who had gone along with hatred and, given another chance, probably still would do? For the post-war generation of European democrats, the solution appeared simple: liberal censorship. In Germany, I found a large building, constructed in the style of a 1960s campus, from which the activities of over 13,000 spies were supervised, every one of them busy assembling material on the far right, or practising the white arts of bugging or infiltration. It was a Friday, and the researchers were sensibly dressed down in sandals and t-shirts adorned with progressive slogans. The liberal censor quoted Joseph Goebbels to me, explaining that democracy must be saved from itself. This was what I had expected and was, reluctantly and with some misgivings, prepared to accept from Germans. But I had not been prepared for the spectacle of a book on trial in France, in a courtroom adjacent to the one in which Emile Zola testified 100 years ago on behalf of himself and Captain Alfred Dreyfus. Nor was I ready for the sight of the piece of paper, resembling a parking ticket, on which the latest fines levied on the Holocaust denier Albert Faurisson were inscribed.

'Anti-semitism,' wrote Jean-Paul Sartre in 1955, 'is not within the category of thought which must be protected by the right to free opinion.' He meant that there were many things which people should not be encouraged to think, let alone say; and that these opinions should be countered by legal means or, if these proved insufficient, by the establishment of a civic culture of anti-racism. In Europe, alas, one can still see the late flowering of Sartrean thought categories everywhere. A prominent French intellectual showed me summarily to the door when I suggested that such ideas were no longer relevant in the age of the Internet, and should perhaps be abandoned in favour of a more robust belief in freedom. I was an Anglo-Saxon, he suggested by way of response. This meant that I believed in globalisation, which implied the power of commerce over democratic principle. I must understand that I had no real principles.

At the end of the nineteenth century, reason dictated, simply, that hatred must be deplored. 'Civilisation', Zola declared, 'consists of restraining those who are slightly different from getting at each other's throats.' He was writing at the time of the Dreyfus case, but there is no sign of panic here. In 1944, George Orwell remarked testily that the word 'fascist' had been used about 'farmers, tobacconists, Chiang Kai-Shek, homosexuality, astrology, women and even dogs'. And yet he couldn't bring himself wholly to reject the word. 'Underneath all this mess there does lie a kind of buried meaning,' he said. 'Even the people who recklessly fling the word "fascist" in every direction attach at any rate an emotional significance to it. By "fascism" they mean, roughly speaking, something cruel, unscrupulous, arrogant, obscurantist, anti-liberal and anti-working class.' Orwell was bored with the attention given to ex-fascists at a moment when the danger appeared to come from elsewhere. In 1948, he declined to support the banning of Oswald Mosley and his followers on the grounds that they posed no discernible danger. 'No one should be persecuted for expressing his opinions, however anti-social, and no political organisation suppressed,' Orwell concluded, 'unless it can be shown that there is a substantial threat to the stability of the state.'

There is no perceptible crisis of democracy in Europe, actual or future. But this is not what one might think. The bannings of the far right are as demeaning as the prosecution of Internet Service Providers for harbouring peddlers of Nazi memorabilia. They are not effective, creating as they do a mythology of martyrdom, and a black chic for the supposedly oppressed. In the end, they tell us more about our own bourgeois fears of deviance. The language of 'anti-racism' and 'anti-

Denmark 1998: Nicholas Fraser (right) and Jonni Hansen, a Danish Nazi. Credit: BBC

fascism' reeks of old, half-forgotten quarrels. The ceaseless invocation of the state as the guardian of democratic propriety is not specially effective. Nor does so much petty censorship offer a specially persuasive argument in favour of the democratic practices it purports to safeguard.

It would be attractive to propose a radical overhaul of the progressive vocabulary applied to the right, but it would also be less than realistic. But if we are lumbered with these less than useful archaic terms, I would like to suggest that some of them at least can be reclaimed and given their original meanings. The need is greatest with respect to the idea of multiculturalism. Nothing is new about the idea that people of different origins and beliefs can somehow rub along together, given prosperity, good luck and an adequate legal framework of rights. Yet the word has recently assumed threatening overtones. Among neo-conservatives in the United States, it implies the annexation of educational standards by previously excluded traditions or groupings: gays, blacks, etc. In Europe, multiculturalism has become the prime hate word among the far right in particular. In their cheapskate oratory, it goes with such words as 'melting pot' or 'patchwork'; and it is used as an omen of what might befall an Americanised Europe randomly filled with aliens.

Europe can be said to have first invented multiculturalism, and then burned the idea (along with many human beings) in the fires. In 1700, 20% of Berlin's population consisted of Protestant exiles from France. No one complained. The British and Hapsburg empires claimed with some conviction to stand above ethnic differences; and in a different way. 'They are my Jews,' said Emperor Franz Josef, when courtiers proposed the expulsion of Ruthenian exiles from his park in Schonbrunn. French Republicanism did even better by formally affirming the non-existence of ethnic or religious differences. True European civilisation, and I believe that it still exists, resides here. If one acknowledges the extinction of this tradition, most recently in places like Kosovo, Bosnia and Croatia, there are nonetheless less dispiriting instances of Europeans creatively rubbing along together. It is easiest to entertain this perspective from Britain. At the time of the first race riots in 1954, who could have entertained the idea of a Britain no longer definitively 'white' and, it would appear, not excessively exercised by the disappearance of the old Christian-patrician order? The grey skies over London have not fallen in. Fewer each year would quarrel with the notion that Britain is better for its 'foreignness'.

My brief life with the far right makes me overwhelmed by the spectacle of poor Orwell coughing his life away in his sanatorium bed, fussing about past horrors. It is not always exciting to find oneself defending the right to free speech of those whose ideas are not only obnoxious, but for the most part without interest. I admire, too, Noam Chomsky for his defence of Holocaust deniers; but I would not expect many to go out of their way in following his example. The best argument in favour of the tolerance of hatred is that it does, in the end, allow us to see the outline of what threatens us. It does stop us from buying into a fictional, atrocity-free world. One might say that it reminds us of what we are like – some of us, at least. Fascism, as it once existed, is no threat to us. But hatred is; so is intolerance, our own or anyone else's. With reason, we live in fear of epidemics. Even if we don't see the mid-century pandemic repeated in Europe, it would seem inconceivable that minor epidemics will not continue to take their toll. As indeed they do already.

Are we responsible for those who can conveniently be called 'foreigners'? Why should we be? Who are 'the foreigners' these days? In 1927, the novelist Joseph Roth travelled around the scattered Jewish communities of the Diaspora in order to write about the difficulty posed to the Europe of 'flush toilets and elevators' by the presence of so many importunate, noisome eastern European Jews. (This was no excessively comfortable assignment in those days; the contemporary equivalent might consist of a series of visits, in short order, to Priština, Soweto and Gaza.) Roth was born in Galicia and had fought loyally for the Empire only to see the foundations of his world disappear in a matter of weeks. The experience caused him to apprehend the imminent prospect of catastrophe without offering much in the way of hope. But his message isn't entirely bleak. He did manage to indicate how much what we now call the developed world requires new arrivals, unceasingly and on a large scale. This wasn't merely because the Germany of his day required street cleaners and household helps. Roth saw that bigotry was a consequence of self-habituation. Societies must seek to alter themselves, or expire from over-familiarity. He understood that these newcomers alone, by their ragged presence, appeared capable of overcoming 'the sheer hatred that like a life-prolonging (though lethal) drug, is so powerful that it is tended like an Eternal Flame, at which these selfish people and nations warm themselves'. On the face of it, an argument for immigration resting on the idea that hatred, to be conjured out of existence, must first be stimulated, would appear to be perverse. But Roth was right (as he was on many other things, with the notable exception of the lethal absinthe he consumed in huge quantities, and which ultimately led to his extinction, in a Paris pauper's hospital, at the age of 45) to insist on this point. I remember sitting in the midst of the Le Pen legions, wondering how anyone could ever think that so narrow, fanatically held attachments might stand for a real European future. And I suppose I am still enough of a rationalist to believe that blind stupidity must ultimately lose out.

These days, the Eternal Flame finds expression not so much in elaborate ideological fantasies of purity as in the nightly TV images of ships run aground, disgorging cargoes of the unwanted, or container trucks revealing human loads hidden amid vegetables. Here are our new-century nightmares. They suggest that we will ultimately be overcome by the illegitimate traffic in humans, and that it is our moral right – our duty even – to refuse them. And this is what we are told over and over again. Against these threats we are invited to set the fake promises of one-world visual rhetoric. The wan, waif-like teen 'multicultural' fantasies of popular culture – Benetton, Gap or Nike – proffer a vision of the future from which all difference has been excised, which is in its way as definitively misleading as our contemporary visions of chaos.

And yet there is another way of looking at the world, which consists of recognising difference without wholly abhorring it. In New York, you can take a boat past the Statue of Liberty, alighting at Ellis Island. There, beautifully preserved, is a record of the largest, most benign and most successful social experiment of modern times: the taking of so many people by sea or land, from one world to another. Hugely enlarged, the faces of Lithuanian, Swedish, Caribbean or Balkan peasants look down at the visitor, and they express fear of the unknown as well as hope. These are not depressing images. Without quite knowing it, their faces seem to sustain some belief that people can be thrown together without excessive harm, and nonetheless survive, retaining some past portion of what they and their forebears once were. They will be allowed to remain human beings. Is that so banal a text for the future? ❏

Nicholas Fraser is author of The Voice of Modern Hatred, Encounters with Europe's New Right *(Picador UK). He is the editor of* Storyville, *BBC TV's acclaimed series of international documentaries*

ANNELIESE ROHRER

Inside story

**International and domestic perceptions of Jörg Haider and his
Freedom Party differ sharply. A leading Austrian journalist urges
a closer look at the record of previous governments**

On a crisp, clear winter morning in February 2000, thousands of
Austrians are demonstrating noisily in an enchanting small square
at the centre of Vienna with the prime minister's office on one side
and the president's office in the Hapsburg palace on the other. Cries of
'*Widerstand*' (resistance) fill the air. Thousands of police in full combat
gear are also present. A new government is about to be sworn into office
by an unwilling but obliging president.

But the demonstrators who have come to express their anger face
to face with the new cabinet are frustrated: Prime Minister Wolfgang
Schüssel from the conservative party Österreichische Volkspartei (ÖVP)
and his deputy, Susanne Riess-Passer from the Freedom Party
(Freiheitliche Partei Österreichs, FPÖ), plus all the other ministers have
chosen to cross the square from the prime minister's office to the palace
via a secret tunnel. While they pass back and forth underground, in the
square the people cry 'Resistance'.

But resistance against what? Against the outcome of a flawless
democratic election in October 1999 which had turned into a disaster
for the ruling Social Democrats (Sozialdemokratische Partei Österreichs,
SPÖ) and conservatives, but brought the FPÖ and Jörg Haider
triumph and 27.2% of the electoral vote, the same as the conservatives?
Resistance against the fact that the conservatives plus the FPÖ had a
12-seat majority in parliament? Against the fact that their leaders
Wolfgang Schüssel and Jörg Haider were determined to translate that
majority into a change of government? Against Jörg Haider who is
perceived as a right extremist by international politicians and observers
but not by the Austrian political establishment, let alone the majority
of the people?

Wolfgang Schüssel. Credit: Die Presse / Clemens Fabry

A populist? Yes. A demagogue? Most certainly. The leader of a party
with xenophobic policies? For sure. A man of extreme rhetoric? No
doubt. A politician who uses coded language that will be understood by
the remaining Nazi sympathisers, or tolerates such words used by others
in his party? All without doubt true. But research into the continuous
growth of the FPÖ since Haider's coup in 1986 shows that from the
1990 election on he made his biggest gains at the polls by attracting
the votes of the SPÖ faithful. In the 1999 general election, he collected
well over 232,000 votes – 5% of the FPÖ's gains – from people who
had previously voted for the Social Democrats. Only 1% was won from
the conservatives. By contrast, Vienna's recent municipal election on
25 March this year reversed that result. No longer in opposition to the
national government but part of it, the FPÖ lost more than 7% of its
former Viennese voters, dropping from close to 28% to little more
than 20%. Traditional SPÖ voters returned to their party, giving it an
unexpected absolute majority in the local chamber.

If Haider and his Freedom Party are indeed the right-wing extremists international observers claim, the disparate results of these two elections allow only one conclusion: the number of voters with extremist tendencies who have and still do support the SPÖ is disconcertingly high – a conclusion Social Democrats would reject out of hand. This is one reason, at least, why international and Austrian perceptions of the nature of the Freedom Party differ so sharply.

Perhaps the most accurate and fitting description of the Freedom Party is that in the report commissioned by member states of the European Union and written by the former President of Finland, Martti Ahtisaari, when they were looking for a face-saving way to end the sanctions they had imposed on Austria in February 2000 as a consequence of the presence of the FPÖ in that government. 'The nature of the FPÖ its that of a right populist party with some extremist elements,' the report stated in September 2000, paving the way for the unconditional removal of sanctions. And that is much what the Austrians themselves believe.

The Austrian government remains firmly in place and its loss of popular support since last year is not a result of overt extremist tendencies but of a severe austerity programme combined with stunning political blunders – both in the process of law-making and in the area of political appointments. However, the truth of Ahtisaari's definition has been driven home to Austrians on at least three occasions since February last year.

The first was a statement by Haider himself in which he suggested that members of any democratic institution, parliament or otherwise, who issue statements detrimental to the country or the government should be brought to court and sanctioned with the loss of their seats in these institutions. After a public outcry and an apology by the minister of justice, Dieter Böhmdorfer, who had previously been Haider's attorney and had not refuted the statement immediately, public discussion died down.

The second was after the publication of a book by an FPÖ insider when it appeared that members of the FPÖ and Haider himself might have gained illegal access to data in the security force's computer to use to their advantage. Haider blamed the ensuing scandal on 'the fevered imagination of sick journalists' but, after an official investigation, police officers were suspended and a number of politicians lost their immunity.

Taking a stand, Vienna: The Embassy of Concerned Citizens, part of continuing resistance to the FPÖ in Austrian government. Credit: Die Presse / Clemens Fabry

The cases, which are the responsibility of attorneys under the authority of that same Dieter Böhmdorfer, have yet to come to court.

The third incident came during the acceptance speech of a newly elected chairman of the FPÖ branch in Lower Austria. Claiming to be ignorant of its significance, he used the coded language of its sympathisers to hark back to the Nazi era. When challenged, he neither apologised nor resigned.

While the eyes of international observers remain fixed on Haider's more extreme, sometime intolerant and xenophobic statements, and the occasional Nazi quote by others in his party, attention might be more profitably directed elsewhere: to developments in the law and the media. Both originated in policies which were sponsored and implemented by the previous coalition governments of the SPÖ and ÖVP, but have been exploited by Haider.

The early 1990s saw the passage of a law designed to sanction Nazi-related activities and statements. It was supported by all parties in parliament, including the FPÖ. Since coming to power, Haider and the FPÖ have used the same law to silence their critics in the media and elsewhere by taking them to court by the hundreds. The mechanism is simple: since Nazi-related ideologies, statements and activities are illegal, those who imply that Haider and his supporters have indulged in such activities are sued for libel. In most cases, proving the breach of law by them – according to the exact words of the law – is difficult to do, especially if journalistic or political judgements are involved.

The most prominent case recently was that of professor Anton Pelinka. In televised interviews with foreigners, Pelinka drew attention to the similarity of Haider's language on foreigners to that of the Nazis: the word 'parasite' featured in both, he claimed. Haider sued for libel, but the case was dismissed. On appeal, however, the case was referred back to the original court where the same judge sentenced Pelinka. Pelinka appealed and was finally acquitted; but not before public outrage found expression in a heated debate on free expression.

Haider has taken innumerable politicians and journalists to court in the last decade without exciting any serious public interest. Even a recent attempt to take the author of a letter to the editor to court has passed largely unremarked, even though the implications for the average Austrian who seeks to express a view in the media could be serious.

In a recent, disturbing turn of events, the department of justice sponsored plans for an amendment to the criminal law which would penalise the publication of unofficial documents with terms in jail for journalists who make these documents known to a wider public. As with other provisions, a similar proposal had been worked out by the previous government under Social Democratic leadership, but never came into effect. Moreover, the previous amendment stipulated fines for violation of the law, not for imprisonment. An enormous public outcry has greeted Böhmdorfer's plan but no final decision has been made. Discussion continues with grounds for deep concern.

There are other disconcerting tendencies in the media which, though the present administration may exploit them more aggressively, were initiated by previous Social Democratic governments. At the root of the problem is the peculiar structure of the Austrian media. Electronic media are the almost exclusive preserve of the government-run and -dominated ORF. Private TV is non-existent, private radio marginal. Over the past 30 years, political intervention, political appointments and political pressures on journalists have been the order of the day. It was common practice under the Social Democrats to appoint party faithful to run radio and TV stations or to exercise influence behind the scenes and this has continued since. As with the law, the only difference is the more blatant and aggressive manner of the present government.

The professional and personal implications of such a structure are not hard to work out: with no alternative radio or TV outlets to turn to, journalists who refuse to toe the line have been confronted with losing their jobs or leaving the profession.

The degree of concentration of ownership in Austria's print sector is unique. The biggest daily, *Die Kronen Zeitung*, has 41% of the market. Previous governments have dropped any anti-trust actions to avoid further concentration with the result that the two biggest daily newspapers plus smaller ones are now owned by the same company. The present government has also decided not to invoke the anti-trust laws to prevent further media mergers with the result that the four leading political magazines with a combined market share of nearly 100% will all be owned by a single company. At least two are destined to disappear. Worse: ORT is already collaborating closely with this group to the benefit of the present government.

Where do Austrian journalists turn if they insist on their fundamental right to free expression? Instead of reacting hysterically to Haider's scandal-seeking words, Europe might do better to pay attention to the undercurrent of the Austrian political system. It only takes a little refinement to render overt censorship unnecessary: it can be achieved without anyone being any the wiser. ❑

Anneliese Rohrer is *senior editor* at Die Presse, *Vienna*

WOLFGANG THIERSE

Problems of integration . . .

The speaker of the German federal parliament, interviewed by Toralf Staud, reveals his anxieties about the growth of neofascist youth culture in the eastern Länder since reunification

Herr Thierse, you have long been disturbed by right-wing extremism in East Germany. What, of all that you see in your journeys around the country, troubles you most?

I'm most shocked by the fear of violence among young democrats and left-wingers. When you talk to youngsters between 15 and 20, they tell you the clubs they cannot go to, what they cannot do, because they have

TORALF STAUD

. . . and a small school in Saxony

Ronny is not right-wing, he says. He just doesn't like foreigners. 'Turks stink,' he says. Ronny, 15, lives in a village close to Leipzig. For him, disliking foreigners is normal.

Jennifer, who is 14 years old and lives in a small town in Saxony, is certain that 'the foreigners are living here at our expense'. Her mother works in a supermarket where, reports

Jennifer, 'the foreigners steal'. This raises prices, she claims, so the 'Germans' ultimately pay more. Her classmates agree with her and also with the view that Germany is being 'flooded' by foreigners.

Ronny and Jennifer are completely 'normal' kids: Ronny wears trainers not military boots; Jennifer has beautiful long hair, not already been intimidated. They have been beaten up because, in the eyes of right-wingers, they don't conform, don't wear the right insignia – the haircut, the clothes. Anyone who is recognisably left-wing has good reason to be afraid in many parts of East Germany. What also shocks me is the mixture of blindness, the refusal to face facts and general helplessness among many local authorities in the face of manifestations of right-wing extremism. I understand that these people are worried about their town's reputation, but anyone who refuses to admit what is happening is playing it down.

I'm not saying that people in local government are on the side of right-wing extremists, but there is a secret sympathy across a broad spectrum of society. It starts with the sentiment, 'These are our boys, after all,' and goes on to state, 'There are really far too many foreigners.' It's not surprising if children and young people start to believe the prejudices they hear all around them.

Hostility to foreigners in the East is dramatically different from xenophobia in the West. Having something against foreigners is already commonplace in the day-to-day awareness of a considerable number of East Germans. The fact that people are not the least bit ashamed is another, alarming difference.

a skingirl's shaven head. Nevertheless, the same right-wing prejudices are firmly fixed in their minds. They are amazed when people from the 'Showing Courage for Democracy' project arrive from Dresden to talk to their school on racism. This is the first time anyone has tried to counter their views. Even the project's simplest comment plunges the kids into confusion.

Paul, 13 years old and also in Ronny's class, asserts with conviction that it is a known fact that all Poles steal. 'How many Poles do you know?' asks Jörn, a member of the project. 'None.' 'How many Germans do you know who steal?' 'Plenty.' 'Then wouldn't it be truer to say that all Germans are thieves?' Paul hesitates, uncertain what to say. Jörn persists. 'Do you always repeat what other people say?' 'No, but . . .'

The Courage project, largely made up of students little older than the schoolchildren they are visiting and dressed in the same trendy gear, has been visiting Saxony's schools for a couple of years. Their work is supported by the German Trade Union Federation (DGB). They have worked with over 220 classes and constantly discover that no one is challenging right-wing extremism

Of course there are real problems of integration in the West. Inter-cultural understanding isn't an idyllic state that happens naturally; it's hard work. But that is not at all the issue in East Germany. Here, hatred of the foreign exists almost regardless of the presence of foreign cultures. And this is suddenly taking on institutional forms, particularly among young people. That is what is so dangerous compared with the West. There, right-wing extremism mainly involves former military comrades. Knowing that values develop slowly and that change, too, takes a long time, one sees what enormous problems face us.

What are the causes?

Mainly the profound upheavals in East Germany since 1989. Right-wing thugs are not necessarily unemployed, but the experience of radical change has generated social anxiety, insecurity and a sense of moral uprooting. That is fairly typical. In a highly complex situation that individuals feel powerless to change, there has to be someone to blame: foreigners.

But there is a second factor: the authoritarian legacy of the German Democratic Republic (GDR). There was always anti-semitism and

and related violence. Most teachers avoid taking a stand because, after the end of the GDR, they were accused – rightly – of having indoctrinated their pupils. They are, in any case, overburdened and struggle to maintain their authority. Ralf Hron, youth secretary in the Saxony DGB and co-ordinator of the Courage project says his group is 'trying to fill a huge gap'.

There's already one shaven-headed youth in the class wearing a t-shirt boasting the Nazis' military cross; he swears at a member of the project for being a 'filthy Jewish pig'. The female teacher finds nothing wrong with the Nazi insignia; her son has one at home hanging in his room. In a Middle School, two boys boast of having attended banned skinhead concerts, listened to illegal music at home and of having older brothers who belong to the German Nationalist Party. Another pupil, who was encouraged by one of the project to criticise neo-Nazis, was beaten up in the next break.

There are, of course, schools – mainly in the bigger cities like Leipzig – where the atmosphere is quite different, but classes like Ronny's and Paul's are the norm. Nadine says foreigners have brought many diseases to Germany; Robert believes they all

Berlin 1994: on the t-shirt the slogan 'White Aryan Resistance Germany'.
Credit: Christian Jungeblodt

work illegally, adding, 'Foreigners are taking our jobs.'

Team members show kids how much tax is paid by foreigners in Germany and demonstrate that even after all the necessary costs are deducted, they still contribute a surplus. They describe the centres in Saxony that house applicants for asylum and list the items in an average food parcel on which refugees may depend for many years. They explain to these East Germans how 'our West German predecessors' brought Turks, Italians and Yugoslavs into the country as 'guest workers'. And so on. They make little impression on dyed-in-

the-wool hardliners, but the aim is to strengthen the resistance of the average kid by giving the data with which to argue back.

In some parts of East Germany, particularly in the countryside, the propaganda of the extreme right articulates a common consensus: this is the only way to explain unemployment and the rise in crime. The foreigners are to blame. The fact that there are few to be found in the East – the figure for Saxony is just 2.3% – is irrelevant.

In much of the East, the extremists affect public attitudes, shape the climate of opinion and dominate xenophobia in the GDR, but they were swept under the carpet and never publicly dealt with. This authoritarian legacy includes the inability to cope with conflict. It is also significant that the average citizen of the GDR had little chance to experience foreigners or the unfamiliar. It was a narrowly confined, closed society.

And third: part of the legacy of the GDR, an aspect that I am sympathetic to, is its emphasis on equality and social justice. Many East Germans felt they had personally lost out with reunification. Moreover, one of the fatal aspects of Marxism-Leninism was its rigid categorisation of friend and foe: us and the class enemies; us and them. To a certain extent, the basic pattern persists in the form of anti-system hostility: a crazily distorted combination of socialism and nationalism.

What can politicians or the state do about this?

The most important thing is to reduce unemployment in the East. We must find policies that generate confidence and reduce the present anxiety. And we must all, politicians as well as the general public, reject any form of violence, xenophobia and hatred of the unknown more vigorously than we have to date. The judiciary and the police should

youth clubs, making their particular brand of sub-culture the only option for teenagers. A key strategy of activists connected to the most extreme right-wing party, the National Democratic Party (NDP), since the mid-90s has been the creation of so-called nationally liberated zones; in other words, no-go areas for non-believers, foreigners, dark-skinned Germans and anyone else who does not conform to their ideology. These include school playgrounds, marketplaces, railway stations and even small companies.

The extremists are by no means social outcasts; often they are well-regarded members of their town or village involved in day-to-day community affairs. They look after public monuments, collect money for child-care centres, play the guitar in old people's homes. Right-wing culture has become the fashionable form of teenage rebellion; racist views are openly voiced and excite no resistance. In this environment, it's not unusual to see nine- and ten-year-olds in bomber jackets. Skinhead bands are surprisingly popular and starting to seep into the mainstream music scene. Germanic runes and pagan mythology create a bogus cultural tradition that generates a good deal of interest.

work to bring cases to a conclusion more quickly. Proceedings against those allegedly responsible for the death of a young Algerian in Guben have been dragging on for a year now. People there told me that delays like this encourage the extremists.

Local journalists often feel threatened and so don't cover this particular problem.

I've discovered that if a journalist writes bluntly about what's going on, his piece is not published on the grounds that if the paper in question prints an aggressive piece on the complacency of the local community, it could lose its readers. But what really annoys me is the way the media deals with xenophobia and right-wing extremism. It's always the same: something happens and for a day or two the papers are full of it; then silence. Nor is it right only to focus on those who use violence – the aggressors. Where are the reports on many people's everyday commitment to democracy? Or the quiet courage displayed by others? These are less spectacular, but should not be ignored or taken for granted. I'd like to see more songs of praise to ordinary, decent folk. ❑

TS An edited version of an interview published in Die Zeit

The main town in the district that houses Ronny's school, Wurzen, is a hotbed of extremist activity. Paul moved from Wurzen to the country. 'Only then', he says, 'did it become obvious how right-wing Wurzen is.' But it is not only in Wurzen that Nazi cadres stand and chat at school gates handing out cigarettes and leaflets.

The son of Petra Schegel, liaison teacher at the school, was beaten up by Nazis in Wurzen a couple of years ago. He ended up in hospital with severe head injuries. When he started legal proceedings, the family received murder threats. The perpetrators have still not been brought to book.

Ronny thought the day's proceedings with the team 'pretty meaningless'; all the speakers had done, he claimed, was badmouth the right-wingers. He still says he's not an extremist himself, though his cousin Lars – who has fallen behind at school and will now leave after the ninth grade – is. He calls Lars over. 'Yes,' says Lars proudly, 'sure I'm a nationalist.' Then he starts to complain about school. Not about work, but about the headmaster who has banned the wearing of military boots. ❑

Toralf Staud is a journalist with Die Zeit *for which this piece was written*

HÉLENE LÖOW

Music to hate with

Aided by the Internet, racist music has made inroads on European youth culture

It was in the first half of the 1990s that White Noise music became the symbol of the growing racist subculture around Europe. Between 1990 and 1995, the music industry, then in a period of rapid expansion, gradually replaced the badly copied tapes, records that were hard to come by and roughly photocopied magazines with professionally produced CDs. The number of CDs on the market grew steadily; production became increasingly professional with Swedish White Noise record labels among the world's most active producers.

By 1996, the first phase was over; for the next two years, production maintained its levels but there was no significant increase. By 1999, however, it was once more on the rise, along with white-power magazines, and other propaganda material. In 1988, for instance, there were only six white-power magazines in Sweden, all of them circulating in photocopy format. In 1999, this number had risen to at least 25, half of them professionally published. Given the size of its population, the volume of racist and anti-semitic material produced in Sweden is high compared with other countries, as is the number of people active in the various movements within the racist subculture.

By the late 1990s, the white-power movement around the world had acquired a new medium for disseminating its propaganda and marketing its music and other products: the Internet. Websites replaced the mail-order companies that had served a hard-core clientele but were difficult for those outside the movement to locate. The sites rapidly attracted vast new audience of potential members, customers and like-minded sympathisers. They also served another purpose: that of linking formerly isolated individuals and small local groups of racists and anti-semites who had previously lacked any easy means of communication. Racist

organisations are not, on the whole, given to advertising themselves or
their wares in the mainstream media, are seldom listed in phonebooks,
and few would risk starting a conversation at work or with a stranger
with, 'Hi! I'm an anti-semite. What are you into?' The Internet changed
all that: all anyone with the inclination had to do was start surfing. There
are plenty of sites, well linked and active.

In the case of Sweden, there are a number of factors that underlie the
growth of its racist subculture. In the late 1980s and early 1990s, the ban
on printing racist and anti-semitic material was lifted. More accurately,
it was not officially lifted, but simply faded away without anyone really
noticing as printers agreed to print the formerly offending material.
The ban had been imposed in the 1960s, but as recession hit the Swedish

Saalfeld, Germany, 1998: skingirls at a neo-Nazi demo. Credit: Christian Jungeblodt

economy in the late 1980s, not only did printers become less discriminating, the press began to accept advertising from various White Noise companies, enabling them to reach a large mainstream audience.

Another factor at work in the present growth of the extremist movement is the age of its ideologues. The movement is dominated by the 1960s and 1970s generation, one for whom the use of modern information technology is as natural as breathing and which they use to advantage. While it is difficult to put a precise figure on the number of activists and sympathisers in in any country, the estimated number of racist activists in Sweden is around 3,000, the majority men born in the 1960s and 70s.

Establishing a direct link between the music industry and racist and anti-semitic groups is difficult, it is evident that not only has the music enabled the subculture to reach out far beyond its normal recruiting ground, but that royalties and fees paid by the music industry has made activists financially independent and given them the resources to finance new projects.

Over the past couple of years, the music of hate has become a hotly debated subject in the media as well as among government officials. Schools have banned the music, local councils have become more restrictive when it comes to letting organisations rent public venues for concerts, the police have made several large busts against concerts and record companies and there have been convictions for incitement to racial hatred. As a result, the number of larger public concerts has gone down and the music industry has been forced to adopt more discreet marketing methods as well as to tone down the 'messages' put out by their groups. Song writers have, to some extent, abandoned their openly racist and anti-semitic language in favour of a coded message.

But the music still plays an important role in the subculture of white power, particularly as a seductive way of spreading its message and as a popular recruiting tool. Meanwhile, the recording companies continue to put out a steady stream of White Noise. Their latest asset is a string of female groups and, with the latest technology for downloading music from the Web, much of the industry has moved to its shelter. Debate has died down, a sign, perhaps, that White Noise is becoming just one among many pop and rock genres. ❏

Hélene Löow is a member of Sweden's National Council for Crime Prevention

DIRAN ADEBAYO

Cost of conforming

'Britishness' is now officially anti-racist, but the price exacted for membership in the club is the denial of difference

There's currently an ad on UK television for McCain's chips. Three UK black lads – quite sporty, hip-looking – have a few moments of banter, then wonder what they're going to have for dinner, before one of them goes to slip the chips in the oven. They don't use slang – or 'jive', as Sebastian Coe, the athletics great turned Tory aide and Linford Christie scourge might put it – nor engage in any other loudly 'black' behaviour, nevertheless the ad is something of a development in the cultural positioning of black Britain. Whereas once the sight of three black guys bonding might have carried the whiff of some militant separatist conspiracy, or been deemed to be otherwise threatening to the prime-time audience the ad is aimed at, such a group is now evidently perceived as being less problematic. The message of the ad is: 'You don't need to be frightened of these guys. Look, they love chips, they're as British as you.'

As such, the ad is a close relative of what I call the 'Queen Vic' take on multiculturalism. In the long-running UK soap *EastEnders*, the Queen Vic pub has always been the place where locals – white, black, Asian – have come to quaff their pints, chill and chat. This despite the fact that, in my largely London experience, pubs have rarely reflected the demographic make-up of their locality. Pubs remain a largely white domain, a place where Anglos and those who work or have been socialised with them repair to at the day's end, while most of their non-white neighbours pass by on the other side of the windows, enjoying their downtime elsewhere.

Chips, pubs; more English than tikka masala, as English as . . . football. Although the game has become probably the most powerful lingua franca the world has seen, the enduring role it plays in the English nationalist project – the Englishness of its origins, the 'Englishness' that others must take on board for them to prosper in the English leagues, 1966 and all that – has also been apparent to anyone who has grown up here. Until a decade or so ago, it was still common for football pundits and managers to hint that these new black players who were coming into the English game were OK as far as they went – natural flair and strength – but that they lacked the grit and bottle that teams needed to take them through the long winter months of the English season, when pitches were hard and the weather was cold. It was no surprise, then, to see that the first England regular, Nottingham Forest's Viv Anderson, was a defender – as if only by playing in a 'gritty' position could a black player show that his original sin had been washed out of him.

And then along came Ian Wright. Here was a great player (whose first club chairman, Crystal Palace's Ron Noades, was, ironically, one of the 'black players dodgy in the winter' brigade), a striker no less, who brought to his game a loud – it seemed defiant – black joy, black expressiveness. When he used to score – pretty much every week in the early 1990s – he would run to the corner flag, and there execute little 'bogling' movements with his arms to the crowd – the bogle then being the big new reggae/ragamuffin dance. Black folk loved him for it – bringing our secret Saturday night codes to the spotlight of a Saturday afternoon! – and he's probably the main reason why black Londoners now overwhelmingly support Arsenal, his main club. I wanted to write his biography 'Ian Wright – Ragamuffin', and felt that if the British public, and the tabloids, could take this representative of the new school to their hearts, if he could supplant old blondie Alan Shearer in the iconic centre-forward position of the national team, then the concept of 'Englishness' would truly have been widened.

But it didn't happen. Wright never did supplant Shearer, making only a few starts for England when he was way past his prime; and when the media did finally get round to embracing Wright, our ragamuffin seemed quite a different boy altogether. Wright, the radio and TV talk-show host, is the superpatriot, a man whose voice was among the loudest denouncing the appointment of a foreigner, Sweden's Sven-Goran Eriksson, to manage England's football team, 'our boys', the Wright persona of the 'Chicken Tonight' ads, buzzing about on a kids' bike with a mock posh accent, a cheeky chappie of hallowed British tradition, his bogling aspects quite shorn off, his 'difference' ignored. 'Oh dear,' I thought to myself, 'I guess this is what it still takes to make it big in this country. Co-option: the British way of doing things.'

And now comes Michael Duberry, the black Leeds player who found himself caught up in the aftermath of a drunken night-time brawl when his best friend at the club, the white Jonathan Woodgate, fellow England international Lee Bowyer and a couple of their friends, allegedly assaulted some Asian students outside a club in the town. As the whole drama of Duberry backtracking on the initial 'alibi' he gave his friends was played out at the spring trial, it struck me that, if the chips ad and the Queen Vic tell us mainly about the liberal fantasies of advertising and media folk, the limits of their 'progressive' vision, then Wright's trajectory, and the Duberry business in particular, speak much more to the lived, everyday contradictions of belonging, the gains and the costs, as it's been experienced by many non-white Britons over the past 40 years, and will continue to be in our increasingly mixed-up nation.

It all felt so 1970s: white lads beating up on a 'Paki'. And Duberry's role, albeit restricted to the aftermath, brought memories of another 70s story, quiet as it's kept – black involvement in such activity. In Andrea Levy's novel *X*, set in 70s north London, she tells the story of two teenage mixed-race sisters, one of whom starts running with a local skinhead gang. In the 1980 Britflick *The Firm*, Y plays the black member of a group of thuggish football fans, based on West Ham's notorious Inter-City firm, who takes part in their hooligan activities. Cut to the present, and one or two black British acquaintances of mine are as vociferous as anyone in their distaste for the various asylum seekers 'infesting' our towns. One of them recently had an altercation with a Somalian: 'You fucking refugee!' he called him. While an Anglo-Asian lady I know – once, would you believe, a 13-year-old skinbird in late-70s Southall, since married into a dyed-in-the-wool English family – now has a daughter whose paternal grandmother insists she wears a rose on St George's Day.

It's strong, this need to be accepted, to belong; and, as the last instance shows, that wish to fit into the dominant dynamic of one's environment is often matched by the need for representatives of that dominant group to construct a simple story around the potential outsider in their midst that brings them easily, snugly, within it. And if the interior desire to fit in, and the bizarre behaviour it can lead to, tends to be most marked in one's teenage and young adult years, when we're in search of ourselves, then the group's desire tends to be strongest in groups with the strongest internal dynamics – in large institutions such as the army, the police force (check former policeman Ike Eze-Anyika's recent novel *Canteen Culture* for black officer complicity in beat patrol viciousness) and football clubs.

So what are we to make of Duberry, his initial attempt to protect his best friend Woodgate, then subsequent decision to 'grass' him up in court, against the strong advice, so he claims, of Leeds United's solicitor Peter McCormick? His lawyer said, after Duberry was cleared on conspiracy charges, that he would have plenty to say when this whole affair properly ends, but for the moment we must make do with what we can learn about the man from his website and interviews and, if you'll allow me, read a little, not so simple story around it.

The 26-year-old Duberry grew up in Enfield, in the suburbs of north London. I grew up in inner-city Haringey, just a couple of miles to the south. The 70s was the period when black 'pioneer' families began moving from Haringey to the whiter Enfield in search of greener pastures, and better education for their children, etc. Every now and again, some of these families encountered racial grief in the 'burbs, and I remember there was a fair amount of *Schadenfreude* displayed when a couple came grovelling back.

But Duberry's family stayed there, and their youth was a schoolboy athletics international before moving on to football. Such prestigious peer groups, with their attendant rewards, tend to foster an even greater desire to 'fit in' among initiates and so from this, from Enfield, from the fact that at his teenage club Chelsea, too, Dube's closest ally was a white midfield player, Jody Morris, we must imagine Duberry is integrated, happy.

But he is a conscious brother too. He's told the Leeds club programme of his admiration for Muhammad Ali, Martin Luther King and Mike Tyson, and this 'gentle man' also bears a large tattoo from *Exodus* across his shoulder blades, in homage to the tattooed militant rap artist Tupac Shakur, who saw the lines as applicable to the international black liberation struggle. Could it be that Duberry, no doubt the veteran of dodgy light-hearted dressing-room banter down the years, found himself dwelling on the Leeds fight after his initial honouring of the group code, and found his racial hackles rising? Like Sammy Davis Jr after a bad day with the Rat Pack? That even if the incident had no racial dimension it could be so construed by the public, and he wished to put clear blue water between himself and any such understanding? Perhaps Duberry would have felt no need to change his story in court if Bowyer or Woodgate had simply made a statement in the intervening period condemning racism, but no such statement came.

Clearly something happened, for Duberry was not so committed to the truth as to tell it the first time round, and if it was something of this nature, then the Duberry affair really is symbolic, for most non-white Brits would have had this 'worm-turning' moment at some point. And if, for many of us, it doesn't begin, or end, in fisticuffs on the street, then it is only because other groups, other classes, don't tend to do such things.

But it is in these other places, specifically the middle class, with their institutions and ideologies the most potent of all, that the bigger battles around race and integration remain to be fought. The first-order injury of physical assault is a much less common issue now for black people at least – long more physically feared than Asians by whites – than the second-order injuries that can arise when a black person, entering, say, the world of employment and white colleagues, feels himself not really known or not fully wanted, by the pack. A former colleague of mine in the national media, frustrated as I'd been by bootless attempts to get certain stories past her editors, and the narrow range of what counts as a 'national' or 'universal' story, has recently moved into film. The first two things she was told on her well-known screenplay course was not to use slang and not to use African names for characters. The UK public aren't up for it, she was told, and the international audience don't expect that from Britain. We want the pleasure of multiculturalism, you see, of everybody eating chips or curry in the same pub, without the 'pain' of having to go that little bit further, having to extend our parameters and so truly appreciate, truly include.

Not so much has changed post Lawrence. Britishness is now officially anti-racist but, as it's manifested in its elites and its peer groups, in what it seeks to promote as true-Brit behaviour and what it chooses to ignore, its narrowness, its demands, remain. But difference, sooner or later, will make a difference; and confronting it honestly and fearlessly will ultimately determine how cohesive this society is. Try as some might, the centre cannot hold. ❏

Diran Adebayo's latest book is My once upon a time *(Abacus 2001)*

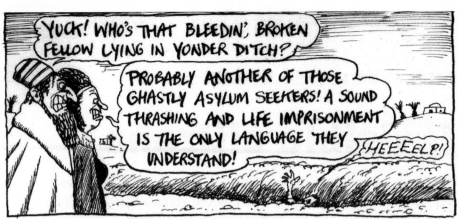

STEPHEN BATES

Invisible citizens

All European countries have their far-right groups but few have been as successful in recent years as the Vlaams Blok, the right-wing nationalist – and separatist – party in Belgium

In a country which usually likes to depict itself as being at the benign, bourgeois heart of Europe, Belgium's Vlaams Blok has been extremely successful in capturing protest votes in the Flemish north by exploiting not only separatist discontents in an increasingly fissiparous society, but also a traditional fear of coloured immigration and historical divisions, still raw after nearly two centuries of statehood.

Arguably, the Blok has been even more successful than Jörg Haider's Freedom Party (FPÖ) in Austria and Jean-Marie Le Pen's Front National in France, which have both captured international attention because their leaders have become national – if sometimes buffoonish – political figures. By contrast, the Vlaams has concentrated on achieving local power – it is the second party in much of northern Belgium, including Antwerp, the second city where it draws a third of the vote, and came within an ace of holding the balance of power in the capital Brussels itself in elections two years ago. Its leader Filip de Winter is more in the mould of Haider than Le Pen, a charismatic, smart-suited, youngish figure and – despite being ostentatiously ostracised by other parties – now leads a significant political force. With even respectable Belgian political leaders speculating gloomily about the long-term future of their federal state, the Vlaams is a significant player.

Many of the jokes about Belgium are overplayed but they do address a certain impulse in the national character: a diffidence about a land often occupied by foreigners in uniform – French, Austrians, Spaniards, Dutch, Germans to name but a few over the centuries – and a cynicism about authority and government in a state cobbled together (largely at the initiative of Lord Palmerston in 1830) from a population lacking any identity of interest or even a common language. It is somehow characteristic that you often see bumper stickers on Belgian cars proclaiming defensively, 'Belgium Will Remain One Country' in three languages. You can imagine how long the king's Christmas broadcast lasts.

A state you can drive across from west to east in three hours and from north to south in one has developed a complex federal structure to accommodate and ensure equal treatment for the French speakers of its southern half, the Flemish of the north (speaking a dialect of Dutch) and the Germans tucked into a small enclave in the distant east.

Filip de Winter: 'charismatic' leader of the Vlaams Blok. Credit: Senepart / Rex / Sipa Press

The constitutional compromises involved in making the political system work – compromise being the supreme political virtue in Belgian society – are now starting to come apart at the seams and it is into those interstices that the Vlaams has successfully burrowed. It exploits historical grievances – over such myths as that of French-speaking officers sending Flemish troops to their deaths in the trenches of the World War I – and encourages regional divisions, sometimes in incomprehensibly petty ways. And, of course, it features immigrants as the source of all crime in its election publicity – coloured outsiders being one group not incorporated into the federal settlement.

To this, you can add an economic division. Historically, the French-speaking south of Wallonia was the country's heavy industrial powerhouse, site of mines and steel mills – making Belgium the fourth-largest economy in the world in 1900 – while Flanders was a rustic backwater. But in the past 30 years, the balance of power has changed: the old industries have declined while high-tech industry has moved into the north to exploit a population happy to speak English in preference to the hated French.

There is a distinct whiff of We Are The Masters Now about much Flemish triumphalism, even from politicians from parties much more moderate than the Vlaams. The political balance of power has shifted too: a primarily French speaker has not become prime minister since the 1960s. While the francophones bleat about social and national solidarity and point out how heavily they used to subsidise the peasantry of the north, Flemish voters moan that their tax transfers amount to the equivalent of each family in the north buying their Wallonian equivalents a new car every four years. It is not hard for politicians to convince them that they would be better off on their own. This is a society which reads newspapers in different languages, watches different television channels, listens to different radio stations – and increasingly has fewer friends or relatives on the other side of the divide. Families living near the language boundary often never visit towns the other side, even two or three miles away.

The struggle is at its most acute around Brussels itself, a capital largely of francophones floating like an island surrounded by Flanders. In Brussels, both languages are officially recognised as part of the constitutional compromise: all street signs carry names in French and Flemish and, confusingly, so do route signs. As soon as you get to the ring road, however, the signs revert to Flemish – disconcerting as Mons suddenly becomes Bergen – and then revert to French again as you enter Wallonia about ten miles south of the city.

In that little doughnut of local authorities around the capital you find Flemish councillors governing largely French-speaking residents with interesting results as the Flemish grow more insistent in the use of a language that francophones have proved remarkably allergic to learning. You may, for instance, find school bus drivers sent to pick up handicapped youngsters attending special schools in Wallonia being denied permission to enter Flanders by the police because their permits are in French, leaving children in wheelchairs waiting by the side of the road. Or you may find that if you wish to receive documents from the commune in French you have to travel to the town hall each time to make a separate, written application.

In Brussels itself, they try to keep a balance in employment opportunities: about 70% going to French speakers and 30% to Flemish, even though the actual make-up of the population is nearer 85% to 15%. Even so, when Flemish firefighters went on strike a few years back to try to boost their percentage, the French resisted and between them they brought the city to its knees – and eventually settled, honour satisfied, for a compromise: 29.48% of jobs in future to be allocated to Flemish-speaking firemen – the equivalent of less than one post a year. No wonder a francophone local paper published a cartoon showing a woman screaming from an upper storey of a burning building with a fireman standing passively on a nearby ladder saying: 'I can't understand what you're saying – you're talking French.'

Brussels is probably the one insuperable obstacle to the division of the state – for it to become the capital of Flanders as the Flemish demand,

Brussels, 13 June 2001: the fascist New World Order clashes with other anti-Bush demonstrators.
Credit: AP / Virginia Mayo

ethnic cleansing on a huge scale would be required and the place would be left a ghost town. It is a tribute to Belgian phlegm that no one – yet – has actually been killed in inter-communal violence. Nevertheless, into the phoney theoretical argument about splitting the state stumps the Vlaams, which has now started to try to appeal across the language divide. Because of the political compromise which requires a majority of each language group on the city's regional government before anything is done, it does not require many seats to block all decision-making.

And the issue it sees as uniting potential voters most satisfactorily is that of the hapless immigrants. Until recently these were an almost invisible group, entirely absent from the fields of Flanders though present in the cities and outside – indeed excluded from – the network of political connections and patronage without which little gets done in Belgian society. Useful for doing menial jobs of course, like cleaning the streets, but otherwise unwelcome.

In a city where you can still see aged pensioners wearing solar topis in the weak summer sun – souvenirs of their time as employees in Belgium's once mighty Congo empire, which ended 40 years ago – equatorial Africans are common. You can even eat monkey in some of the shadier city restaurants. But the inhabitants of Brussels were surprised to learn that there were also 70,000 Muslims in their city – 7% of the population, mainly from north Africa – a year or two back.

The biggest jolt to the system emerged from the Belgian paedophile scandal in 1997. Stung by accusations of corruption and incompetence following their failure to rescue children from the molester Marc Dutroux, who had been kidnapping girls on an almost industrial scale and who was eventually captured by accident – four years on he still awaits trial, but that's another story – the police eventually reopened the case, long overlooked, of an eight-year-old Muslim girl, called Loubna Benaissa, who had disappeared without trace five years earlier.

They discovered her mummified body hidden in a trunk in the basement of a known paedophile only a couple of hundred yards from her front door. In the stinging words of an official inquiry, they had devoted less attention to her case when she was reported missing in 1992 than they would have done to a missing wallet. When the little girl's teenaged sister Nabela – who had done much to keep the case in the public eye in the face of massive police, official and media indifference – was eventually named by a local newspaper in a spasm of national guilt as

Brussels citizen of the year, there were complaints that she did not qualify as, despite having been born and lived all her life in the city, she wasn't really Belgian.

In such circumstances it was understandable that the Vlaams' chief candidate in the following year's local elections, Johan Demol, should hope to succeed by defying electoral law and appearing on posters in his uniform as a former local chief of police. He failed – but not by much.

To their credit, other political parties refuse to entertain any deals with the Blok, maintaining what is known even in Flanders as a cordon sanitaire around them, but how far this will hold in the face of Vlaams' onward march, particularly if community divisions exacerbate, is open to question. That this should be happening in the country which is proud to be at the heart of Europe is troubling and strikes all sorts of resonances in the ongoing debate about the sort of European Union that is being built just across the road in Brussels. ❏

Stephen Bates *was the* Guardian *European Affairs editor, based in Brussels,* *1995–99*

MICHEL SAMSON

Portrait of a town

**Vitrolles, a small town in south-eastern France, is the far right's
shop window in the region. In this year's municipal elections,
voters re-elected the incumbent mayor on her record in office,
knowing – and approving – what to expect**

In March 2001, in the second round of the French local elections,
Catherine Mégret, the MNR's (Mouvement National Républicain)
sitting mayor managed to hold on to the town hall in Vitrolles
(Bouches-du-Rhône, near Marseilles), a town of 37,000 inhabitants.
She got 7,292 votes (45.32%), beating her Socialist opponent – who had
the support of the Communist candidate in the second round – by 201
votes. The centre-right candidate of the RPR (Rassemblement pour la
République), who had managed to stay in for the deciding round, lost
7% of the vote, with the first-round total of 2,365 (17.47%) dropping
to 1,707 votes (10.61%) in the second. The two sides agreed that this
spectacular drop had benefited the sitting mayor: it was in the most
right-wing wards that the RPR suffered its biggest losses, demonstrating
that the far right owes its victory here to its ability to pull right-wing
voters together to see off the left.

Above all, her re-election proves that France's far right, despite the
fact that its dominant party, the FN (*Front National*), has split into two
sharply competing wings, is still a force to be reckoned with, especially
in south-eastern France. On the same day, Daniel Simonpiéri, the MNR
mayor of the neighbouring town of Marignane (Bouches-du-Rhône)
was also re-elected and Jacques Bompard, an FN member, was re-elected
in the first round in Orange (Vaucluse), just 100 kilometres further
north. In Toulon (Var), however, the largest town to be controlled by
the far right, the sitting mayor, whose majority had fallen apart halfway
through his term of office, was beaten. Another item to be chalked up
is the success in various seats in the south-east of followers of Bruno

Mégret, the MNR's national leader, as well as his own good results in his Marseilles seat. In the working-class areas in the north of the city he won more than 20% of the vote.

What follows is an attempt to provide an analysis of the policies of Mme Mégret in Vitrolles and to understand the significance of this vote for a platform which is so obviously based on social exclusion.

In this new town, which has only a huge shopping mall for a town centre and is cut in two by a motorway, a major arterial road and a railway line, there are two main areas of Mme Mégret's local government policy which are of particular importance. The first concerns social policy. The majority group on the town council has been operating a policy that is violently and flagrantly discriminatory. A motion giving a special maternity benefit to couples where one parent was French or from a European country was passed by the town council before being quashed by an appeals tribunal. It resulted in Mme Mégret and her deputy mayor being condemned by a tribunal which is hearing their appeal even as I write this report in April 2001.

Another striking example of this segregationist policy concerns the social centre in the Cité des Pins, a housing development which the town hall detests because it has a large immigrant population made up of many nationalities but mainly North African. In July 1997, this municipally funded centre, which served as a meeting place for all the most active social or cultural associations in the community, was closed down, supposedly for repairs. This was at a time of year when children and adolescents needed it most, because many of them cannot afford to go away on holiday. The centre was burned down at the end of August 1997 and has been left in ruins ever since, making it quite clear that policies to provide any kind of social assistance to the poorest had been completely abandoned.

The town hall then proceeded, as a matter of declared and official policy, to do absolutely nothing further about this area and its inhabitants who are regularly vilified in speeches by members of the town council. Other social centres suffered a similar fate. Meanwhile, the number of social workers on the town's payroll was reduced from six to two, both recruited by Mme Mégret's team. The town council has repeatedly proclaimed this uncompromising and sensational policy from the rooftops and boasted about it in its official publications and posters. Far from bothering the majority party, judicial or political censure has actually been seized on as an electoral resource and used to demonstrate how they have been unjustly attacked by all the other political parties and by the judiciary, even though they were democratically elected on the same basis as all other local councillors throughout France.

Cultural policies have been just as radical. No sooner was Mme Mégret's team in office than it set about destroying the Sous-Marin, a 'café-musique' run by young people. Like a number of others, this place had been loaned by the previous town council and supplied with a grant. Local rock and rap groups performed there; it was a place you could sit and chat over a beer or two, solving all the world's problems; above all, it was a place where you could dream.

On the morning of 6 October 1997, the place was bricked up by a gang of local heavies on the orders of the town council. The young employees were thrown out and the windows were concreted over because the local authority claimed that drugs had been found on the premises. Subsequently, the local authority was censured because its debate on the seizure of the premises, and consequently the seizure itself, had been illegal, but also because it had slandered the Sous-Marin's employees. Just previously they had sacked the manageress of Vitrolles' only cinema – which had also been in receipt of a grant. This was because she had organised a programme of films about Aids that had already been shown on Arte, the Franco-German television channel. She was compensated by an industrial tribunal but, in the meantime, the cinema was closed down and has remained so. The local council tried to go on the attack by staging 'white pride' rock concerts but, when this didn't work, switched their efforts to supporting classes at the municipal conservatory for classical music: a discreet way of favouring children of the middle classes rather than those of the poorest groups. It has also approved a number of measures intended to promote traditional Provençal culture as an inducement to the older, more traditionalist members of the population.

Catherine Mégret's victory in Vitrolles in 2001 is thus one symptom of a quite radical new departure: the implantation of an extreme right-wing tendency firmly founded in control and management. Indeed, it is notable that the usual torrents of abuse from the FN president, Jean-Marie Le Pen, who never gets beyond the level of screams of frenzied protest, found so few echoes during these municipal elections, in which he was not standing. Bruno Mégret is right to stress that, on Sunday

18 March, his movement, the MNR, broke through the credibility
barrier for the first time, because his supporters now have the benefit of
the 'sitting member effect'. As far as his wife or his second-in-command
Simonpiéri, mayor of Marignane, are concerned, this year it really isn't
just a matter of battles won as a result of random, unexpected three-way
elections: the electorate know what they are doing when they vote for
these candidates; they know the policies, the pros and cons, the style
to expect. In addition, in the three far-right towns, the battles with
the judiciary and the political establishment brought in the media, both
written and spoken, local and national, in a big way, which helped to
make voters even better informed about the day-to-day running of their
towns than those elsewhere.

This factor relates to the most important feature of this extreme
right-wing electorate: it is based on 'victimhood', a feeling widespread

*Marseilles 1997: demonstrators attempt to disrupt a rally with Jean-Marie Le Pen
and Catherine Mégret, mayor of Vitrolles. Credit: Florian Launette / AP*

in this area that you are the victim of those in power, of those in Paris, of foreigners and – of course – of the press and the judiciary. Playing on this narrow-minded chauvinism is something the FN and MNR councillors have got down to a fine art. Catherine Mégret issued a leaflet entitled *A Manifesto just for us*, and this is echoed by the little Astérix figure on the signs you find on all the roads leading into Orange (in the *Astérix* cartoon books, the hero and his friends inhabit a small enclave, the only bit of Gaul that the Roman occupiers have never succeeded in conquering). Moreover, the three mayors never miss a chance to denounce the 'demonisation' they have to put up with; they use it as a code word for all the resentment felt by their supporters, and it thus becomes a vehicle for the political expression of the social ills from which they suffer.

But although such 'victimhood' is by no means confined to the extreme right, among this electorate it goes along with a quite blatant desire for anti-Arab racial discrimination. It had already shown itself to some extent when Mme Mégret was twice found guilty of discrimination in respect of her racist declarations in a German newspaper soon after she came to power. One of these, currently under appeal, could cost her her right to stand for election. Far from regarding such cases as a problem, she and her friends exploited the situation by appearing in a third trial – on the maternity allowance – as sacrificial victims, assuming an attitude of defiance towards the majesty of the law and successfully provoking their ejection from the courtroom.

The *Manifesto*, also censured by the court, provided more recent evidence. It proposed nothing less than the expulsion from the town of any immigrants 'found to be a source of trouble or insecurity'. It went even further in proposing that 'any French people living in the Cité des Pins who wished it should be rehoused in another area . . . The Mégret party will therefore offer them new, purpose-built housing, at an equivalent rent, elsewhere in the town.' It would be difficult to find a clearer statement of intent to go the way of separate development.

These leaflets were widely distributed: for example, the inhabitants of the better-off residential area of Vignolles which gave the sitting councillors 60% of their vote, knew what the leaflets said. Similarly, the inhabitants of Orange know perfectly well that when, at the end of the year, free Christmas dinners are given to the elderly, they contain pork: a neat way of excluding any Muslims. They know, too, that the people living in the housing estates of Fourchesvielles feel completely cut off from the rest of the town. People in Marignane are well aware that the only social centre in the town, which happens to be situated among blocks with a large immigrant population, has had all its financial aid cut off and that their mayor is once more going to have to stand up in court to explain his actions in connection with the ongoing story about the pork provided for school dinners: yet another sly method of excluding young children from Muslim families.

These two elements, the 'victimhood' and the anti-Arab racism, are part of a coherent plan, a logical process: they form the basis for public spending. This is perfectly well understood by those of the electorate who believe that any aid, direct or indirect, to anyone worse off than themselves constitutes a direct threat. They are the same people who, on the level of political philosophy, think that national sovereignty – something to which they are all the more attached because they rarely have a chance to be proud of themselves – begins at the gates of their little villas.

In his account of how the memory of Algeria as French is transformed into anti-Arab racism, the historian Benjamin Stora speaks of the 'southernism' which grew up in Algeria and then transferred to France, on the model of the poor whites in the southern United States. In his view this 'recollection of exclusion will gradually transform itself into a latent sense of vindictiveness'. Allowing for the fact that not all the MNR or FN electorate are *pieds-noirs* (European colonists formerly living in Algeria, now resettled in France), even if the extreme right-wing militants often are, this phrase chimes well with what seems to be happening in these towns: the relationship with the immigrants and children of immigrants is still typified by the insecure poor white's attitude of colonial superiority. One of the Vitrolles militants summed it up in an image, which is picturesque if a little limited in its range: 'We bought those electors with nothing more than a street light outside their houses.' His explanation is limited in range only in the sense that a street light is never enough unless it forms part of a wider policy. But, when you see it in the context of the illegal pamphlet, it speaks loud and clear: nothing for the Cité des Pins, everything for the areas that want a street light. ❏

Michel Samson *is a journalist with* Le Monde *based in Marseilles*

ANNA BIKONT

Neighbours

On 10 July 1941, after two years of Soviet occupation, German troops arrived in the small Polish town of Jedwabne, north-east of Warsaw. That day, 1,600 Jews were herded into a barn by their Polish neighbours, doused with petrol and burned alive. The massacre went on record as a Nazi atrocity and, eight years later, a regional court found 22 Poles guilty of collaboration in the killing. A man of German origin was sentenced to death. Everyone else got between 8 and 15 years in prison and a memorial went up in Jedwabne putting the blame squarely on the Nazis; it will be replaced this summer with a new monument attributing the massacre to the Poles.

Last year, Jan Tomasz Gross, a Polish historian working in New York, published a book based on accounts by witnesses of the massacre, including Jews who had taken refuge in fields outside Jedwabne. Sasiedzi (Neighbours) appeared in an edition of only 2,000 copies but it provoked the most candid public debate on Polish–Jewish relations Poland has ever seen. President Kwasniewski acknowledged Polish responsibility for the killings and the Catholic Primate, Cardinal Jozef Glemp, issued an apology. The major weekly Wprost published a survey of anti-semitism in Poland's history. It concluded that during World War II, when 6 million Polish people died, 3 million of them Jews, not enough had been done to protect the country's Jewish population. Extreme right-wingers still deny that Poles participated in the Jedwabne massacre but, more generally, there is acceptance that local people were involved. The debate, initially fuelled by anxiety over public response in the US where Neighbours was due for publication in English, has taken on an unprecedented momentum as Poles and Jews reach out for surviving witnesses of the crime that has shattered Poland's long-cherished perception of itself as the innocent of European history.

IM

'Those Jews in Jedwabne, whether they were burned then or not, their fate was sealed,' said Zygmunt Laudański, trying to explain to me what happened in Jedwabne on 10 July 1941. 'The Germans would have killed them sooner or later. It's such a small thing, and someone is trying to stick it on Poles; my brothers what's more. We feel hurt.'

There is elegant china on the table and an excellent home-made gingerbread cake. Together with his brothers, Kazimierz Laudański is well known in the area; he is a bee-keeper, and clients come all the way from Germany to buy his honey. He has two brothers. Zygmunt Laudański was sentenced to 12 years for having taken part in the murder of the Jedwabne Jews, but served only six. Jerzy Laudański was sentenced to 15 and served eight. Zygmunt, now 82 years old, and Jerzy, 79, both living in Pisz, are the only two of those convicted still alive. When the press began to mention the Laudańskis in connection with Jedwabne, their elder brother Kazimierz, also living in Pisz, wrote to Adam Michnik, editor-in-chief of *Gazeta Wyborcza*, protesting against the slander against their good name: 'Like the whole nation, we too suffered under the Germans, the Soviets and the People's Republic of Poland.'

When I came to Pisz, it was Kazimierz who organised my meeting with his brothers. 'We come from a family of real Polish patriots. Many of us have been killed and tortured,' says Kazimierz Laudański. 'Pity you didn't meet our great-grandfather. It is no accident that all three of us are still alive. It's because we don't smoke, we don't drink. How can anyone say my brothers are hooligans? Whatever we did, we did out of patriotism, none of us has ever allied with the enemy against the nation.' 'It's a lie,' Zygmunt adds, 'that my brother and I killed over a thousand Jews. We are an honest family and always have been. This tragedy cannot be allowed to obscure our honesty.'

According to Szmul Wasersztajn, who was saved from the pogrom in Jedwabne and testified before the Jewish Historical Committee on 5 April 1945 (five years later, his report became the starting point for the investigation and trial of 1949): 'The order [to annihilate all the Jews] was given by the Germans, but it was Polish hooligans who took it up and carried it out in the most horrible ways; after all kinds of persecutions and tortures, they burned all the Jews in a barn. During the first pogroms and in the slaughter itself, the following scum distinguished themselves by their cruelty . . . The bandits searched Jewish homes, looking for the sick and the children left behind. The sick they carried to the barn themselves, small children they roped a few together by their legs and carried them on their backs, then put them on pitchforks and threw them on to smouldering coals.'

Among the 14 names Wasersztajn lists is Jerzy Laudański.

Sławomir S, a retired lawyer who left Jedwabne in the 1950s, says, 'Please don't mention my name; the Laudańskis are still alive and I do my shopping in Pisz. I met one of them once on the street and it sent shivers down my spine. I don't want any trouble. Maybe this fear has been in me since that time, but even now friends warn me about talking with you. I was ten years old in 1941. Some mothers wouldn't let their children out on that day, but I was the kind that would poke his nose into everything. And so I found myself in front of that barn. There was no big crowd, maybe 50 people, all men. Me and my friends were standing a little to the side. There was some fear that they would take us for Jewish kids and throw us in. Józef Kobrzyniecki, who had led the crowd when the Jews were made to carry the statue of Lenin, who'd beaten them the hardest and was going around houses to find the ones still trying to hide so he could finish them off with a bayonet, was there. He was throwing children into the burning barn. I saw it with my own eyes. A horrible crime was committed by Polish hands. When I grew up, I left Jedwabne immediately; since then I don't want to have anything to do with that place.'

'Our people organised the gathering of the Jews, but took no part in the burning,' says Kazimierz Laudański, who came to Jedwabne after the event. 'Their attitude was normal and peaceful. There was fear, pity and a terrible stench spread 300 metres beyond the site. Shocked Poles were saying it was a punishment from God. It was a devilish trick of the Germans: they directed the whole thing and used the Poles like actors in a theatre. But that the Poles wanted to burn the Jews: no, it was nothing like that.' He doesn't, however, deny that between 22 June 1941, when the Soviet occupation ended, and 10 July, Jews were murdered.

'There were many acts of revenge,' he says. 'But who were the victims? Only the spies and the communists would get lynched. Those got what they deserved, indeed. But the Jewish community and a gang of communists are two different things. Still, the communists, Polish and Jewish, shouldn't have been collaborating with the NKVD [Soviet People's Commissariat for Internal Affairs]. Treason is punishable by death.'

Jerzy Laudański: 'The mayor was giving orders, but it was the Germans' initiative. I was near the bakery and mixed with the crowd.'

'How come you were there at all?'

'Curiosity. There was something going on, the Germans were driving out the Jews. There was a huge Lenin statue, it must have weighed a ton and a half, and the Jews were carrying it. No one was crying over Lenin being taken away, except maybe some of his followers; after all, thousands of people had been sent to Siberia.'

'Were the Jews beaten at that point?.

'There were Poles in the market square, but I saw nothing of that sort. There may have been 500 Jews where I was standing, but I didn't see a single one beaten. The Jews were calmly talking and weeding the soil between the cobblestones. The Germans like to have things in order so the marketplace had to be weeded. And then everything went on by itself and seemed spontaneous.'

'How do you mean, spontaneous?'

'The Jews went spontaneously, obediently; the Poles were spontaneously behind them, because nobody was expecting that kind of tragedy. When they say that the Poles committed the murder, it's a slur on Poland and it's not true.'

'How were the Poles reacting?'

'Some were happy, some not, but people were curious. People were laughing and saying that just a little while ago, under the Soviets, the Jews wouldn't have been cleaning the marketplace.' He stuck unwaveringly to his 'spontaneous' version of events throughout our lengthy conversation.

It is only after many more conversations in Jedwabne that I notice a curious anomaly: those who now accuse the Jews of collaborating with the NKVD during the Soviet occupation and with the UB after the war, saw lots of Germans on the scene; those who feel sorry for their murdered neighbours did not see a single German taking part in the round-up of the Jews that day. They do not question the fact that the murder took place with the Germans' consent or at their suggestion. They simply say the Germans did not participate directly in the crime, just that one or two of them took photographs of the market square.

Kazimierz Mocarski remembers the stories told by his mother about how some people left town that day because they didn't want to get involved, while others from the area harnessed up horses and carts and came to Jedwabne, because there were houses, workshops and stores waiting to be plundered.

Both in eyewitness and second-hand accounts – for it is common knowledge among the older generation in Jedwabne who murdered and who got rich off the Jews – certain names recur persistently: Eugeniusz Kalinowski, Józef Kobrzyniecki, Czeslaw Mierzejewski, Stanislaw Sielawa, Józef Sobuta, Michal Trzaska – and the Laudański brothers. But even now, 60 years on, those who witnessed the crime are afraid to testify under their own names.

Marianna K from Jedwabne: 'They had clubs and rubber bars. They must have cut up the rubber the night before when they had decided on the murder. My father had said they were going to kill Jews two days earlier. He'd worked for the Jews helping them buy grain. When they drove the Jews out into the market square, I saw 12-year-olds chasing them, and many 17- or 19-year-olds. Sometimes they had been schoolmates. How could they have looked in their eyes when they were killing them? The Jews were so defenceless, so sad; they were so enraged.'

Kazimierz Mocarski: 'A few days later, one of my friends invited me to his place, he wanted to show me the Jewish flat he'd taken over. He told me how the Jews were beaten before the burning, how they were pushed around and forced to say Polish prayers.'

Jan Cytrynowicz, a harness maker, lived in Wizna before the war and was baptised there as a child: 'I came to Jedwabne after the war and lived with my Polish stepmother. My drinking buddies didn't know about my origins, so after a few drinks they'd start their stories: "I chased that one. I stabbed that one hard." They were proud if they had killed two or three Jews.'

Janusz Lech Dziedzic, a farmer from Przestrzel, a settlement two kilometres from the town, whose grandparents kept Szmul Wasersztajn hidden for sometime before he ended up in Antonina Wyrzykowska's place: 'I can't even imagine it, I mean the burning alone is so painful, and then the suffocating . . . And these people had never done them any harm. My father, Leon Dziedzic, had been a friend of Szmul Wasersztajn before the war, he would visit the synagogue with him, even though my father's friends said you have to trample on a cross on the way in. One day, some time in the 1970s, a man came to our yard when my parents were gone, and I knew it had to be Szmul, because

I remembered my grandmother's stories about his big protruding ears. He had come from Costa Rica. I showed him Grandma's picture in the family album; he kissed it, and cried like I'd never heard any child cry before. He said, "My mother gave me my life, but she couldn't help me keep it, and this woman risked the lives of her own eight children to save my lousy Jewish life."'

Before the war, Zygmunt's and Jerzy's father, Czeslaw Laudański, was active in the National Party, known in the area as the *narodówka*. The Nationalists had their own repertoire of songs such as: 'Beloved Poland,/You have millions of people,/But your land/Is still full of Jews./Rise, oh White Eagle,/Strike the Jews,/Let them no longer/Be our lords.' The NP shaped the consciousness of most Poles in Jedwabne and other towns and villages in the area. Its influence spread through the local church papers, the chief source of news and opinion. The bishop, Stanislaw Kostka Lukomski, well known for his anti-semitism, made sure this was reflected in the diocesan publications under his control.

Slawomir S: 'A little before the war, they'd already stopped the Jews trading in Jedwabne. They would stand in front of Jewish shops with crowbars. On Wednesdays, market day, the *narodówka* would usually come from Lomźa and locals joined them.'

Zygmunt Laudański: 'Of course I heard the slogan "Do not buy from a Jew" in church. There was another one: "Buy from your fellow

Roman Vishniac, Warsaw street vendors, 1938. Credit: © Mara Vishniac Kohn/Courtesy Howard Greenburg Gallery, New York City

countrymen." What's wrong with that in your own country? How can you call it anti-semitism? It was just advertising.'

According to reports taken down by the Jewish Historical Committee immediately after the war, Poles were murdering their Jewish co-citizens and stealing their property in many places in 1941. In a report from Tykocin, written in 1946 by the survivor Menachem Turek, we read: '[In July 1941] a crowd of Poles led by a group of nationalists, veterans of the pre-war boycott action, stormed Jewish houses and emptied them completely. With wild shouts of vengeance, threats and curses, the drunken mob robbed Jewish shops, taking whatever they could get their hands on.'

'It was the mob that killed the Jews on 10 July 1941,' Janusz Lech Dziedzic says, 'but had the priest stood in their way and said, "You'll go to hell for this and the devil will be squaring up with you," they would have listened to him, except, maybe, a couple of rogues who were already drunk at that point.'

When you go to Jedwabne today, it is not so difficult to imagine what might have happened 60 years ago. The local priest, Edward Orlowski, speaks the same language as his predecessor from the pre-war period. The local 'negationists' have consolidated around him.

'All this is intended to present us as murderers,' he said at a meeting with the population of Jedwabne. 'The Jews used to live on very good terms with the Poles. Those good relations were destroyed by the Jews during the Soviet occupation. And what's going on now? A continuation of that. When Poland was conquered in 1939, Jedwabne was probably the first town to organise a resistance movement. Poles were getting killed in Auschwitz. Why are they talking now about Jedwabne and not about those sufferings? It's not just Jedwabne that's being slandered, but the Polish nation as a whole. We have to defend ourselves.'

When I met him at the parish office, he said: 'If this Jedwabne thing is settled the way Gross wants it, it will be like piercing a hole in a ship and waiting for it to sink. The truth is, it was the Germans who committed the murder, not the Poles.'

'Do you ever come across anti-semitic statements in your parish?'

'There is no problem of anti-semitism here.'

Janusz Lech Dziedzic: 'Whenever anything bad happens in this particular community, it always turns out to be the Jews. I have

been hearing this since I was born – whether it was a matter of bad
government, bad weather or a dying cow, it was always the Jews' fault.
My father had money because he was a good farmer and a prudent
manager; my mum used to get up at night to pick strawberries and carry
them to the market in the morning. And the people would say we had
Jewish money for helping the Jews. Now I keep hearing that the Jews
got what they deserved, because they had been denouncing Poles to
the NKVD. I no longer have the energy to tell them that the Poles did
that too, I just ask, "And what were those children guilty of?" When
journalists started to come and my father talked with them, people
would ask me, "How much money did the Jews pay your father for that
interview?" I asked one of them, "And how much was your father paid
for murdering the Jews?" He turned beet-red. It hurts to know that your
father has raped a Jewish woman, cut her head off. One of my colleagues
visited me three times to reread Professor Gross's book and see if anyone
from his family was mentioned there. He said, "I have to know whether
any of my ancestors had bloody hands."'

'Do you remember the screams that day?' I ask Jerzy Laudański.

'When they were being shut in that barn, they did shout something
in Yiddish. I don't know what. It was a spontaneous scream, maybe to
be let out, maybe they were praying that way. And then they suffocated
from the smoke right away. When they went quiet, it was to the end of
time.' Zygmunt Laudański says he couldn't hear anything, because he
was standing more than 200 metres from the barn.

Kazimierz Mocarski: 'I was scything hay on the Biebrza banks, a few
kilometres from Jedwabne as the crow flies. The sun was going down,
so it must have been afternoon, when I heard a frightful screaming as if
from a large group of people. High-pitched-dominated so it must have
been women. It was getting more and more desperate and when it
stopped, there was thick black smoke rising into the sky. When I came
home, my mother told me: "They have burned the Jews."'

'Didn't that scream ever wake you up at night?' I ask Zygmunt
Laudański.

'A young body doesn't react that way, I never woke up at night.'

'What did you think about the whole thing?'

'What was I supposed to think? It happened and it's over.' ❑

Anna Bikont *is a Polish journalist with* Gazeta Wyborcza

JAN TOMASZ GROSS

Remembrance

Jedwabne is part of something bigger. The main defect of Polish historical narrative about the German occupation is the absence of the Jewish issue. According to the Polish historiographical canon, the Jewish and Polish experiences run parallel. I fell victim to this view myself. I wrote two monographs about Polish society under the German and Soviet occupations with no reference at all to the Jewish dimension. It was only with time that I began to understand that the destinies of Poles and Jews can't be treated separately. They share a common history tied in appalling knots, as in Jedwabne, where one half of a village murdered the other. Exploring the truth about Jedwabne will lead to a breakthrough in our mythologised historical consciousness . . .

Jedwabne follows the pattern of atrocities committed by neighbours throughout the world – from Yugoslavia to Rwanda – more than 50 years after the Holocaust. It's a huge challenge to modern civilisation . . .

The most important thing has to be the evolution of Polish social attitudes towards the tragedy experienced by the Jews under the German occupation. Of course it's important to honour the victims and the place with a memorial and an appropriate plaque. But the main thing is an open public debate in the Polish media. This has already begun . . . The fact that it is taking place at all was received with disbelief at first, and then with enormous relief. But it's a pity that so few of the people who are following the discussion on *Neighbours* know what it's about, even though it affects them directly. My book is practically unavailable in Polish bookshops – though you can find it on the Internet (www.pogranicze.sejny.pl). I see this kind of wide public discourse about ourselves as a potentially cathartic experience . . . Some shocking voices have been raised, of course, such as the piece in *Rzeczpospolita* where a murderer from Jedwabne is presented as a martyr . . . I'm concerned by the interview Slawomir Radon, head of the council of the Institute of National Memory (IPN), gave to *Gazeta Wyborcza*. The IPN is preparing a book about Jedwabne. If this publication turned out to be in any way an attempt to vindicate the crime, it would be an outrage . . .

Poland is one great Jewish cemetery. This was where – for logistical reasons – Hitler chose to localise all Nazi mass murders. The images Jews have retained

Jedwabne, 23 February 2001: the war memorial blaming the Nazis and the Gestapo for the massacre of 10 July 1941 is to be replaced this summer. Credit: AP Photo / Czarek Sokolowski

of the most tragic moments in their history have been passed from generation to generation. They remember not just indifference, but pleasure, delight on the faces of their Polish neighbours as they were hounded into ghettos, loaded trains and driven to their deaths. That's why an anti-semitic image or piece of graffiti anywhere near Auschwitz or Treblinka is far more painful that the same image in Paris, for example. Anti-Polish feeling in the US Jewish community – whose ancestors mostly left Poland long before the Holocaust – stems from the scorn they encountered there. This was what encouraged them to emigrate. The Jewish population in Poland was proportionally higher than anywhere else and there are more people of Polish-Jewish descent in the USA than there are Jews from other countries. Many of them also happen to be opinion formers. I didn't want to publish *Neighbours* in the US first to avoid generating anti-Polish feeling there. I was keen for the message of the book to get to the Poles before it went anywhere else. Because this is first and foremost a Polish issue, a matter of personal conscience. ❑

*From an interview by **Jerzy Slawomir Mac** published in* Wprost, *11 February 2001. Translated by Irena Maryniak. Sasiedzi* (Neighbours) *was published in Poland by Wydawnictwo Pogranicze (Borderlands Publishing House) in 2000. The English-language version is published in the USA by Princeton University Press (US$19.95)*

SLAVENKA DRAKULIC

Who's afraid of Europe?

A committed European voices new-felt doubts about the 'European project'

I live in Sweden, Croatia and Austria. Europe is my home.
Living as I do on both sides of real and imagined European borders,
constantly crossing them back and forth, as little as a year ago my faith
in the construction of a united Europe was far stronger than it is today.
That was before the elections in Austria, in Norway and Switzerland, in
the city of Antwerp; before the referendum on the euro in Denmark, or
incidents such as that in Malaga where a mob, mobilised by a neo-Nazi
website, chased Moroccan workers for three whole days. Similar events
are happening throughout Europe. A different Europe is emerging
before my eyes. This is not déjà vu: I belong to a generation that had
no experience of fascism. But I see xenophobia, nationalism and racism
growing everywhere. Moreover, because I come from Croatia, I can
tell when simple fear of the 'Other' becomes something different and
dangerous. Are what I see simply isolated incidents, or are they signs
that the European project is in danger?

I was born after World War II and grew up on a sleepy continent
divided by the 'iron curtain' and dwelling in the shadow of a possible
nuclear war. As school children, we would practise what we had to do
in the case of such an attack. We learned to recognise its characteristics
by heart: first a mushroom cloud would appear on the horizon, followed
by a blast of heat and ashes. You should hide behind any barrier, pull the
gas mask over your face and under no circumstances drink water (the bit
with the water was particularly strongly impressed upon us and I always
wondered why). Although only children, we understood that these
preparations would give us little protection if the horror described in

our textbooks really happened. Still, we practised dutifully. It did not help us. When the next war, the war in the Balkans, erupted much later, we were taken by surprise. Little did we know in the late 1950s that the war we would witness would be a local one, limited and low intensity – the war that would catch us totally unprepared.

My generation grew up with the idea that after WWII, such a war with its genocide, concentration camps and forced resettlement of entire populations was simply not possible. Europe had learned its lesson, the history teachers told us; such horrors could not happen again. Today, after the war in my country, in Bosnia and in Kosovo, I no longer believe Europe has learned that lesson. But perhaps I am wrong. Ours was a Balkan war. Are the Balkans Europe? Today the answer seems to be yes; tomorrow could bring a different answer. In which case, what exactly constitutes Europe? Where does it begin and end?

Berlin, 12 May 2000: NPD demonstrators with a banner declaring 'Prussian Law and Order' mark the anniversary of Hitler's takeover of Austria. Credit: Christian Jungeblodt

Even that seemed clearer in my schooldays: Europe was where the Soviet Union was not. The political changes of the last ten years blurred that childish certainty. The peoples of Europe have witnessed the collapse of communism and the disappearance of the common enemy; the speeding up of the integration process within the EU; its planned enlargement into the East; and the war in the Balkans. At the same time, globalisation threatens to engulf the entire world. These changes have happened too fast for people to grasp. They react as people always react to the unknown: with uncertainty and fear. While the known world is dissolving in front of their eyes, the shape of the new one is not yet clear. What is Europe? How far can it spread eastwards and still remain Europe? Is Turkey Europe? What about Russia?

These are not abstract questions. What is at stake is the effect of these changes on the life of Europeans, their work, income, education, language and so on. Increasingly, people feel they are losing control of their lives. Anxiety undermines their confidence in the world around them and their sense of certainty. This anxiety is vague, to be sure. But although it is not entirely identified or specified, often not even recognised as such, it is out there, palpable, measurable in opinion polls, referendums, election results; articulated as doubts about the necessity of a common currency, of integration and enlargement; about the free circulation of the workforce. Yet vague as it is, this anxiety is already having its effect on the political life of some countries and might perhaps soon bring substantial changes to the political landscape of Europe.

The mechanism of exploiting fear is simple and well known. As an individual, you may feel lost and confused, swept away by the speed and magnitude of historical events. Suddenly, there is somebody offering you shelter, a feeling of belonging, a guarantee of security. We are of the same blood, we belong to the same territory, our people first, so goes the rhetoric. To scared ears it is soothing to hear old-fashioned words like 'blood', 'soil', 'territory', 'Us', 'Them'. You feel stronger, no longer alone, confronted with the 'Others', with too many immigrants, Muslims, Turks, refugees, Africans, asylum seekers, Gypsies, or even with too much big bureaucracy that wants to rule your life from Brussels. Once you have found the pleasure of belonging, 'Others' don't frighten you any longer. From the fear of the unknown to the creation of the 'known' enemy is often only a small step. It doesn't need much more than that vague sense of anxiety, plus a political leader who knows how to exploit it: the media will do the rest.

It looks as if the new, darker picture of Europe started to surface with the victory of the Freedom Party and Jörg Haider in Austria. The truth, however, is that his electoral success simply made that anxiety more visible. Haider has been the most successful, but others such as Umberto Bossi, Christoph Blocher, Karl Hagen, Edmund Stoiber, Filip de Winter, Pia Kjersgaard or Jean-Marie Le Pen are catching up. Belgium's ultra-nationalist Vlaams Blok recently celebrated the biggest victory for the extreme right in Europe since the Freedom Party entered the Austrian coalition government (see p64). The success of Bossi's Northern League in Italy, now in government with Silvio Berlusconi, is based on xenophobic immigration politics. The Danish People's Party got 18% in the last polls thanks to aggressive xenophobic propaganda. Pia Kjersgaard openly says that immigrants, especially Muslims, are threatening the safety of families and the Christian values of genuine Danes, 'their very Danishness', as she puts it. She went as far as comparing cultural pluralism to the Holocaust. The recent referendum rejecting the euro in Denmark was no surprise. In France, the extreme right is being re-elected on the basis of its anti-immigrant policies in towns it controls (see p70).

Even in Germany, Prime Minister Gerhard Schröder suffered a defeat in opinion polls after having suggested that Germany 'import' 10,000 computer experts, mostly from India. Although it has been estimated that Germany needs some 70,000 computer experts to catch up with international advances in information technology, 56% of the population opposed his plan. In another poll, only 4% of the Germans expressed enthusiasm for the free circulation of labour within the EU. The rise in popularity of Norway's Progress Party is part of the same movement to close borders and build new walls; as is the success of Blocher's Swiss People's Party, which jumped to 22.6% in the latest federal elections; up from 14.95% in 1995. 'People are feeling insecure in a brand new globalised world; they think isolation makes them more secure,' explained an official from the Swiss foreigners commission.

Even such a cursory survey indicates the growing success of ultra-right-wing parties across Europe. What emerges is not necessarily a pattern of brown and black shirts again, but a new pattern of the exploitation of people's growing anxiety by the populist rhetoric of right-wing parties. These parties do not invent the anxiety; but they are the only ones to have their fingers on the people's pulses, to recognise their fears and give shape to inchoate feelings of dissatisfaction. Focusing it on xenophobia is easy: there are 'Others' in every society. As long as this xenophobia expresses itself only in polemic, it is not so alarming. More alarming is something like the opinion poll published in *Der Spiegel* last year showing that the majority of Germans agree with some views on the extreme right, particularly its attitude to immigrants. And it is alarming, too, that this kind of rhetoric has translated into election results in the last year or so. It cannot be dismissed as a purely marginal phenomenon.

Anxiety is sweeping over post-communist Europe as well. The enthusiasm of the first years after the fall of communism has been replaced with disappointment. Once more, a united Europe looks distant: new walls are springing up to replace the old Berlin Wall, conditions for joining the EU are hard to meet and the date is pushed further into the future. This opens up room for nationalists and anti-Europeans, who argue that the newly won sovereignty should not be given up so easily. They spread fear of multinational companies that will buy their country, of the Americanisation of their culture, of globalisation. It is not surprising when somebody like Slobodan Milosevic uses this kind of language. Yet democrats like Vaclav Klaus, the former Czech prime minister, are speaking out against the EU as well. 'Europe is now fundamentally challenging the nation state, particularly its sovereignty,' he said, speaking in Austria in June 1999. Klaus, too, speaks of assimilation and the loss of national identity: 'We don't want to become Euroczechs!' Hungary's Prime Minister Viktor Orban is also sceptical about the EU, not to mention the Slovak populist Vladimir Meciar or the Hungarian nationalist and anti-semite Istvan Csurka. Post-communist Eastern Europe is far away from a united Europe in another sense as well: 67% of Poles, for example, believe that when their country joins the EU they will become second-class citizens.

The success of right-wing nationalist, xenophobic and anti-European parties and populist leaders presents a danger to integration in both western and eastern Europe as their leaders tell people their national, cultural and social identity is in jeopardy. Not only will foreigners take all their jobs, but – and this seems more important – society itself will be transformed beyond recognition. In the language of the right wing, a multicultural society means cultural disintegration. This does sound threatening to people. It is irrelevant whether we call this political egocentrism, regional nationalism or new regionalism; the result is the same everywhere: homogenisation, mobilisation of defensive mechanisms and isolationist politics.

Research done last March at the Institut für Demoskopie Allensbach on the fear of losing their identity in a united Europe, over 50% of Germans said they thought a German identity would be lost – compared with 35% in 1994. But what is the identity they would like to protect so much? In general, the question is not asked until that identity is challenged or threatened in some way. From a personal viewpoint, national identity is a given, something as 'natural' as the colour of the eyes. Culture, history, language, myth, memory, mentality, values, habits, cuisine are all part of the national identity that dominates our sense of personal identity. Recently, in the small French town of Millau a man was imprisoned for destroying a local McDonald's restaurant. But the process turned into a manifestation of support for José Bové. He became a national hero because he had articulated the French fear of US domination of their culinary tradition and their right to make cheese out of non-pasteurised milk. Anything else would threaten their national identity. You cannot ask the Germans to stop drinking their beer or the Dutch not to grow tulips. When they were negotiating their entry into the EU, the Swedes were particularly keen to make sure that chewing-tobacco would not be forbidden for them – it is a matter of their national identity.

On the other hand, in newly established states like Croatia, for example, one can actually observe the process by which a national identity is constructed and its symbols invented by using a clutch of national myths and rewriting its history. It only proves what modern anthropology argues: that national identities do not represent a set of eternal, ready-made cultural, historical or social characteristics, but are no more than cultural construct, inventions, not 'natural' at all. The archaic, populist rhetoric of Croatia's Franjo Tudjman didn't want to know that identity is always constructed in relation to the Others; it wanted only to exclude these Others, the Serbs.

Yet there are many examples that demonstrate it is possible to identify with more than one nation and one culture. I met a Turkish *Gastarbeiter* on a train in Germany, and he complained: 'When I'm in Germany, they consider me a Turk, but when I visit Turkey, they don't take me as one of them, they consider me a foreigner, a German. I always feel I have to choose between the two, and I don't like that.' 'Well, how do *you* feel? What do *you* think you are?' I asked. 'I am both,' he replied. It was only others who had a problem with his identity. But in a nationalism culture, identity is made up of borders, territory and blood and one is forced to choose one nation, sometimes with unexpected results.

Some years ago, two small villages in Istria were caught in a dispute between two newly founded states, Croatia and Slovenia. When Slovene journalists asked people there if they were Slovenes, they said yes. But when Croatian journalists asked them if they were Croats, they offered the same response. Confused journalists sought an explanation. Finally somebody told them that 'either/or' was the wrong question. They felt strongly about their identity, but defined it in regional not national terms: they were Istrians. In a 1991 census, about 20% of people in that region declared themselves Istrians though, according to the regulations, they should have declared themselves 'Others'. This anti-nationalist demonstration against Tudjman's government carried a clear message: for Istrians, nationality and identity do not necessarily overlap. Nation, as a political category, was only one aspect of their identity, and less strong than the transnational regional one. 'The EU will only achieve a solid basis of legitimacy when Europeans perceive a European political identity. This does not imply that they would no longer feel themselves to be Swedes, Finns, Frenchmen, Portuguese, Czechs, Poles or Hungarians, but that the sense of a common European destiny has been added to these,' writes Ingmar Karlsson.

I recall the earlier census of 1981 in Yugoslavia when almost 10% of the population declared themselves Yugoslavs. Further analysis demonstrated that this was the voice of the post-war, young urban generation. Was this the beginning of the Yugoslav nation? I don't think so. I think people were still very much aware of their ethnic identities. In my own experience, this was simply a matter of adding one common Yugoslav identity to another – Serbian, Croatian or Bosnian.

If nations are not eternal, and national and personal identities are a construct, then they can be reconstructed. Another kind of imagined community can be created. Perhaps this is the right time to think about a new model of identity to balance the growing anxiety in Europe. Instead of using cultural exclusion, can identities be created by combining the sum of ethnic, regional, national, transnational elements of identity? If identity can be reconstructed in terms of a multiple identity, can this be used to establish a European identity? Not as a standardised and globalised community, but as a non-hierarchical community of diverse cultures with people feeling they belong to a specific culture but not to a state – like the Istrians. Can transregionalism help to overcome the anxiety people feel about integration?

Because of the way I live, a united but diverse Europe is a possibility that enriches me and gives me greater freedom. But to create such a Europe, people need to be convinced that they, too, are gaining, not losing something. We are at the point when losing seems more obvious, when fear overtakes hope in the future. Who is afraid of Europe? Bronislaw Geremek, the former Polish foreign minister has already answered that question: 'Europe is afraid of itself.' ❏

Slavenka Drakulic is a Croatian writer and journalist. This is an edited version of her speech to the Meeting of European Cultural Journals, Vienna & Bratislava, November 2000. © eurozine

FLASHPOINT

Z

Algerians are bracing for further upheaval as revelations about civilian
murders by the anti-terrorist services combine with a nationwide
revolt instigated by the 6 million Berber minority and general disquiet at the
government's policy of 'harmony' with former Islamist guerillas (*Index* 1/01).

Two years into a doubtful mandate, President Abdelaziz Bouteflika has
introduced a draconian revision of the criminal code that will punish reporters
or publications found guilty of slandering the president or any other 'constituent
body' of the state with fines of between US$700 and US$70,000, and prison
terms of up to three years. The press corps dubbed it the 'Dilem' Amendment
after a cartoonist who regularly lampoons Bouteflika. The new legislation
skilfully undermines the 1990 Information Code, which nurtured a far
more varied media here than in Morocco or Tunisia, in spite of the state of
emergency that has existed since the cancellation of the 1991 elections.

On 18 June, media lawyer Khaled Bourayou told algeria-interface.com:
'What's the point of the enormous fines the amendments levy unless it's to hit
the pocket? Publishers and managing directors will be judged on the ability to
avoid costly court cases, rather than on their ability to run a newspaper. The
aim is to kill the media, to end journalism.'

As one of the 'constituent bodies' to benefit from the new code, the security
forces that rule energy-rich Algeria will henceforth tolerate far less scrutiny
of their role in the 10-year conflict with Islamist forces which continues to
kill 200–300 people every month, according to Amnesty International. *La Sale
Guerre* by Habib Souaïdia, published in Paris in February, is just the most recent
in a series of testimonies that directly implicate the military in the massacres of
civilians that were hitherto ascribed to Islamic guerrillas.

Souaïdia, a former counter-insurgency officer now living in Paris, names
the killers, torturers and officers responsible for well-documented raids against
civilians suspected of Islamic sympathies in Lakhardia, 80km east of Algiers. 'If
we closed with terrorists,' he writes, 'we used to cut off the heads of the ones
we shot and bring them back. We'd leave the bodies to scavengers . . .' His
detailed accounts of atrocities executed by special mobile units have horrified
both the military establishment and public opinion.

The security forces confront a different challenge now after several hundred
thousand Berbers descended on Algiers in mid-June to protest against police

brutality and demand that Tamazight, the Berber language, be officially recognised. Four people died and 1,000 were injured in clashes that pitted rural Berbers, wearing the Tamazight symbol for 'Z' on their green and yellow shirts, against the majority Arab-speaking Algérois. The demonstration occurred after two months of rioting triggered when police killed a teenager in Beni Douala, in the Berber stronghold of Kabylia, on 20 April. Some 60 unarmed protesters were subsequently killed by paramilitary forces.

'They shot people, tracked them down, killed them in the forest, on the edges of villages well away from the protests, using live ammunition and machine guns,' reported French Green MEP Hélène Flautre at a Paris press conference on 31 May. She had escaped her minders during an EU trade trip to Algeria and gone to Kabylia to hear what had happened. 'This was no urban guerilla warfare,' she continued. 'All these acts were driven by hate. It is my conviction that they acted on orders to kill.' Significantly, President Bouteflika made no public comment on the killings until ten days had elapsed.

When he did, it was to acknowledge that Tamazight should be recognised in the constitution, a move he had determinedly ruled out three years before when Arabic was made compulsory in all official transactions. Berbers were promised education in their own tongue in 1994 and 1995, but recognition of Tamazight is seen as threatening an Algerian identity rooted in Arabic and Islam.

More violent protest was expected on 25 June, the third anniversary of the assassination of Berber folk singer and nationalist Matoub Lounes, who was mown down on a mountain road in Kabylia shortly before President Bouteflika opted for Arabic (*Index* 5/98). Matoub's next album, released after his death, contained a parody of the national anthem that accused the government of colluding with the Islamists – a message equally pertinent today.

The more secular Berber minority was often seen as providing the government with a political counterweight in its fight against Islamic fundamentalism. But the balance of power is changing. President Bouteflika's programme of 'civil harmony', which gave former guerrilla fighters an amnesty in exchange for their confessions, is proving deeply unpopular. He may be seeking to strengthen his hand by sacrificing his Berber partners for allies of a more conservative, confessional stamp.

But he may have underestimated the Z factor. ❑

MG

A censorship chronicle incorporating information from the American Association for the Advancement of Science Human Rights Action Network (AAASHRAN), Amnesty International (AI), Article 19 (A19), Alliance of Independent Journalists (AJI), the BBC Monitoring Service Summary of World Broadcasts (SWB), Centre for Journalism in Extreme Situations (CJES), the Committee to Protect Journalists (CPJ), Canadian Journalists for Free Expression (CJFE), Glasnost Defence Foundation (GDF), Information Centre of Human Rights & Democracy Movements in China (ICHRDMC), Instituto de Prensa y Sociedad (IPYS), The UN's Integrated Regional Information Network (IRIN), the Inter-American Press Association (IAPA), the International Federation of Journalists (IFJ/FIP), Human Rights Watch (HRW), the Media Institute of Southern Africa (MISA), Network for the Defence of Independent Media in Africa (NDIMA), International PEN (PEN), Open Media Research Institute (OMRI), Pacific Islands News Association (PINA), Radio Free Europe/Radio Liberty (RFE/RL), Reporters Sans Frontières (RSF), the World Association of Community Broadcasters (AMARC), World Association of Newspapers (WAN), the World Organisation Against Torture (OMCT) and other sources

AFGHANISTAN

Saboor Salehzai, the BBC World Service translator in Kabul who was arrested on 16 December, was released four days later (*Index* 2/2001). (RSF)

On 14 March Taliban Minister of Information Qadratullah Jamal ordered the closure of the BBC office in Kabul and gave correspondent **Kate Clark** 36 hours to leave the country. The expulsion was in response to Clark's interviews with ordinary Afghans who said they disapproved of the planned destruction of two 1,400-year-old statues of the Buddha carved out of cliffs in Bamian, 100 miles northwest of Kabul. Pictures on Al Jazeera TV in Qatar on 19 March showed scenes of a huge explosion and plumes of smoke rising from the mountainside. A Taliban spokesman said that Islamic 'scholars' had debated for months, finally deciding that the Buddhas were 'idolatrous' and must be destroyed. (RSF, CPJ, *New York Times*)

ALGERIA

Arab Izarouken, publication director of the daily *Voix de l'Oran*, and journalist **Aouari Abdelkrim** were sentenced to six months' imprisonment for libel on 7 April. The charges arose from the publication of remarks by a member of an organisation of war veterans' children who named 14 people as 'a local Mafia, responsible for the squandering of land in Oran'. (WAN)

On 17 April **Ahmed Benaoum**, publication director of the daily *Al Raï*, was informed by Oran's tribunal that the supreme court had confirmed the two-month prison sentence for defamation originally imposed on 12 December. On the same day, the same court told him that he would not be imprisoned as he had received

a presidential pardon on 30 October last year. *Al Raï*'s director asked the minister of justice to open an inquiry into the case. Benaoum was prosecuted for publishing an article which implicated a senator in a corruption case. (RSF)

ANGOLA

On 22 February unidentified gunmen entered the home of **Isaias Soares**, journalist with independent Catholic Radio Ecclesia and Voice of America, opening fire on him. The gunmen were forced to flee when Soares's two brothers, both policemen, returned fire. No one was injured. The attack may have been triggered by Soares's recent reporting on criminal gangs in Malanje. Fearing that it could lead to further aggravation Soares did not lay criminal charges. Soares has previously faced a ban which prevented him from entering official institutions and has been detained by police (*Index* 6/1999). (MISA)

ARGENTINA

The government has imposed a swingeing 21% VAT on newspapers and magazines, it was reported on 4 May, despite the fact that President Fernando de la Rua maintained as recently as 15 March that taxes on the press endanger plurality of information. (IAPA)

AUSTRIA

On 18 April, **Anton Pelinka** won his appeal against Jörg Haider, who had successfully sued him for libel in May last year over Pelinka's comment that Haider's description of the

Simon Davies on

PRIVACY

Ursula Owen on

HATE SPEECH

Patricia Williams on

RACE

Gabriel Garcia Marquez on

JOURNALISM

John Naughton on

THE INTERNET

... all in **INDEX**

SUBSCRIBE & SAVE

UK and overseas

○ **Yes! I want to subscribe to *Index*.**

❏ 1 year (4 issues)   £32   Save 16%
❏ 2 years (8 issues)   £60   Save 21%
❏ 3 years (12 issues)   £84   **You save 26%**

Name _____

Address _____

                                              BOB5

£ _____ enclosed. ❏ Cheque (£) ❏ Visa/MC ❏ Am Ex ❏ Bill me
(*Outside of the UK, add £10 a year for foreign postage*)

Card No. _____

Expiry _____ Signature _____

❏ I do not wish to receive mail from other companies.

INDEX   ✉ Freepost: INDEX, 33 Islington High Street, London N1 9BR
             ☎ (44) 171 278 2313   Fax: (44) 171 278 1878
             e tony@indexoncensorship.org

SUBSCRIBE & SAVE

North America

○ **Yes! I want to subscribe to *Index*.**

❏ 1 year (4 issues) $48   Save 12%
❏ 2 years (8 issues) $88   Save 19%
❏ 3 years (12 issues) $120   **You save 26%**

Name _____

Address _____

                                              BOB5

$ _____ enclosed. ❏ Cheque ($) ❏ Visa/MC ❏ Am Ex ❏ Bill me

Card No. _____

Expiry _____ Signature _____

❏ I do not wish to receive mail from other companies.

INDEX   ✉ Freepost: INDEX, 708 Third Avenue, 8th Floor, New York, NY 10017
             ☎ (44) 171 278 2313   Fax: (44) 171 278 1878
             e tony@indexoncensorship.org

Nazi concentration camps as 'punishment camps' trivialised the nature of the Third Reich (*Index* 4/2000, 1/2001). The Vienna Supreme Court overruled a lower court's decision that Haider had been defamed by the statement. (*International Herald Tribune*)

AZERBAIJAN

On 23 March in the Salya region, police arrested local *Express* reporter, **Gylynjkhan Nesirili** after he tried to meet local residents who objected to agricultural reforms in their region. (CJES)

On 3 April **Idrak Abbasov**, a journalist for the newspaper *Impuls*, was beaten by police after photographing them illegally trying to remove a newspaper booth owned by distribution company Qaya. **Iltifat Babashov**, Qaya's deputy director and other employees tried to block the police. Abbasov was subsequently taken to Baku's Binagadi police station. (JuHI)

Police harassed, attacked and arrested a number of journalists covering a protest rally by the opposition Democratic Party of Azerbaijan on 21 April. **Suleyman Mammedli**, editor-in-chief of tri-weekly *Hurriyet* was beaten and insulted by Yashar Aliyev, deputy chief of the Baku senior police department. Two other *Hurriyet* journalists, **Heidar Oguz** and **Jesur Mammedov**, were also beaten and insulted. Nesimi District Court ordered Oguz to be imprisoned for seven days and Mammedov for 12. (Journalists' Trade Union, RFE/RL)

An application by the Journalists' Trade Union (JuHI) to hold a street rally for World Press Freedom Day on 3 May was rejected by the Baku authorities on the grounds that 'the streets will be very busy'. (JuHI)

On 11 May a Baku court sentenced **Shayin Djafarli**, deputy editor of the independent daily *Yeni Musavet* to one year of corrective labour on charges of 'hooliganism'. He was freed immediately under the terms of an amnesty. Djafarli was arrested in November 2000 after a confrontation in the editorial office with residents from Mashtaga who were protesting the paper's coverage of political developments in Azerbaijan. (RFE/RL)

BANGLADESH

On 25 February nine journalists were assaulted by police during a press conference organised by students in Tangail, northern Dhaka. Three were hospitalised. (RSF)

The unnamed correspondent of *Dainik Bhorer Kagoj* in Rajbari was arrested on 26 February after a complaint by the officials of the hospital whom he accused of corruption. He was beaten by police, splashed with boiling water and forced to sleep in a four-foot-wide room. (RSF)

On 9 March **Panthanibas Barua**, daily *Purbakon* correspondent in Chittagong, was arrested for publishing articles on corruption in the local police. On 19 April the Chittagong office was attacked by a group of ruling Awami

League cadres, led by Mamunur Rashid Mamun, the city's ward commissioner. **Iskander Ali Chowdhury**, *Purbakon's* chief sub-editor, and journalist **Jalaluddin Ahmed Chowdhury** were assaulted. Mamun had apparently taken exception to an article published about him. Chowdhury has filed a case against Mamun under the Public Safety Act. On 7 May Mamun reportedly surrendered himself to police. (Media Watch, CPJ, RSF)

In late March it was reported that **Tipu Sultan**, the United News of Bangladesh journalist who was severely beaten in January this year (*Index* 2/2001), may lose the use of both his hands if he does not quickly receive specialist orthopaedic treatment. Despite identifying his attackers, no one has been arrested. (RSF)

Sawkat Jamil, photographer with *Sangbad*, and **Jewel**, photographer with Agence France-Presse, were attacked by police on 1 April while covering opposition activists on the first day of a 48-hour general strike in Dhaka. The police initially blamed the journalists for throwing a home-made bomb. They were eventually released. (Media Watch, Hotline Bangladesh)

Later that day **Samrat**, Dhaka University correspondent for the daily *Prothom Alo*, was assaulted by members of the government's student wing. The Chatra League activists were angry with his reports on campus politics. (Media Watch)

On 2 April reporters **Galman Safi** and **Mashiur** of *Dainik Bangla Bazar* and **Fazle Azim** of *Dainik Inquilab* were assaulted by supporters of Mirza Abbas, a prominent leader of the opposition Bangladesh National Party, while collecting information for a story in Shahjahanpur. (Media Watch, RSF)

The same day, opposition activists burned a *Bangladesh Observer* vehicle, injuring its driver, and bombs were thrown at the office of the pro-government newspaper *Ajker Kagoj*. The blasts only damaged property, but the journalists inside had to evacuate the premises. (Media Watch, RSF)

Prabir Sikder, Faridpur correspondent for the daily *Janakantha*, was critically injured by gunmen who shot and stabbed him on 20 April. Local journalists believe that Sikder, who had to have his shattered right leg amputated, was attacked because of his recent stories about Musa-bin-Shamsher, brother-in-law of the present health minister, and two other prominent individuals who collaborated with the Pakistani army during the 1971 liberation war. (Media Watch, CPJ)

On 21 April **Nahar Ali**, correspondent for the Khulna-based *Dainik Anirban*, died in hospital from injuries he suffered at the hands of kidnappers on 17 April. Ali had his arms and legs broken before being left for dead. It is believed that Ali was kidnapped from his home for reporting on local criminal gangs. (CPJ)

Shaidul Alal Imran, correspondent for *Manavjamin* in Feni and editor of the local daily *OTO-EB*, was attacked by supporters of a local politician. Imran's left arm was broken, but he avoided being wounded when his assailants shot at him three times. Imran had recently reported that the politician's supporters had been fraudulently collecting money. (WAN)

Nazmul Imam, district correspondent for *Manavjamin*, narrowly escaped being kidnapped by a group of eight to ten masked men while on his way home on the night of 6 May. Imam had recently written reports about a local terrorist group, a drug smuggler and underworld activities. (Media Watch)

Iqbal Mansoor, a photographer for the daily *Shyamol Sylhet*, was kidnapped while covering a story in Sylhet on 7 May. Mansoor was released after he agreed not to publish photos he had taken, tell the police who his kidnappers were or file a case against them. (Media Watch)

On 21 May, 16 people were charged with the murder last July of **Shamsur Rahman**, special correspondent for the daily *Janakantha* and freelance reporter for the BBC (*Index* 5/2000). Among the accused are five journalists, including Mizanur Rahman Tota, Jessore bureau chief of the daily *Inquilab*. Eight of the accused are still at large, including Nasiruddin Kalu of the governing Awami League. (Media Watch, BBC)

After a persistent harassment by the authorities, the independent printing house Magic was forced to cease business on 12 March. Affected publications include many of the leading state newspapers, such as *Belarusskaya Delovaya Gazeta*, *Nasha Svaboda* and *Narodnaya Volya*. (RSF)

Dmeitri Yegorov, a 17-year-old photojournalist, was detained, beaten and threatened by police while covering the opposition-organised 'Freedom March' in Grodno on 25 March. His camera and dictaphone were broken and he was taken to hospital suffering from severe concussion. (*International Herald Tribune*)

Czech journalist **Michal Plavec** was detained and expelled on 13 April for what the foreign ministry said was 'improper conduct'. It said Plavec 'co-ordinated the work of a foreign organisation in Belarus and has time and again been involved in unsanctioned mass actions accompanied by arrests.' Though an official of the Czech-based People in Need Foundation, Plavac was working at the time for the Czech weekly *Respekt* newspaper. (RFL/RL)

The authorities announced on 11 May that they had arrested members of a gang suspected of having kidnapped ORT cameraman **Dmitri Zavadski**, who disappeared at Minsk airport in July 2000 (*Index* 1/2001). The suspects, who are all current or former security agents, carried out the abduction for the Russian far-right Russian National Unity, according to official reports. Zavadski was formerly personal cameraman to the president. He was imprisoned for two months in 1997 with ORT journalist **Pavel Sheremet**, following their report on smuggling and poor security along the Lithuanian border (*Index* 5/1997, 6/1997, 2/1998, 4/1998). (RSF)

BELGIUM

Interior Minister Johan Sauwens in the Flanders region was forced to resign after it was revealed that he attended a meeting of SS veterans and Nazi sympathisers, it was reported on 11 May. Sauwens tried to shrug off his presence as an 'error of judgement', but a videotape showed him enthusiastically singing Nazi songs. (*International Herald Tribune*)

BOTSWANA

Chris Bishop, the British head of news and current affairs at Bostwana TV, resigned on 1 May, complaining at excessive government interference. His resignation was prompted when officials blocked a documentary due to be aired about Mariette Bosch, the first white woman to be hanged. (*Press Gazette*)

BRAZIL

Journalists at the daily *Zero Hora* in Porto Alegro were pressured at police headquarters to reveal their sources in a case involving police commissioner Pedro Urdangarin, it was reported on 8 March. Journalists **Nilson Mariano** and **Altair Nobre** had pub-

lished official documents about an investigation by Urdangarin's department which included an accusation of 'passive corruption' by Urdangarin in reference to extortion by his officers. (Periodistas)

Sao Paolo's state-owned weekly *O Debate* is threatened with closure as a result of longstanding lawsuits by magistrate Antonio José Magdalena and prosecutor Carlos Aparecido Rinard. The newspaper reported that Magdalena lived in an expensive house paid for with public funds, while Rinard felt slighted by a number of articles. Director **Sergio Fleury Moraes** states that he has been the victim of legal persecution for ten years. He cited the time when Judge Magdalena jailed him for seven months in the municipal prison which was especially reopened for him. It had been used as a kennel for years. (Periodistas)

BRITAIN

The *Sunday Times* is seeking to gain clarification in the High Court over procedures for dealing with cases of breach of confidence involving members of the armed forces. Since November 1999, the paper has been restrained by injunctions from reporting allegations by a former member of the Force Research Unit, who uses the pseudonym **Martin Ingrams** (*Index* 1/2001). His allegations include conspiracy by army personnel to murder and to pervert the cause of justice. (www.cryptome.org)

The Scottish Freedom of Information Bill, published on

1 March, has been praised for allowing greater openness than its English and Welsh counterpart. The bill requires that the disclosure of information may only be refused when it would '*substantially* prejudice' the effective conduct of public affairs, law enforcement, national security or defence. The British equivalent requires only that 'prejudice' be established. (*Guardian*)

In March it was reported that Conrad Black, owner of the *Daily Telegraph* and *Spectator*, had written an article to the magazine accusing contributor **Taki Theodoracopulos** of anti-semitism and contributing to Britain's 'anti-Israeli bias'. (*The Times*)

Ann Robinson, presenter of BBC 1's *Watchdog* and *The Weakest Link*, was accused in March of racial hatred for her attempt to eliminate the Welsh in BBC2's spoof *Room 101* programme. Martyn Jones of the Welsh Select Affairs Committee has complained: 'If [her] remarks had been about black people, Pakistanis or gays it would not have gone out.' (*The Times, Guardian*)

In early March the vice squad raided the Saatchi Gallery in London in a bid to seize two photographs taken by US photographer **Tierney Gearon**. One of her children is depicted standing naked on a beach in a 'scary' cartoon mask while, in another, her son pees in the snow during a family holiday. The photographs, part of the gallery's *I am a Camera* exhibition, were declared to 'depict children in sexually compromising positions and likely to encourage paedophiles'. The gallery refused to remove the photographs from the exhibition. The police announced on 16 March that no action would be taken against either gallery or author after the Crown Prosecution Service found that no offence had been committed. (*Guardian, Daily Telegraph*)

On 22 March three prison inmates launched a High Court battle to win the right to vote for the 52,000 prisoners in custody in England and Wales. Nineteen European states allow prisoners to vote, with a further eight extending the right to certain categories of offenders. Edward Fitzgerald QC, representing the inmates, called the disqualification from the vote an illegitimate punishment and maintained that it was illogical to deny those found guilty and jailed the right to vote when those found guilty, but not imprisoned, could still participate. Allowing prisoners the right to vote would ensure MPs became more involved in prisoner issues, he said. (*Guardian*)

On 4 April Dame Stella Rimmington, the former head of MI5, announced her decision to proceed with publication of her memoirs in spite of opposition in Parliament. She has been offered a six-figure advance and has been in consultation with her successor Sir Stephen Lander over the contents. However, MI6 head Sir Richard Dearlove and defence officials are strongly opposed to publication. (*Guardian*)

On 26 April Trade and Industry Secretary Stephen Byers announced his decision to drop threats to sue the *Daily Mail* over allegations that he 'buried' an official report into former Labour Paymaster-General Geoffrey Robinson's financial affairs. A biography, *The Paymaster*, by Tom Bowyer, which alleges that he denied receipt of a £200,000 payment from fraudulent tycoon Robert Maxwell, went on sale on 22 March despite government efforts to suppress it. Byers has come under increased pressure to publish a classified report referred to in the book, an extract of which was published in the *Daily Mail* along with criticism of Byers' conduct. (*Daily Telegraph*)

The shadow cabinet was criticised on 14 April for failing to declare to the Register of Members' Interests a sum of £1m raised to maintain their offices. The figure, amounting to £50,000 per cabinet member, was raised by the Front Bench Club, a 200-strong group who donate £5,000 each in return for invitations to political functions. (*The Times*)

Sunday Mirror editor Colin Mayler announced his resignation on 12 April after the collapse of the trial of Leeds United footballers accused of seriously injuring an Asian student in the city. Mr Justice Poole discharged the court following publication in the *Mirror* of an interview in which the father of the victim gave the opinion that the attack had been racially motivated. Mr Mayler could faces criminal charges for contempt of court, which may include a prison sentence of up to two years. (*Guardian*)

In a pre-trial hearing on the **David Shayler** case (*Index* 5/2000), ending 16 May, Mr Justice Moses ruled that the defendant has no defence under the Human Rights Act for allegations of breaching the Official Secrets Act. The judge's ruling means that Shayler will be unable to invoke a public interest defence in his trial. The defence argued that it should be for the jury to decide whether the sanctions imposed under the act are 'proportionate to the aim pursued' and necessary in a democratic society, in accordance with tests established at the European Court of Human Rights. In a preparatory hearing on 26 April, Shayler pleaded not guilty to charges of disclosing classified information and documents obtained as a member of MI5. The trial has been delayed until November to allow the defence to appeal. (*Daily Telegraph, Guardian*)

The editor of the *Sunday Express*, **Michael Pilgrim**, was officially sacked on 22 May by its new proprietor, Richard Desmond. Pilgrim's departure followed publication of a leaked memo in which he complained of Desmond's interference in editorial decisions, suppression of legitimate stories, pressure to run unjustified stories to settle scores and refusal to publish stories critical of advertisers. (*Guardian*)

BURUNDI

Gabrielle Nikundana, a journalist with independent Bonesha FM and Deutsche-welle radio, has been held by the intelligence service, Documentation Nationale, since

12 March. Nikundana was arrested on 7 March after Bonesha broadcast an interview with **Anicet Ntawuhiganayo**, spokesman for the armed opposition group FNL. (AI)

CANADA

On 20 April **Charles East**, a photographer covering the Summit of Americas for *Time* magazine, was arrested and detained for three days after being mistaken for a violent demonstrator. He had regular press accreditation and a press inscription on his helmet. Freed on bail, he faced charges for 'conspiracy to hide his identity' by wearing a gas mask, conspiracy to participate in a riot, contempt for a police officer and resistance during his arrest. (RSF)

CHAD

On 17 April the High Commission of Communications announced a ban on 'political debates' and 'programmes of a political nature' at all private, community radio stations in the run-up to the general election on 20 May. Commentary to back up information bulletins was also prohibited. (RSF)

CHILE

On 5 February senator and businessman Francisco Javier Errazuriz initiated legal action against **Enrique Alvarado, Javier Urrutia** and **Mireya Muñoz** of *El Metropolitano* for refusing to publish a front-page version of events pertaining to a case being heard in a Santiago criminal court involving the senator in the falsification of a public document. (Periodistas)

CHINA

Five overseas Chinese scholars have been detained between last August 2000 and April this year, two of whom are full US citizens, while two are US residents. All have close affiliations with foreign universities, and all have written on sensitive topics such as the 1989 Tiananmen protests, ethnic minorities or Taiwan. US Secretary of State Colin Powell has expressed concern over the lack of legal representation afforded those detained, and described as 'particularly outrageous' the treatment of the five-year-old son of **Dr Gao Zhan**, held incommunicado for 26 days despite being a US citizen. Following the detention in April of **Wu Jianming**, rumoured to have had a hand in the publication of the 'Tiananmen Papers' (*Index* 2/2001), the State Department warned Chinese-Americans intending to travel to China that they risked detention if they had already published works critical of the government. Beijing reacted immediately, describing the warning as 'extremely wrong and irresponsible', and demanded its retraction. Many scholars had already cancelled plans to work in China. 'It's just not worth the trouble of going there,' said Harvard sinologist Roderick MacFarquhar. (*International Herald Tribune*, Agence France-Presse)

Feng Zhaoxia, a journalist known to have investigated links between gangsters and officials in his hometown of Xi'an, died on 15 January in suspicious circumstances. Police concluded that he slit his own throat. His family is urging authorities to reopen the case, insisting the wound was too deep to be self-inflicted and his death was an act of revenge. (RSF)

Eight members of a reading club in Shaodong, Hunan Province, were arrested on the morning of 4 March by 40 police officers who also confiscated several books. Four were released the following day, but **Xiao Qianming** – whose home was used for the meeting – **Yang Guoxin**, **Li Liming** and **Luo Jianxin** were 'temporarily held' with no reason given. Xiao's wife **Peng Caixiu** said the group's weekly discussions were about literature and sometimes current affairs. (Agence France-Presse, Associated Press, Reuters)

Lu Xiaolan, a senior member of the China Democratic Party (CDP), was detained in Wuhan on 10 March. Lu was one of the last CDP leaders known to be at large and his whereabouts are now unknown. (AFP)

Lu Xinhua was arrested on 11 March in Wuhan having posted articles on the Internet promoting political reform. He was formally charged on 20 April with 'incitement to subvert state sovereignty'. **Jiang Shihua**, 27, a teacher from Sichuan Province who was arrested in December having posted the phrase 'down with the Communist Party' on a bulletin board, was reported on 12 March to have been sentenced to two years' imprisonment on charges of subversion. **Yang Zili**, a software engineer, was detained on 13 March in Beijing. His homepage carries politically sensitive essays, instructions on how to view banned sites using proxy servers and a condemnation of the 'soul of communism'. Three graduates, **Xu Wei, Jin Haike** and **Zhang Honghai**, were arrested on the same day in Beijing before setting up a weekly Internet forum to discuss political reform. All three were charged on 20 April with subversion and, if convicted, face up to ten years in prison. The Shanghai Administration of Radio, Film and Television published a notice on 23 March in the *Liberation Daily* prohibiting dissemination over the Internet of TV and radio programmes without the prior approval of a government official. **Guo Qinghai**, an economist from Wuhan City, was sentenced to four years in prison following a short closed trial on 3 April. Guo wrote articles and editorials for foreign news sites. **Wang Sen**, a known member of the outlawed CDP, was arrested on 30 April in Dachuan, Sichuan Province, having posted an article on the Internet 'defaming' police. Wang alleged the city's medical centre was selling Red Cross-donated TB medication at an inflated profit. He was charged with subversion. (Agence France-Presse, Associated Press, Information Centre for Human Rights and Democratic Movements in China, Reuters)

Beijing has led a chorus of protest over plans in Japan to publish a school history book which glosses over its imperial past and wartime atrocities. In response, the Japanese education ministry's screening panel made 137 revisions, but China and both Koreas said the book still sought to justify Japan's annexation of the Korean Peninsula, made no mention of the 100,000 Korean 'comfort women' and described the Nanjing Massacre in which 300,000 Chinese died as an 'incident'. The book was compiled by the nationalist Japanese Society for Textbook Revision, which claims current Japanese histories are too 'masochistic'. (Agence France-Presse, Associated Press, Reuters, *Washington Post*)

Shen Hongqi, a lawyer from Henan Province, was sentenced on 18 April to three years in prison on charges of subversion. He had written two articles advocating democratic elections and calling for the legalisation of opposition parties for submission to newspapers. (Agence France-Presse)

The Cardinal Kung Foundation (CKF) reported on 24 April the arrest and detention of several members of the underground Catholic Church. **Bishop Mattia Pei**, 83, was arrested in early April. **Bishop Shi Enxiang**, 79, was arrested in Beijing on 13 April – Good Friday – having spent five years in hiding. Bishop Shi has already spent 30 years in prison. Also arrested on Good Friday were **Fr Feng Yunxiang** in Fujian Province and **Fr Liao Haiqing**, 70, in Jiangxi Province. Thirteen of Fr Liao's followers were also arrested. **Fr Lu Genjun**, 39, was detained on 15 April along with three other unidentified priests in Hubei Province.

Fr Li Jianbo, 34, was arrested on 19 April in Inner Mongolia. CKF also reported that a priest, known only by his family name, **Yin**, was sentenced to three years in a labour camp in April following his arrest in January. Thirty-five Christians were detained in Inner Mongolia on 26 May for 'illegal religious activity'. (Cardinal Kung Foundation, Agence France-Presse, Associated Press)

COLOMBIA

Soraida Ariza Mateus, a correspondent for Voz de Cinaruco radio station, escaped unhurt when her house in Saravena was destroyed by an explosive device attached to the door on 27 February. She had received no previous threat. (IFJ)

For the first time in many years the trial of a journalist's alleged assassins is to go ahead in the High Court, despite an acquittal in a lower court. Charges against businessman Fernando Bermudez, Victor Felix Trujillo and Alvaro Quintero Alvarado for the murder of Radio Sur journalist **Nelson Carvajal** on 16 April 1998 (*Index* 4/1998) were dropped in Neieva lower court in December 2000 because of lack of evidence and dubious witness credibility. The prosecutor's office has since appealed to the high court to have the verdict overturned. In January 1999 attempts were made to bribe an investigator in the prosecutor's office. Carvajal had reported on incidents of corruption involving Bermudez who, according to witnesses, issued threats. (RSF) Sixty-nine-year-old **Guil-**

lermo **Angulo Pelaez**, a
commentator, former consul,
film-maker and friend of
Nobel Prize-winner Gabriel
García Márquez, was kid-
napped outside his country
house on 16 March. The authorities attribute the snatch of
'Professor Angulo', as he is
popularly known, to the Revolutionary Armed Forces of
Colombia. (IPYS)

No sooner was it established in
March that Colombia topped
the world's list of murdered
journalists – 10 in the previous
year – three more were assassinated in less than a week.
Flavio Bedoya, correspondent of the Communist Party
daily *Voz*, had reported on the
presence of paramilitaries from
Autodifesas Unidos de Colombia in the southern region
around Tumaco, and of their
collusion with the armed
forces. He was gunned down
on 27 April. The next day, the
chief of press in the Bogotá
mayor's office, **John Portela**,
was shot in the face by an
unknown individual for no
apparent motive. On 1 May
**Carlos Alberto Trespalacios
Yali**, director of communications for the Medellin munici-
pality sports and recreation
institute, was murdered for
unknown reasons, though he
had previously been threatened. On 3 May – World Press
Freedom Day – sportscaster
and law student **Yesid Maru-
landa Romero** was fatally
shot six times by three men in a
Cali street. No threats had been
made. (IPYS)

Police bomb-disposal experts
defused a 550-pound cluster
bomb packed in a pick-up
truck outside the office of *Voz*

in central Bogotá on 21 May.
Police said the bomb could
have caused widespread destruction across a two-block
radius. Editor **Carlos Lozano**
believes the bombers were
waiting for his arrival at the
office before detonating it. He
blamed outlaw paramilitary
groups, and suggested a connection with the killing three
weeks earlier of *Voz* journalist
Flavio Bedoya. However,
Lozano had recently been
appointed to a commission set
up to monitor official efforts to
curb paramilitary attacks
around the country. (CPJ)

COOK ISLANDS

On 17 April **Jason Brown**,
senior editor of the islands' only
independent daily, *Cook Islands
News*, was banned from covering parliament till 31 May, following a complaint by the
deputy prime minister who
claimed that he had been
misrepresented in one of his
articles. (PINA)

COTE D'IVOIRE

On 12 April the Commission
Nationale de la Presse (CNP)
imposed a ban on the bi-
monthly Burkinabé newspaper
Solidarité Paalga. The Commission cited three reasons for its
actions: the nationality of publishing director **Nicholas
Sahouidi**, who is from Burk-
ina Faso; the newspapers failure to comply with the legal
deposit system; and the lack of
professional journalists on staff.
Sahouidi argued that his
nationality had appeared on all
official documents submitted
to the CNP and the legal
deposit department. He admitted, however, that none of the

staff possessed press cards.
(RSF)

On 8 May two journalists were
sentenced in absentia to three
months' imprisonment and
fined CFA100,000 (US$134).
Meite Sindhou, editor-in-
chief of the daily *Le Patriote*,
and his publications director,
Patrice Lenonhin, were
charged with defamation in
connection with an article
published last June implicating
Martin Bléou, president of the
Ivoirian League of Human
Rights in a fraud case involving
the illegal transfer of funds to
a Swiss bank account. Bléou was
later exonerated and the court
ordered that his innocence be
publicised in the local press.
(RSF)

CUBA

On 22 February, RSF correspondent **Ricardo González
Alfonso** (*Index* 1/1998) was
arrested at his home in Havana.
Police interference with a
seminar organised by the independent Jorge Mañach Library,
which he runs from his home,
suggests that his arrest is linked
to library work, rather than his
journalism. (CubaNet)

Journalist Manuel **Antonio
González Castellanos** (*Index*
1/2000), independent reporter
for the Holguín-based Cuba
Press Agency, was released
from prison on 26 February
shortly before he would have
fully served his 31-month
sentence. He suffered contin-
ual harassment, assault, restric-
tion of visiting rights, forced
labour, isolation and medical
neglect during his incarceration at the maximum-security
Cuba Sí prison and at the pro-

visional prison in Holguín. (PEN, RSF)

On 17 March, members of the Communist Party Department of Religious Matters in Palma Soriano, Santiago de Cuba, physically assaulted Catholic **Elena Macias** in her home and destroyed her religious images. (Destaque Internacional)

RSF journalist **Ricardo González Alfonso** was placed under house arrest on 9 April, after being arrested and released earlier that evening on charges brought by his ex-wife. The imposition of house arrest in a domestic dispute case in which the complainant lives in the same house raises doubts about whether this is merely a pretext for another incident of police harassment. The reporter has faced harassment from police since giving interviews to a Miami radio station. (CPJ)

CZECH REPUBLIC

The three-year suspended sentence and large fine imposed in December 2000 on **Michal Zitko**, publisher of Adolf Hitler's *Mein Kampf*, was overturned on 20 February when a Prague court ruled that serious judicial mistakes had been made. (RFE/RL)

DEMOCRATIC REPUBLIC OF CONGO

The journalist **Mayimbi** of the daily *Forum* newspaper has been detained since 5 April in the central prison of Matadi. His arrest relates to an article, entitled 'Imported wheat flour of questionable quality for sale

in the cities of Boma, Moanda and Banana'. Mayimbi was arrested after a complaint was filed by the company in question. Journalist **Washington Lutumba**, correspondent with the daily newspaper *Le Potentiel*, has been detained over the same story since 30 March. (WAN)

The libel trial of **Jean-Luc Kinyongo Saleh**, publisher of the bi-weekly *Vision*, resumed on 20 April at the Kinshasa/Gnombe Tribunal. The case was originally brought by former internal affairs minister Gaetan Kakudji, following publication of an article, signed by **Berlin Atu-Atu**, which accused him of having 'benefited most from the war economy, which allowed him to scandalously become part of the bourgeoisie in a flash'. On 16 March Saleh – who had gone into hiding – was sentenced to four months' imprisonment and fined US$2,500, but the defence appealed the decision on grounds of procedural defects. Kakudji, who has since been dismissed, was mentioned in a recent UN report on the pillaging of resources during the war, and a Kinshasa paper recently published a receipt, signed by the minister, for a gift of US$2.5m in cash from the Mina diamond company. (Journaliste en Danger)

Reporter **Kasongo Mukishi**, journalist for the Kinshasa-based newspaper *L'Avenir*, was assaulted on 23 April by Dido Kitungwa, director of Kinshasa's Penitentiary and Re-education Centre. The incident took place at the conclusion of a day's free assistance organised by the Human

Rights Institute. Allegedly Kitungwa attempted to take away the journalist's notes and ordered guards to detain him. Editor-in-chief of *L'Avenir* **Mondo Pellet** was later detained in Kinshasa by six soldiers who, before robbing his belongings, threatened to 'take him to the Congo river'. (Journaliste en Danger)

Communications Minister Kikaya bin Karubi has ordered the closure of the newspaper *Le Libre Afrique*, its supplement *Le Derby* and the associated satirical review *Incognito*, it was reported on 15 May. The decision was justified on the grounds that the newspapers had been founded on false declarations as to their addresses, and the director's status as a professional journalist. (Journaliste en Danger)

ECUADOR

Wilson Cabrera, *El Observador* journalist in the remote Amazonian region of Morona Santiago, has been vindicated by an anti-corruption inquiry into the activities of the mayor of Morona, the three judges and the court president at his trial, where he was sentenced to three months' imprisonment on 28 November last year. (IPYS)

EGYPT

On 20 March the Administrative Court confirmed for the eighth time that the Labour Party's bi-weekly newspaper *Al Shahab* had been officially authorised to reappear having been banned in May 2000 after an editorial against censorship at the ministry of culture (*Index*

4/2000). The Supreme Press Council, however, rejected the ruling saying that as long as the Labour Party remained suspended, its paper could not be published. (*Cairo Times*)

The Supreme Court lifted the travel ban on former army colonel **Mohamed el-Ghanam**, only for police to prevent him from entering the airport on 28 March. El-Ghanam has been banned from leaving the country since 1997, officially because of a pending court appeal, though he claims it is to prevent him from publicising human rights abuses. As head of the interior ministry's legal department he uncovered attacks on the Christian minority and political prisoners, as well as President Hosni Mubarak's grant of pardons to police officers convicted of murder. (Digital Freedom Network)

On 28 March the government announced that it would 'no longer receive foreign commissions which investigate religious freedom'. No direct reference was made to the US Commission on International Religious Freedom whose visit, two weeks earlier, was criticised by parliamentarians and journalists; it condemned the use of torture, arbitrary arrests and military courts against Copts and Muslim extremists. (*Cairo Times*)

On 12 April a computer programmer and an accountant were given three-month jail sentences for creating a website that hosted personal ads for homosexuals. (*Cairo Times*)

On 13 April lawyer Nabih Al Wahsh filed two petitions against feminist author **Nawal Al Sa'dawi** (*Index* 9/1987, 9/1990, 8/1992) after the publication of an interview in the weekly *Al Midan* in which she criticised Islam and its laws concerning women. Al Wahsh accuses her of 'defaming religion' and has sued for her to be forcibly divorced from her husband under a *sharia* law which states that a Muslim man can only marry a believer in one of the three monotheistic religions. In 1996 **Nasr Abu Zaid** and his wife were forcibly divorced on the grounds that his writings were anti-Islamic (*Index* 5/1996). (*Cairo Times*)

Journalist **Mohammed Abu Liwaya** (*Index* 1/2001) was sentenced to one month in prison and fined US$2,000 on 29 April for libelling the head of the Journalists' Syndicate, Ibrahim Naffie. The appeals court reduced the six-month sentence he had received last November. (*Cairo Times*)

Veteran sociologist **Dr Saad Eddin Ibrahim** was sentenced to seven years' hard labour on 21 May, following an unparalleled smear campaign in the television and press. Ibrahim, a sociology professor and founder-director of the Ibn Khaldun Centre for Development Studies, was first arrested on 30 June 2000 (*Index* 5/2000, 6/2000) and charged with accepting EU donor funds without permission, 'deliberately disseminating false information and malicious rumours about the internal affairs of the state' and harming its image abroad. Prosecutors

characterised Dr Ibrahim and 27 other defendants from the centre as 'criminals ready to sell their nation and people for money', and accused him of 'using his intelligence to jeopardise this country's stability and sow the seeds of disunity'. The Ibn Khaldun Centre had used the EU's US$160,000 grant to finance a project intended to increase public awareness about voting rights that included a documentary which mentioned past instances of electoral fraud. Dr Ibrahim had expressed his intention of forming an independent observation and monitoring unit to assess the fairness of last November's parliamentary elections. Amnesty said the defendants 'were tried before a court that fails to meet international standards of fair trial', adding: 'We fear that the decision to convict had already been made prior to the conclusion of the trial.' (*Cairo Times*)

EL SALVADOR

Five journalists were charged with 'crimes against honour' in a case brought by National Reconciliation Party's former vice-president Francisco Merino on 6 March. **Alfredo Hernández, Mauricio Bolaños, Gregorio Morán** and **José Zometa**, from the daily *Prensa Gráfica*, and **Camila Calles**, from *El Mundo,* had reported allegations by Judge Ana María Gúzman Morales that Merino had threatened her while she was investigating a case involving him. (IAPA)

ETHIOPIA

Eletawi Addis, the largest private daily in the country, has been forced to close because of a dispute between the editor and owner over political reporting. Most newspapers have recently given prominence to a continuing crisis within the Tigray Liberation Front, the dominant party in the government coalition. Editor-in-chief **Solomon Abate** and his deputy **Dereje Desta** resigned over what they called 'violations of editorial freedom' by the paper's proprietor, **Fissesha**. (EFJA)

Some 3,500 students were detained for eight days following riots in Addis Ababa on 17 and 18 April which left 30 dead and 250 seriously injured. An estimated 10,000 students joined the protest to remove police from the campus. The University of Addis Ababa reopened on 24 April after students were forced to sign a declaration that said: 'Participation in the illegal movement of the university's students from 10-18 April was wrong.' (AI)

Seifu Mekonnen, journalist for the Amharic weekly, *Mebrek*, has disappeared and **Ashebar Bekele**, journalist for the Amharic weekly *Genanaw* has been detained. Mekonnen was first detained after attending the Ethiopian Human Rights Council conference at the Jerusalem Hotel, where officials denied any connection between them and the violent riots taking place outside. Bekele was arrested under suspicion of involvement in the riots and held in detention in the Addis Ababa police headquarters. (RSF)

The European Court of Justice has ruled that the EU can lawfully suppress criticism of its institutions and leading politicians by employees. Bernard Connolly, an EU official sacked for publishing a book criticising the single currency, had his dismissal upheld by the European Court of Justice on 7 March. Connolly was ruled to have been 'bound to end his career' by writing the book. (*Guardian, Daily Telegraph*)

The EU's Freedom of Information Bill has been widely derided as against the 'spirit' of the Amsterdam Treaty in which commitments were made to 'enshrine' the citizen's right of access in law. The deal, agreed in secret meetings on 4 and 5 April, has been criticised for incorporating articles that deliberately circumvent freedom of information. The definition of 'sensitive documents' is broad and provisions remove certain agencies and bodies created by the EU from inclusion. Decisions on which documents are to be withheld – under the stipulation that they may 'prejudice the public interest – are to be made by bureaucrats. The rules also grant member states the power to veto access to any controversial documents that they submit. The bill was overwhelmingly accepted by the European Parliament on 3 May. (Statewatch News Online, *International Herald Tribune, Financial Times*)

FRANCE

President Jacques Chirac's refusal to obey a summons to give evidence in a corruption scandal dating from his time as mayor of Paris has thrown the country into constitutional confusion. Provisions that protect the head of state from facing charges or trial during his time in office do not preclude appearance for questioning, but the constitution prevents the summons from being enforced. It was reported on 29 March that the summons by Judge Eric Halfen concerned allegations that Chirac's Gaullist movement received Fr280 million (US$36.4m) from kickbacks in the Paris region in the 1980s and 1990s. (*The Times*)

General Paul Aussaress, who confessed to running an execution squad during the Algerian civil war, claimed on 2 May that details of torture and summary executions were regularly transmitted to François Mitterrand, justice minister at the time. He further reported that the government acquiesced in the use of torture during the Battle of Algiers in 1957. (*Daily Telegraph*)

GEORGIA

Late on 24 February, **Tamaz Tsertsvadze**, chief editor of independent weekly *Meridiani*, was attacked by assailants armed with steel rods on his way home. He was taken to hospital suffering from concussion, a broken nose and several broken ribs. Tsertsvadze and his colleagues had received several threatening telephone calls, warning them to stop publishing articles critical of the authorities. (RFE/RL, IPI, OUAN, CJES)

On 1 April, five weeks after the attack on **Tamaz Tsertsvadze**, staff at the *Meridiani* came to work to discover that the office had been broken into and equipment had been stolen. Among the missing items were two computers containing the templates, back-up files and the complete current issue. *Meridiani* was forced to suspend publication. (CJES, IPI)

GHANA

In April the defeated National Democratic Congress (NDC) issued two writs against **Jake Obaseki**, editor of the *Daily Evening*, and its publisher, the New Times Corporation (NTC), seeking damages for two articles titled 'NDC attempted to withdraw 7.2b cedis for post-election violence' and 'Rawlings to refund 116m cedis … He is not qualified, neither is Ato Dadzie'. (Free Expression Ghana)

GREECE

On 2 February **Sotiris Bletsas**, a member of the Society for Vlach Culture, was sentenced to 15 months in prison and a fine of US$1,400 for distributing a publication which numbered the Macedo-Vlach Aromanian language among the country's languages. Bletsas was charged with the 'dissemination of false information' by Eugene Haitidis, a member of the New Democracy Party. (Greek Helsinki Monitor)

GUATEMALA

On 20 February the offices of the Guatemala City daily *El Periódico* were attacked and its staff and publisher were threatened by a group of 50 supporters of Communications, Infrastructure and Housing Minister Luis Rabbé. The attacks were in response to a series of articles tracing corruption in public works contracts. More recently, a number of journalists with *El Periódico* and *Prensa Libre* have been threatened both verbally and physically. On 27 March, *El Periódico* journalist **Silvia Gereda** was told that she and her two colleagues, **Luis Escobar** and **Enrique Castañeda**, would be killed if they continued to report on alleged corruption at the National Mortgage Credit Bank. Three days later, journalist **Walter Martín Juárez** was held at gunpoint and similarly threatened. (IAPA, CPJ)

GUINEA

On 14 March **Aboubacar Sakho**, editor of the weekly *Le Nouvel Observateur*, who was sentenced to ten months' imprisonment in February (*Index* 2/2001), was released in response to journalists' campaigns. (RSF)

On 8 May **Tibou Camara**, publications director of the private weekly *L'Observateur*, was arrested outside his offices by Conakry's anti-gang police and beaten before being taken to the central prison. On 24 April he and five other journalists from the paper were tried on charges of defamation following a complaint by Malick Sankhon, secretary general of the ministry of tourism, after an article accused him of plotting Camara's kidnapping. Camara was sentenced to six months' imprisonment and a fine of GF1m (US$ 523). The five remaining journalists remain at large. (RSF)

GUINEA-BISSAU

On 15 February journalist **Athizar Mende** of *Diario de Bissau* and the newspaper's photographer were detained for one night. The deputy public prosecutor threatened to prosecute Mende over his investigation into two diplomats who have been repeatedly summoned by police. On 8 March 30 journalists signed a motion against censorship and the arbitrary detention of journalists. (RSF)

Military bosses have threatened journalists over their coverage of the 23 November coup d'état. On 30 March Brigadier General Melciades Lopes Fernandes entered the private radio station Bombolom FM where a programme was being aired on the subject of 100 soldiers accused and detained for their involvement in the coup. The next day soldiers attacked the public radio and television network, RTBG, threatening that 'the time of tolerance' was finished and that if war broke out the radio station would be 'the first target'. (RSF)

HUNGARY

On 11 February the first Roma radio station, Radio C, started broadcasting on a temporary lease to an estimated 150,000 Roma in the Budapest area. The station features Roma news, music, culture and social issues and is almost entirely run by Roma. Radio C is funded by the EU, the US Embassy, The Open Society Institute and Levi Strauss jeans. (*New York Times*)

INDIA

In late April novelist **Arundhati Roy**, lawyer **Prashant Bhusan** and environmental activist **Medha Patkar** were charged with criminal contempt and ordered to appear before the Supreme Court in connection with the Narmada Dam controversy (*Index* 3/1999. 1/2000). The case stems from a controversial 2–1 Supreme Court ruling in October 2000 which allowed work to proceed on the dam. During a demonstration last December, Roy is alleged to have called the court a 'sold institution', and she and her co-accused are alleged to have made 'vulgar slogans' about the court and to have threatened the lives of the three lawyers who filed the case against them. (*Sunday Times*)

The Delhi High Court on 26 April asked the police to confiscate all copies of *Wah India* magazine's 16–30 April issue, which included a survey that evaluated judges' integrity, understanding of law and courtroom behaviour (*Index* 2/2001). A division court bench also issued notices to the magazine's editor-in-chief **Madhu Trehan** and its printer, publisher and editor, **Rahul Mishra**. (United News of India)

In early May police in Delhi claimed to have uncovered an assassination plot against

Tarun Tejpal, managing director and editor-in-chief of news website Tehelka.com, and **Aniruddha Bahal**, Tehelka's senior reporter. Six alleged gangsters from Bihar and Uttar Pradesh were arrested in connection with the alleged plot. In March this year, Defence Minister George Fernandes and Bangaru Laxman, president of the ruling Hindu nationalist Bharatiya Janata Party, were forced to resign from the government after Tehelka secretly filmed Laxman and a large number of senior bureaucrats, army officers and politicians accepting bribes for a media arms sting. (*Independent*, BBC)

On 10 May 17 journalists were attacked by security forces as they attempted to cover the funeral procession for three victims of a suicide bombing the day before in the town of Magam, Jammu and Kashmir. The injured journalists are: **Kumaramanglam** and **Sanam Anjum**, cameramen for southern India's Enadu TV; **Aijaz Rahi**, photographer for Associated Press; **Meraj-u-din**, an Associated Press cameraman; **S. Irfan** of the Press Trust of India; **Fayaz Ahmad** of the *Daily Aftab*; **Sheikh Mushtaq** and **Faya Kabuli** from Reuters; **Nassir Ahmad** of Zee TV; **Shujat Bhukhar** and **Missar Ahmad Bhat** of *The Hindu*; **Bilal Ahmad Bhat** of *Asian News International*; **S. Tariq** of New Delhi Television; **Tauseef Mustafa** of Agence France-Presse; **Sanam Aijaz** of ETV; **Javid Ahmad Shah** of the *Indian Express*, and **Sayed Muzaffar Hussain** of the Urdu daily *Srinigar Times*. (CPJ, RSF)

INDONESIA

On 27 March reporters from TV stations RCTI and TPI were banned from reporting in Ternate Island by governor Muhyi Effendi, who claimed the stations' reports 'provoked' the community and disseminated criticisms of government. (Alliance of Independent Journalists)

On 23 April **Rudi P. Singgih**, photographer for *Pilar* magazine, was shot dead by police in Bandung, allegedly for car theft. According to police, he was killed after stabbing an officer on his way to the station. Though on leave, Singgih was conducting an investigation into a confidential case. The magazine declined to reveal who was being investigated but it plans to file a complaint against the police. (*Jakarta Post*)

On 12 May, in two separate incidents in the province of Aceh, journalists **Murizal Hamzah**, from the tabloid *Media Kutaraja*, **Umar H N**, from TV station RCTI, and **Abbas Gani**, of *Fakta* magazine, were beaten up by government troops and had their equipment confiscated. (Agence France-Presse)

IRAN

On or around 12 February writer, editor and human rights lawyer **Mehrangiz Kar** (*Index* 2/2001) was allowed to seek medical treatment abroad for the breast cancer that was diagnosed since her release from jail in June 2000. (WiPC, PEN)

On 12 February, **Mohammed-Bagher Vali-Beik**, general manager of Jamee-e-Rouz, the company that had published most of the reformist newspapers now banned, was arrested and detained in Tehran. (RSF)

Abbas Dalvand, head of the *Lorestan* magazine, was arrested in Khorammabad on 14 February and accused of 'publishing deceitful articles' and 'insult against the revolutionary and judicial institutions' of the state. He was bailed on 18 February. (RSF)

On 15 February **Farida Davoudi-Mohadjer**, journalist for the banned dailies *Fath* and *Khordad*, was arrested and detained in Tehran by order of the Revolutionary Court. Policemen searched her residence, seizing a large number of documents, and pulled off her chador. She was released on 12 March. (RSF)

Reza Alijani, journalist for the banned monthly *Irane-Farda*, was arrested on 24 February and taken home by security agents who carried out a search. The Revolutionary Court ordered his imprisonment, but provided no reason. (RSF)

The conservative weekly *Harim* was suspended by the judiciary on 8 March for 'defaming' President Mohammed Khatami. The newspaper had mocked the president over his 1997 promise 'to institute the rule of law and civil society in Iran'. (RSF)

Mohammad Hassan Alipour, publisher of the banned weekly *Aban*, was given a six-month suspended sentence and banned from working for the press for five years. He was convicted of 'spreading lies to disturb public opinion.' (RSF)

On the evening of 11 March, security agents raided the home of **Mohammad Bastehnaghar**, son-in-law of a leading liberal cleric, where about 30 people were gathered to celebrate the release on bail of **Ahmad Zeid-Abadi** (*Index* 5/2000). Abadi had been imprisoned since August 2000, charged with, among other things, spreading 'anti-Islamic propaganda.' Those arrested included Ahmad Zeid-Abadi himself, and colleagues **Hossin Rafai** and **Saide Madani** of *Iran-e-Farda*, **Taghi Rahmani** and **Fatemeh Govarai** of the banned weekly *Omid-e-Zangan* and **Reza Rais-Toussi** of the banned daily *Fath*. Zeid-Abadi and Govarai were released the next day. The head of Tehran's Revolutionary Court stated that 'the detainees were conspiring to overthrow the Islamic government.' (RSF, *Daily Telegraph*)

On 18 March the daily *Dorrane-Emrouz*, the weeklies *Mobine* and *Jamee-Madani* and the monthly *Peyam-e-Emrouz* were ordered by the judiciary to stop publishing. The respective managers – **Hamid-Reza Zahedi-Kohnegourabi**, **Mohammad Gharibani**, **Mahmoud Raoufi** and **Mohammad Zahedi-Asl** – have had proceedings started against them. (RSF)

Forty-two people were arrested following a raid on 7 April, including **Reza Tehrani**, editor-in-chief of the banned magazine *Kian*, and **Fazlollah Salavati**, editor-in-chief of the banned Isfahan weekly *Navid-e-Esfahan*. They were charged with 'collaborating with counter-revolutionary groups'. Those arrested all reportedly had connections with the progressive Movement for the Liberation of Iran party, banned since March. (RSF)

There are serious concerns for the safety of theologian **Hojjatoleslam Hasan Yousefi Eshkevari** (*Index* 4/2000, 1/2001) who is believed to have been transferred from Evin prison on or around 12 April. Eshkevari, who is a diabetic, is reportedly held incommunicado and being denied insulin. Eshkevari contributed to the now-banned newspapers *Adineh*, *Neshat* and *Iran-e-Farda*. (WiPC, PEN)

On 15 April **Hamid Kaviani** of the suspended daily *Salam*, was abducted for several hours and released. He was hospitalised with injuries. On 21 May in the afternoon, he later disappeared in a Tehran street. In June 2000 Kaviani had appeared before the Special Court for the Clergy over his book *In Pursuit of the Criminals*, which investigated the killings of dissidents in late 1998. (RSF)

On 17 April **Hechmatollah Tabarzadi**, editor-in-chief of the daily *Hoviyat-e-Khich* and a student leader, was arrested and imprisoned in Tehran. (RSF)

Having published its first edition just four days earlier, the daily *Nosazi* was ordered closed on 9 May. The court said that editor **Hamid-Reza Jalai-Pour** (*Index* 5/1998, 4/2000, 6/2000) was not 'competent' to publish a newspaper. The court also accuses him, as owner of the *Jameh-e-Rooz* publishing house, of having published 'criminal' material. (RSF)

On 9 May **Hamid Jafari-Nasrabadi**, student head of the magazine *Kavir*, and **Mahmoud Modjayi**, one of its journalists, were arrested in Tehran and accused of publishing a 'blasphemous' article in which they used an 'indecent tone' against several state institutions. (RSF)

Between 8 and 13 May, 400 cybercafés were closed down in Tehran, over alleged non-compliance with permit and licensing laws. (RSF)

It was reported on 16 May that an appeal court has quashed three convictions against leading investigative journalist **Akbar Ganji** (*Index* 4/2000, 1/2001, 2/2001), by the Tehran Revolutionary Court, reducing his sentence from 10 years to six months. Ganji was cleared of offences including 'harming national security' and keeping classified documents, but the court upheld a verdict of 'insulting the authorities'. Ganji had published articles suggesting that senior conservatives had ordered the killings of dissident intellectuals and writers in 1998 (*Index* 1/1999, 2/1999). (*Guardian*, Associated Press)

IRAQ

Prominent Kurdish scholar and historian **Muhammad al-Ruzbayani** was murdered with an axe in his Baghdad home on 27 March. Ruzbayani, 88, had been an adviser on Kurdish affairs to the government and was reportedly receiving financial support from institutions in the Kurdish-controlled areas of Iraq, a factor which may have aroused the suspicions of the authorities. (*Al-Sharq al-Awsat*)

ISRAEL

It was reported on 20 April that **Moshe Negbi**, legal commentator for the daily *Maariv* and a recipient of the Sokolov Prize, was dismissed allegedly for refusing to write articles favourable to Ofer Nimrodi, proprietor of the Maariv-Modi Publishing House. Ofer Nimrodi and his brother Yaakov are under criminal investigation (*Index* 2/2000). (IPI)

Poet-columnist **Abdel Hakim Masalha** 40, was questioned by the Shin Bet at Madera police station on May 2 about nationalist poetry published in *Saut al Halk u'al-Huriya*, and reportedly told to tone down his writing. Masalha had written about youths killed in the *al-Aqsa* intifada and the suffering of their parents. (*Ha'aretz*)

Samer Awartani, an administrator for Rafidiyeh hospital in the Occupied West Bank, was detained incommunicado by intelligence agencies on his return from a seminar on patient empowerment and healthcare management in Oxford on 7 May. Israeli participants at the seminar had filmed Awartani's presentation – the only speech to be filmed – on how the hospital was coping with the large numbers of casualties since September. Awartani has no known history of political activism. (*Guardian*)

ITALY

It was reported on 28 February that Jesuit theologian **Rev Jacques Dupuis** has been granted permission by the Vatican to publish his study of religious pluralism, despite receiving a rebuke against its anti-doctrinal content that could lead readers to 'erroneous or harmful positions'. The Vatican's inquisition into Father Dupuis' 1997 book, *Towards a Christian Theology of Religious Pluralism*, silenced the Belgian Jesuit for two and a half years. Under the terms of a signed agreement, Father Dupuis is obliged to publish the Vatican's comments in an appendix to the work, and to abide by its objections, although he claims that he thought he was only required to take the Vatican's views into account. (*International Herald Tribune*)

The landslide victory of Silvio Berlusconi in the May election threw up the vexed question of media ownership and political control. Berlusconi's Fininvest owns 48% of Mediaset group which controls three private channels. Independent analysis during the campaign has shown that, while public broadcaster RAI gave roughly equal coverage to the two leading candidates, Berlusconi's channels gave five times more coverage to his campaign than to his rivals'. (*Financial Times, IFJ, RSF*)

KAZAKHSTAN

On 3 April **Yermurat Bapi**, editor of opposition weekly *SolDat*, was convicted of 'publicly insulting the dignity and honour of the president', charges based on two articles published in the 30 May and 6 July editions (*Index* 5/2000). The first held President Nursultan Nazarbayev responsible for ethnic clashes in Almaty in December 1986; the second, written by historian and dissident **Karishal Asanov**, described him as 'illiterate, incompetent and corrupt', the prosecution claimed. The court acquitted Asanov for lack of evidence but sentenced Bapi to one year in prison and ordered him to pay US$280 in court expenses. (RFE/RL)

On 10 April the state-run newspaper *Egemen Qazaqstan* published an anonymous article, entitled 'Who is really attacking, and who is really defending himself?' The article claimed that journalists hired by NTV general director Yevgeny Kiselev were trying to protect their own interests using slogans about press freedom. (RFE/RL)

KENYA

Milton Omondi of the Kenya News Agency was arrested on 21 April in Garissa after he became engaged in a dispute with a police officer who refused to register his complaint at receiving death threats on 16 April. (NDIMA)

Police were called in after a 26 April raid on the private Citizen radio and TV station (*Index* 2/2000, 3/2000) by the Communications Commission of Kenya (CCK) vandalised broadcasting equipment and took it off-air. **Samuel Macharia**, proprietor of Citizen's holding company Royal Media, has called on the court to issue injunctions against the police and for the CCK to cease interfering with its operations. (RSF)

KOSOVA

Associated Press (AP) TV producer **Kerem Loton** was killed on 28 March in a mortar attack on a strip of territory along the border with Macedonia. The AP crew came to report on armed border clashes. A cameraman had just got out their vehicle, leaving Loton behind, when it was hit by a mortar shell. (ANEM)

KUWAIT

Leading woman journalist **Hudaya Sultan al-Salem**, owner and editor-in-chief of the weekly *Al-Majales*, was killed in a drive-by shooting on 20 March. Her assailants reportedly handed themselves over to police. (RSF, *International Herald Tribune*)

The Cyprus-based magazine *Al-Tadamon al-Arabi wal-Douali* was reportedly banned between 23 and 28 April. Owner and editor-in-chief **Mona Chatilla** has been told she is no longer allowed to visit the country. The publication's Kuwaiti correspondent, **Oulfat Farid**, was also denied the renewal of his accreditation.

The last issue of *Al-Tadamon al-Arabi wal-Douali* featured Saddam Hussein and his son Qusai on the cover. The magazine is already banned in Saudi Arabia, Algeria and Libya. (RSF)

KYRGYZSTAN

On 28 February the Pervomai district court in Bishkek ordered the Uchkun publishing house not to print that week's edition of the opposition *Res Publica*. According to chief editor **Zamira Sydykova**, the paper had failed to pay the balance on two fines imposed in January 2000 (*Index* 2/2000). (CJES)

On 13 March the Jalal-Abad district court reversed its own decision to free journalist **Moldosali Ibraimov**, cleared of criminal libel charges in July last year (*Index* 5/2000). He has since been sentenced to a suspended prison term of two years. Ibraimov's lawyer has filed a complaint with the Supreme Court. (CPJ, RFE/RL, CJES)

The final edition of the bi-weekly opposition *Asaba-Bishkek* was published on 14 March. The authorities confiscated the paper's bank account on 15 March to retrieve a fine of 1m soms (approx. US$22,000) for libelling the Canadian Kumtor Operating Company (*Index* 2/2001). According to chief editor **Bermet Bukasheva**, unknown people bought almost every copy of the last edition which contained articles critical of President Askar Akayev and his family. Since 6 March, articles by *Asaba* journalists had been printed in *Res Publica* but, according to owner **Melis Eshimkanov**, the project has not proven profitable and would be discontinued. *Asaba*'s fines since last October amount to around US142,000 (*Index* 5/2000, 1/2001). On 10 May Eshimkanov was fined a further 1,000 soms (US$20) for participating in a 13 April protest against the paper's forced closure (CJES, RFE/RL. RSF)

LEBANON

Samir Qassir, journalist with the daily *an-Nahar*, is reportedly being harassed over a 16 April editorial criticising the security forces. On 28 March his passport was seized at Beirut airport and only returned on 11 April. (CPJ)

LIBERIA

On 21 February **Joseph Bartuah, Abdullah Dukuly, Jerome Dalieh** and **Bobby Tapson** of the independent *News* were arrested on charges of espionage for reporting that the government had bought spare parts for helicopters while delaying months of back pay for civil servants. The UN believes that the helicopters have been used since 1997 to supply weapons to rebels in Sierra Leone. After international pressure, the charges were dropped on 30 March. (AI)

The government announced on 27 April that media reports on fighting in the north and on other issues of national security should be cleared with the ministry of information before publication. A statement by

Information Minister Reginald Gooderidge described the order as a means of preventing 'disinformation that could cause doubt and panic in the public'. (CPJ)

LUXEMBOURG

The European Court of Human Rights has overturned the conviction of radio journalist **Marc Thoma**, it was reported on 2 April. The national court of appeal upheld Thoma's conviction for quoting a newspaper report which accused forestry workers of corruption. The European Court found a violation of article 10 on freedom of expression and specified that the journalist had a 'right of quotation'. (*IFJ*)

MALAWI

The *Chronicle* newspaper has been threatened with three civil actions for defamation from senior government figures. President Bakili Muluzi brought a complaint in a personal capacity in response to the paper's allegations in September that he was responsible for awarding building contracts in return for donations. The second suit was made by Minister for Health Aleke Banda in regard to an article that suggested President Muluzi intended to dissolve the Cabinet. National Assembly Speaker Sam Mpasu has also initiated a civil action for the *Chronicle*'s charge that he was a 'partisan speaker'. (IPI)

MALI

On 16 May **Sidiki Konate**, head of the Office of Radio

and Television in Mali (ORTM), was convicted of criminal defamation and sentenced to serve 30 days in jail with a fine of US$1,350. The Autonomous Union of the Magistracy filed charges against both ORTM and the mayor of Bamako, **Ibrahima N'Diaye**, after the latter charged in a 26 March TV programme that magistrates were corrupt and inefficient. The mayor received a fine of US$3,000. (RSF)

MAURITANIA

Mohammed Lemine Ould Bah, correspondent for Radio France International (RFI) and Radio Monte Carlo (RMC) in Nouakchott, was summoned by the information ministry over his report on the recent visit of President Maaouiya Sid'Ahmed Ould Taya to Senegal. The journalist's report for RFI suggested that relations between the two countries were improving because of the imminent export of Mauritanian oil to Senegal. The minister accused Ould Bah of 'undermining the country's interests' and informed him that his authorisation to work for RFI and RMC had been terminated. (RSF)

MEXICO

Journalist **Saul Martínez** with the daily *El Imparcial* was assassinated on 24 February between the towns of Matamoros – where the paper is based – and Rio Bravo. He was last seen in San Fernando, where he stopped at the police station before heading to Matamoros to interview Commander Dionicio Flores. Martínez was investigating

Ignacio Coronel, a known narcotics trafficker in the region, and had received death threats two weeks prior to this killing. He may have been kidnapped on his arrival at Matamoros airport, where he had told Flores he was heading. His killing follows closely on that of **José Luis Ortega Mata**, editor of the weekly *Seminario de Ojinaga*, who was shot and killed on 19 February. Many suspect that Mata's murder was also linked to stories on drug trafficking, in this case in the border region of Chihuahua, as well as to a forthcoming article alleging links between drug trafficking and local campaign funding. (CPJ)

MOROCCO

On 1 March **Aboubakr Jammai** (*Index* 6/2000, 2/2001), publications director of *Le Journal Hebdomadaire*, and general director **Ali Ammar** were convicted of defaming Foreign Minister Ben Aissa. They were given jail terms of three and two months respectively, plus fines and damages totalling some US$200,000. The charges related to articles published last year in *Hebdomadaire's* now-defunct predecessor, *Le Journal*, accusing Ben Aissa of corruption while acting as ambassador to the US. (CPJ)

An edition of the Spanish weekly *El Cambio* was banned on 19 March for featuring an article about the Western Sahara. On 6 April an issue of *Rissalat Al Foutouwa* was seized by the authorities and access to the weekly's website, www.fotowa.com, was also blocked. On 17 May an issue of the French weekly *Courrier International* was proscribed without official explanation, having contained a feature on the Berbers. (RSF)

MOZAMBIQUE

On 13 March police arrested two businessman, Momade Abdul Assife Satar and Ayob Abdul Satar, and a former bank manager of the Maputo branch of the Commercial Bank of Mozambique (BCM), Vicente Ramaya, for ordering the murder of journalist **Carlos Cardoso** on 22 November 2000 (*Index* 1/2001). Cardoso was investigating the disappearance of US$10m from the BCM during its privatisation in 1996. The money was allegedly channelled out of the country via bank accounts held in the Satar family name. They were formally charged on 22 May. The investigation was called a litany of blunders by Cardoso's widow, **Nina Berg**. The police did not question eyewitnesses or the pathologist who carried out the autopsy, nor did it prevent onlookers from touching evidence. Prosecuting attorney Diamantino dos Santos stands accused of deliberately destroying evidence against the Satars, but has thus far managed to evade arrest. On 28 February Interior Minister Almerinho Manhenje announced at a brief press conference that suspects had been arrested in connection with Cardoso's murder, but reporters from *Metical* and *Mediafax*, the publications launched by Cardoso, were not invited to attend. On 4 March the official weekly *Domingo* disclosed the identities of the actual killers, information which could only have come from official sources. However, the two illegal immigrants whom *Domingo* named were not among the five arrested in early March for carrying out the murder for the Satars. The accused -Anibal Antonio dos Santos Junior, Manuel Fernandea, Jose Carreira Miguel, Romao Massangaia and Fernando Magne – are all notorious underworld contract assassins. (CPJ, MISA, RSF)

NAMIBIA

On 22 March government representative Mocks Shivute announced that the government intended to make good with immediate effect its decision in December 2000 to halt advertising in the daily *Namibian*. A similarly critical newspaper, *Windhoek Advertiser*, was forced to close previously when income declined following a withdrawal of government advertising (*Index* 5/2000). (RSF)

NEPAL

In early March concern was raised over the disappearance of **Krishna Sen**, editor of the Nepali-language weekly *Janadesh*, who was arrested in April 1999 for publishing an interview with one of the leaders of the Maoist insurgency. Though authorities claim Sen was released from Rajbiraj jail on the night of 10 March, local journalists have reported him missing. After local and international pressure, the government released Sen from Jaleshwor jail in Mahottari district on 15 March. (CPJ, RSF)

Yubaraj Ghimere, editor of the Nepali-language daily *Kantipur*, **Kailash Shirohiya**, managing director of both *Kantipur* and its English sister publication *Kathmandu Post*, and **Binod Raj Gyawali**, director of both publications, were arrested on 6 June in the aftermath of the murder by Crown Prince Dipendra of King Birendra and other members of the royal family. Upon their arrest, they were told that they were being charged with treason because of an editorial written by a Maoist rebel leader that was published in *Kantipur* on 6 June. It called on citizens to reject the newly crowned King Gyanendra as a 'puppet of Indian expansionist forces'. On 11 June the prisoners appeared in court, although the government has so far failed to bring formal charges against them. (CPJ)

NIGERIA

On 25 April **Rockfeller Okeke**, editor with the state-run News Agency of Nigeria, was shot dead by unknown gunmen as he was entering his house in Ukpo, Anambra State. The police have so far failed to establish a motive. (WAN)

PAKISTAN

On 7 March the one-man judicial tribunal of Justice Qaim Jan Khan, of the Peshawar High Court, held that several staff members of the *Frontier Post* were responsible for the publication of a blasphemous letter which appeared in the paper on 29 January (*Index* 2/2001). In his view the incident took place 'due to [the] sheer negli-

gence, rather [than the] personal negligence' of managing editor **Mahmood Afridi**, news editor **Aftab Ahmed** and sub-editor **Munawar Mohsin**. (Pakistan Press Foundation)

Shakil Shaikh, chief reporter for the national English-language daily *News*, was abducted and beaten on 28 March in Islamabad. 'You write too much. Now you will not write any more,' Shaik's attackers said repeatedly. They also threatened to harm his parents, wife and children if he did not 'change his attitude'. (Pakistan Press Foundation, CPJ, RSF)

On 4 May **Ahmed Nawaz Abbasi**, correspondent for the Urdu daily *Nawa-I-Waqt*, was arrested by police in Bahawalpur in the Punjab. Police accused Abbasi of providing Agence France-Presse with an old photograph of a man who had died in the drought in the Cholistan desert. The photograph was published in all the leading national newspapers, raising the ire of the Cholistan Development Authority which complained to the police. (Pakistan Press Foundation)

On 14 May it was reported that **Dr Younus Shaikh** is in jail charged with blasphemy. Shaikh was denounced by his medical students for asserting that Mohammed was not a Muslim until the age of 40; that his parents were not Muslims; that his first marriage, at 25, was made without an Islamic marriage contract; and that, therefore, he had never removed his underarm hair or

been circumcised. For this piece of logic, Shaikh faces the death penalty. (*International Herald Tribune*)

Hadhi Sanghi, photographer for the Sindhi-language daily *Kawish*, was beaten by police in Larkana, Sindh on 14 May. He was covering the release from prison of Sindhi nationalist leader Qadir Magsi when he noticed that prison staff were beating a prisoner. He took pictures of the event, which showed officers attacking the crowd when it tried to protect Sanghi from being arrested by police. Sanghi was eventually captured, beaten and charged along with 28 others for attacking the jail. (Pakistan Press Foundation)

PALESTINE

Gamma agency photographer **Laurent van der Stockt** was shot in the knee on 9 February and seriously injured while covering young Palestinians' demonstrations in Ramallah. He was 50 metres from Israeli Defence Force (IDF) troops. (CPJ)

On 9 March three Reuters journalists were shot at by an IDF soldier in an armoured personnel carrier at the Netzarim junction in Gaza. (CPJ)

The Ramallah offices of the Qatar-based al-Jazeera satellite channel were closed on 21 March by armed officers of the Palestine Authority (PA). Security chief Mohammed Dahlan said al-Jazeera 'did not respect the PA or President Yasser Arafat'. The offending item was reportedly a trailer for a programme on the Lebanese civil war which included a demonstrator holding a shoe over a picture of Arafat. (Agence France-Presse, Independent Digital)

On 14 April **Zakaria Abu Harbeid**, journalist with the Ramatan Press Agency, was shot in the hand in Khan Younis while taking pictures of IDF troops shooting at Palestinians. (RSF)

On 20 April **Layla Odeh** of Abu Dhabi TV was shot in the thigh by the IDF while interviewing Palestinians in Rafah whose homes had been destroyed. Odeh and two colleagues claim that no violent incidents were occurring at the time. The IDF apologised for the incident and said an investigation was under way. (CPJ)

Bertrand Aguirre of the French TV station TF1 was shot while covering demonstrations in Ramallah on 15 May. A bullet from the IDF hit Aguirre's flak jacket, causing a haematoma. At least 20 journalists have been injured since the *al-Aqsa* uprising began in late September. (CPJ)

PANAMA

On 14 March journalists **Rainer Tuñon**, formerly with *Crítica Libre*, and **Juan Díaz**, with *Panamá América*, were sentenced to 18 months in prison for publishing information regarding the issuing of fake medical diplomas given them by a magistrate. Authorities also sought to arrest **José Otero**, a journalist with the daily *La Prensa*, under the same charge of 'crimes against honour'. (RSF)

PERU

The cable channel Cable Canal de Noticias (CCN) has accused the company Telefónica Multimedia, which grants TV frequencies and licences, of halting its news output on 12 April and reinstating it on 7 May for a 90-day trial period 'on condition that the programming content met the quality standards set by Telefónica'. CCN goes on to say that 'Telefónica is trying to turn itself into an institution that will monitor content and the viewers' level of approval and would, in effect, relentlessly censor the content of programming that Peruvians have access to.' (IFJ)

On 16 April journalist **Hermes Rivera Guerrero** was pardoned and released after serving nine years of a 20-year sentence handed down in May 1992 for terrorist activities and membership of Sendero Luminosa (Shining Path). In reality, Rivera was imprisoned because of the critical reports on government corruption that he broadcast on Oriental Radio Station in Jaen, Cajamarca. Four journalists remain in prison: **Pedro Carranza Ugaz**, **Antero Gargurevich Oliva**, **Juan de Mata Jara** and **Berrospi Javier Tuanama Valera**. Their cases are also under review. (IPYS)

Twenty-four hours after journalist **Luís Zevallos Hidalgo** broadcast a tape on Radio La Oroya in which Javier Izquierdo Yantas, chief of provisions of the Yauli, is heard to demand a bribe from a supplier to a children's milk programme in Huancayo, he was brutally

assaulted by four assailants with blunt instruments on 19 April. The incident was reported to the police and the local public prosecutor, but investigations are being held up. (IFJ)

PHILIPPINES

On 24 February **Mohammad Yusop**, commentator for Radio RXID, was shot dead in Pagadian City on Mindanao island, the most recent in a series of murdered journalists. **William Yap Yu**, publisher of *Pagadian City Star*, was killed on 14 May last year (*Index* 4/2000); **Vincent Rodriguez**, correspondent for DZMM on 27 June (*Index* 5/2000); **Olimpio Jalapit**, broadcaster for DXPR, on 17 November (*Index* 1/2001); and **Rolando Ureta** on 3 January (*Index* 3/2001). (RSF)

RUSSIA

NTV reported that **Yurii Vlasov**, head of the Moscow region justice department, and his driver, **Dmitrii Gruzdev**, were found strangled to death early on 11 March. (RFE/RL)

Adam Deniyev, the deputy head of administration installed by Moscow in Chechnya, was assassinated on 13 April when a bomb exploded in a private television studio attached to his Grozny home. He was reading from the Quran during the traditional Thursday recitation. Akhmad Kadyrov, head of the administration, said that the rebel leader Aslan Maskhadov had threatened them both 'in all his media appearances'. (*The Times*, RFE/RL)

Konstantin Zavrazhin, a press photographer for the newspaper *Izvestiya*, was beaten by Captain Dmitry Urvantsev in Moscow on 15 April and had his camera confiscated. The officer then took out his pistol and pointed it at the journalist. (GDF)

Gazprom-media staged a boardroom coup on 3 April, gaining full editorial control of NTV, Russia's only independent national television station, formerly owned by **Vladimir Gusinsky**'s Media-MOST company (*Index* 4/2000, 5/2000, 1/2001, 2/2001). A snap shareholders' meeting culled Gusinsky, NTV chief and journalist **Yevgeny Kiselev**, installing Alfred Kokh as chairman, US banker Boris Jorden as NTV chief and Vladimir Kulisikov, head of the state news agency RIA Novesti, as channel editor. The new management team forcibly occupied NTV on 14 April as Gazprom security officers and the interior ministry's special troops seized the station's offices and control rooms. These had been occupied by 356 employees protesting against the new appointments. All regular broadcasts stopped as journalists and technical staff reported ongoing news, along with live coverage of events inside the studio. The editorial policy of Media-MOST's best-selling publications were also affected as Gazprom ousted staff at the daily *Sevodnia* on 16 April and closed it down. Three days before the decision, a Molotov cocktail was thrown at the car of **Dimitri Biryulov**, director of Media-Most's publishing company, Sem Dnei, though

he wasn't injured. On 17 April staff at the weekly *Itogui* arrived at work to find their newsroom barred by private security guards. **Sergei Parkhomenko**, *Itogui*'s editor, was dismissed and the rest of the staff were forced to resign. Meanwhile, efforts to extradite Gusinsky were thrown out by a Spanish court, allowing the former media magnate to travel for the first time in four months. (*Guardian*, *Daily Telegraph*, RSF, CPJ, RFE/RL)

The regional branch of the Federal Security Service (FSB) in Krasnoyarsk said on 18 April that it had charged a scientist with treason for trying to obtain information on the effects of space on satellites to China. The FSB refused to name him, but colleagues said **Valentin Danilov** of the Krasnoyarsk State Technical University had been held since mid-February. (Reuters)

New York-based financier and philanthropist George Soros announced on 5 June that he was reconsidering his philanthropic activities as a result of a clampdown on academic freedom by the Russian Academy of Sciences. In May the academy ordered its hundreds of institutes to maintain 'constant control' over the foreign contacts of their employees, including trips abroad, and the activities of foreign academics in Russia. (Associated Press)

On 16 April **Moussa Diop**, correspondent with the private daily *Sud Quotidien* in Velingara, was attacked by local activists of the ruling Parti

Démocratique Sénégalais (PDS). Diop was intending to interview a local official when the group began to stone him, forcing him to take refuge in his car. Diop had claimed that there is dissent within the party. In March PDS militants attacked another journalist, **Cheikh Djemg**, from the private paper *Wal Fadjeri* for making similar allegations. (RSF)

New legislation amending section 42 of the Broadcasting Authority Act is seen as the latest move to limit critical reporting. It will declare foreign broadcasting services to be 'engaging in domestic politics' and, therefore, in need of prior government approval and subject to arbitrary suspension or banning. (A19)

On 23 March **Tyrone Seale**, assistant editor and reporter for the Afrikaans daily *Beeld*, was thrown out of the annual congress of the right-wing Herstigte National Party (HNP) in Pretoria. Seale claims that HNP Secretary Louis van der Schyff asked him to leave because the party is 'a racial one' and only Afrikaners were welcome. (MISA)

Nobel Prize-winning author and anti-apartheid liberal **Nadine Gordimer** was among other illustrious names – including Shakespeare – whose works were declared 'too racist or too boring' to be studied in secondary schools by administrators in Gauteng Province. The ban was later lifted and Education Minister

Kader Asmal issued a personal apology to the author. (MISA)

On 14 May photojournalist **Benny Gool**, formerly with the *Cape Times*, was subpoenaed to testify as a witness to the gang murder of Rashaad Staggie in Cape Town in August 1996. Gool took photographs of the killing, allegedly carried out by vigilante group PAGAD. However, Gool refused to testify, citing journalistic principles and fear for his life. Seven state witnesses against vigilante groups have been murdered since May 1998. Judge John Foxcroft refused to issue a warrant for Gool's arrest after he failed to appear in court, but instead pointed to inaccuracies in the subpoena and declared that it should be reissued. (MISA)

SPAIN

It was reported on 3 March that Pepe Rei, the imprisoned *Ardibeltza* editor and former writer for *Egin*, a newspaper closed by the government in 1998, had suffered heart attacks while in prison. Rei was accused of providing information to the secessionist group ETA and faces two to four years in prison although he has not been officially sentenced. (*Index* 6/1994, 5/1995, 4/1996). (*Euskalinfo*)

The Roman Catholic Church announced on 8 April that members of ETA will be excommunicated. The move would prevent the funerals of ETA members from being conducted in local churches. (*Guardian*)

SRI LANKA

On 23 February the state-owned *Daily News* and *Dinamina* newspapers published front-page stories alleging a conspiracy by the opposition United National Party (UNP) and Janatha Vimukthi Peramuna (JVP) to overthrow the government. The *Dinamina* report claimed that **Saman Wagarachchi**, a UNP member and editor of *Peramuna*, and **Sujeewa Gamage**, editor of *Peraliya* and *Iva*, would assist by engaging in anti-government propaganda. Subsequently, on 28 February, the *Peraliya* office was set on fire and Wagarachchi has been receiving telephone threats. (Free Media Movement)

A S M Fasmi, a reporter for the Tamil-language newspaper *Thinakkural* who is based on the north-western island of Mannar, has feared for his life since 21 March. Fasmi's report on the alleged 10 March rape of two Tamil women by members of the security forces was published on that day, and he was arrested by army intelligence officers. He has subsequently received several threatening phone calls. (CPJ)

On 26 March the government used national security as grounds for ordering TNL television not to broadcast a programme on the planned new presidential mansion. The action was highly controversial because the economy is in a serious crisis, and the mansion is expected to cost at least R1.7 billion (approximately US$22 million). (Free Media Movement)

Subramaniam Tiruchelvam (*Index* 2/2001), a 52-year-old Jaffna-based Tamil journalist arrested in Colombo on 2 January and allegedly tortured, was released on 30 March without charge. (*Hindu*)

Marie Colvin, a US correspondent working for the *Sunday Times* in Britain, was hit by shrapnel in the northern Vanni region on 16 April. Colvin had spent two unauthorised weeks in Tamil Tiger territory from where she had filed reports about the humanitarian crisis in the area. She was trying to re-enter government-held land with the aid of Tamil guides when the group was fired upon by Indian troops. In a press statement, the department of information noted that Colvin had overstayed her visa and claimed that she 'had her own secret agenda with the LTTE [Liberation Tigers of Tamil Eelam]'. However, it facilitated Colvin's quick transfer to a hospital in Colombo and her flight to New York. She suffered a serious injury to her left eye as a result of the attack. (*Sunday Times*, Free Media Movement, CPJ, RSF, *Gulf News*, *Hindu*, *The Times*)

On 23 April Judge R T Vignarajah ordered police in the northern Jaffna peninsula to complete their investigations into the assassination of Tamil journalist **Mylvaganam Nimalrajan** (*Index* 1/2001) by the end of May this year, and to hand over their report to the authorities. (Lanka Academic)

In mid-May it was reported that the criminal defamation case against **Victor Ivan**, editor of the Sinhalese-language

Ravaya newspaper, would be allowed to proceed, even though Upali Abeyratna, the presiding High Court judge in the case, had been disciplined by the Judicial Services Commission after Ivan's paper successfully accused him of professional misconduct. On 23 May an army-issue smoke bomb was thrown at the offices of the *Ravaya* and Tamil-language *Athavan* weekly newspapers. Ivan, who used to be a confidant of President Chandrika Kumaratunga and is now one of her most trenchant critics, said: 'You have to look at this attack in the context of a concerted attack against me and my paper by the government.' (Free Media Movement, Agence France-Presse, BBC, Associated Press)

On 30 May President Chandrika Kumaratunga ordered the immediate lifting of the ban on reporting on military issues imposed on local and foreign media for the past three years. Chief censor Ariya Rubasinghe said the government's decision was taken because the censorship was not being practically implemented. 'Even though we had the censorship, it has not been strictly enforced in recent times,' he said. (Associated Press)

SUDAN

Alfred Taban, BBC correspondent and director of the *Khartoum Monitor*, was arrested and detained in the Khartoum army headquarters on 12 April, where he was held without charge under emergency laws. The arrest was reportedly carried out during a church Easter ceremony after police

insisted that it be moved from the centre to a suburb. (PEN)

SWAZILAND

On 2 May the private monthly *Nation* was prohibited from publishing because of its failure to pay registration tax. Five thousand copies were allegedly seized. The High Court later declared the ban 'illegal' and it was lifted on 21 May but, the following day police raided its premises to insist that the journal was still 'technically' banned. Attorney-General Pheshaya Dlamini has appealed against the High Court's decision, thus delaying the reopening of the *Nation*'s offices. (MISA)

The independent weekly *Guardian* newspaper and its staff have been subjected to a series of threats and sanctions. On 1 May journalist **Thulani Mthethwa** was interrogated at length by police. Two days later police raided and searched the newspaper's offices in Mbabane. On 4 May the government imposed a ban, claiming that the *Guardian* had failed to fulfil the legal registration requirements. Copies of the newspaper were seized by police around the country and officials intercepted it as it crossed the border from South Africa, where it is printed. The *Guardian* had recently published articles concerning the royal family and allegations that the king's recent illness was related to rumours about his wife's attempts to poison him. MPs, including Minister for Information Mntonzima Dlamini, regard the articles as an infringement of the king's privacy. (MISA)

SYRIA

Nizar Nayouf (*Index* 6/1992, 8/1992, 10/1992, 10/1993, 6/1994, 6/1995, 5/1996, 3/1997, 1/1999, 4/1999, 4/2000, 2/2001) was released from military prison on 6 May after serving nine years of a ten-year sentence. He was taken to his parents' home in Lattakieh but remained under house arrest. On 21 June Nayouf was kidnapped by six members of the Intelligence service, who put a hood over his head. The abduction occurred as he was about to address a press conference. 'They threatened me over information I was planning to reveal,' he said on his release a day later. Nayouf suffers from a malignant tumour of the glands, and is paralysed from the waist down as a result of torture.

'Adel Isma'il, of the Lebanese daily *Al-Ra'i*, is the last remaining journalist in detention. He was sentenced to 10 years' imprisonment for alleged membership of the banned Democratic Ba'ath Party. (RSF, WAN, WiPC)

TAIWAN

Japanese cartoonist **Kobayashi Yoshinori** was barred entry on 3 March following publication of a non-fiction comic in which he said comfort women in Taiwan had volunteered to associate with occupying Japanese forces as a way out of poverty. Yoshinori had paraphrased the comments of Hsu Wen-lung, a prominent Taiwanese businessman and one-time advisor to President Chen Shui-bian, who said the women had the 'best possible job'. Hsu later withdrew his remarks, but Yoshinori was censured on the grounds he had 'insulted the national dignity'. (Agence France-Presse, Associated Press, Reuters)

THAILAND

On 10 April **Withayut Sangsophit**, director of radio station Home Media, was shot dead in Surat Thani. He had recently denounced the local authority for involvement in financial irregularities and had been under police protection for three months. (RSF)

TOGO

An unspecified number of copies of the weekly *Le Regard* were seized by police officers on 27 March for alleging that the government had refused EU funding for legislative elections, due in October. Under the new press code the minister of the interior and security may order the seizure of any newspaper deemed to be in violation of press laws. Following this amendment six newspapers were seized in 2000 (*Index* 2/2000, 4/2000, 5/2000). (RSF)

TUNISIA

On 21 February RSF's Robert Ménard and Jean-François Julliard were detained and deported after trying to distribute copies of banned publication *Kaws el Karama*, whose publisher **Jalel Zoghlami** (*Index* 4/2000, 2/2001) began a hunger strike on 3 February to demand legal recognition of the monthly. He ended his fast after three weeks. (RSF)

Mokhtar Trifi, leader of the Tunisian Human Rights League (LTDH), was convicted and sentenced to three years in prison for spreading 'false information' on 3 March. The former journalist had signed a petition against a February court decision which declared the new leadership of the LTDH invalid. (*CHR Tunisia*)

It was reported on 16 March that editions of *Salama* and *El Mustaqilla*, published in Paris and London respectively, had been banned. The issue of *Salama* contained an article about the status of women while *El Mustaqilla* included two pieces on human rights. No official explanation was given. (RSF)

TURKEY

A new legal action commenced in 8 February against **Akin Birdal**, vice-president of the International Human Rights Federation (*Index* 4/1998, 5/1998, 1/1999, 4/1999, 6/1999, 1/2000, 2/2000, 3/2000, 6/2000) for having called for Turkey to apologise for the harm it had inflicted on the Armenians and other minorities. Akin Birdal is accused of having openly insulted 'Turkishness' after remarks made in Germany last year. (*Cildekt*)

It was reported on 2 March that **Eylem Tandogan**, head of Mem publishing house, went to trial for printing a book by condemned Kurdish rebel leader Abdullah Ocalan that was deemed to be 'aiding and abetting a terrorist organisation' and 'spreading propa-

ganda'. Tandogan faces from one and a half to four years in prison if convicted. The two-volume book, *How to Live*, was written in 1996, but only published in Turkey last year. (Agence France-Presse)

Swedish-Kurdish writer **Mehmet Uzun**, charged with helping a terrorist organisation on the basis of his novel, *Bright as Love, Dark as Death*, had his case dismissed on 4 April. The Istanbul State Security Court also dismissed the case against **Hasan Oztoprak**, of Gendas publishing house, accused of separatist propaganda on the basis of an essay by the writer entitled 'The Blossoming of the Pomegranate Tree'. Oztoprak faced a three-year sentence. (*Cildekt*)

The pro-Kurdish daily *2000'de Yeni Gündem*, first published in Turkish on 27 March last year, was obliged to cease publication on 31 March, following the examples of *Yeni Ulke*, *Ozgür Gündem*, *Ozgür Ulke*, *Yeni Politika*, *Demokrasi*, *Ulkede Gündem* and *Ozgür Bakis*. *2000'de Yeni Gündem* had been seized 15 times and taken to court in 53 separate cases. **Ragip Zarakoglu**, chief editor of the paper, said: '*Gündem* gave voice to another Turkey and, in one of the most difficult times for Turkey, tried to make its contribution to the democratisation of the country.' (*Kurdish Observer*)

Caskun Ak, of Internet access provider Superonline, was sentenced by an Istanbul court to 40 months' imprisonment on 27 March for 'mockery and insults to the institutions'. He was accused of failing to censor a 24-page contribution of clippings and reports on human rights violations in the southeast, when he was moderator of a chat forum. Caskun was summoned by the police following four complaints filed by the ministries of the interior and justice, by parliament and the armed forces general staff. (*Cildekt*)

Economist and academic **Fikret Baskaya** (*Index* 5/2000), sentenced to 16 months' jail on 13 June 2000 for a crime of opinion, was due to be jailed on 29 June. He was convicted on the strength of an article published in the defunct daily *Ozgür Bakis*. Eight years ago, Baskaya was sentenced by a state security court to one year and eight months for his book *Paradigmanin iflasi* (*Failure of the Paradigm*), a sentence that lost him his university chair. The European Human Rights Court, advised of the case, found Turkey guilty of infringing freedom of expression. (*Cildekt*)

UKRAINE

Radio Continent's broadcasting licence was cancelled on 12 April, and its frequency assigned to another station, Radio Onix. The decision was justified by its non-payment of US$10,000, a debt allegedly due an increase in its broadcasting time in 1997 and the rebroadcast of foreign radio programmes that has been judged illegal. Significantly, the station used to employ murdered journalist **Georgy Gongadze** (*Index* 1/2001, 2/2001). The decision threatens the existence of a station which rebroadcasts Voice of

America, the BBC and Deutschewelle. (WAN)

A team of US experts concluded in May that the headless, charred body discovered near Kiev in November 2000 was that of **Georgy Gongadze**, editor-founder of the online publication Pravda (*Index* 1/2001). An earlier genetic identity test, using some of his mother's blood supplied by the parliamentary inquiry into his disappearance, had proven negative. The cause of death could not be determined because the head was never found. **Mykola Melnychenko**, a former bodyguard of President Leonid Kuchma who made recordings of him apparently ordering Gongadze's murder, has been granted asylum in America after living in hiding since last November (*Index* 2/2001). The tapes are to be subjected to phonoscopic analysis to determine their authenticity. (Associated Press, *Daily Telegraph*, RFE/RL)

USA

In March students at Brown University, Rhode Island, stole nearly 4,000 copies of campus newspaper *Brown Daily Herald* in protest at its publication of an advertisement denouncing reparations for slavery, placed by conservative columnist and salon.com writer **David Horowitz**. Later in April, when Princeton's *Daily Princetonian* ran the advert opposite an editorial describing Horowitz's views as 'racist', the writer withdrew his payment pending an apology, describing himself as the victim of a 'left-wing witch hunt'. (Associated Press)

A First Amendment ruling has granted the Nuremberg Files website the right to continue publishing a list of pro-abortion doctors, with their home addresses and car registration numbers. The site describes abortion as 'Satan's food-source' and calls on volunteers to carry out surveillance duty on the perpetrators. Pro-abortion activists are bewildered at the toleration of what they consider a simple hit list. Ten doctors have been killed for being pro-choice, and a further 17 murder attempts have been made. The names of the dead have been scratched out on the website, but are still visible. (*Guardian*)

On 3 May New York public radio station WNYC broadcast recordings of prisoner executions that took place in Georgia between 1983 and 1998. Six hours of executions are available online at sound-portraits.org. (*Guardian*)

On 7 May **Jeffrey Pierce** left an Oklahoma prison after being cleared of rape by new DNA testing. He had spent 15 years in prison on the basis of evidence from Oklahoma Police chemist Joyce Gilchrist. Gilchrist's work has been heavily criticised during the years to the extent that she was reprimanded by one professional organisation and expelled from another. The cases on which she worked include 11 in which the defendants have been executed, and 12 in which the alleged perpetrator is on death row. The federal Justice Department has started an investigation. (*International Herald Tribune*)

On 6 June Random House agreed to stop distributing copies of a memoir by **Bryan Magee** that accuses Ralph Schoenman, a noted lecturer and one-time confidant of philosopher Bertrand Russell, of being a CIA operative. In *Confessions of a Philosopher: A Personal Journey Through Western Philosophy from Plato to Popper,* first published in the US in 1998, Magee says Ralph Schoenman was planted to spy on Russell, a noted 1960s opponent of the Vietnam War. He also called Schoenman 'appallingly sinister' and 'calculated and manipulative', according to court documents. (Associated Press)

UZBEKISTAN

On 28 February writer **Emin Usman** died in custody at the ministry of internal affairs (MID). He was arrested on 11 February and accused of 'distributing materials that contained a danger to public security'. Usman was taken to the basement of the MID building, a place notorious for torture. Usman's relatives were informed he had committed suicide, but in a medical certificate given to relatives the cause of death was cited as 'brain tumour'. (CJES, WiPC)

On the night of 9 March the apartment of **Elena Urlayeva**, a consultant with the Human Rights Society of Uzbekistan (UHRS), was set on fire while her family slept. No one was injured, but the UHRS believes the incident was revenge for Urlayera's picketing of parliament on 7 March. (UHRS, RFE/RL)

Majid Abduraimov, a journalist for the newspaper *Yangi Asr,* was arrested in Sukhandarya on 10 March for allegedly accepting a bribe of US$6,000. According to RFE/RL, this was the third in a recent series of arrests of journalists writing about corruption. Sources says the real reason for his arrest is his articles about oil fraud involving local officials. (CJES)

VENEZUELA

Omar Estacio, the lawyer representing *La Razon* editor **Pablo López Ulaccio** (*Index* 5/2000), petitioned the 14th Caracas Court on 20 February in relation to evidence that was not admitted in the previous hearing and the lapse of time since legal proceedings began in November 1999. The request was denied. Estacio has also written to President Hugo Chavez charging him with responsibility for the fate of Ulacio who fled, believing he would not get a fair trial. Court inspector **General René Molina**, who last year dismissed one judge on the case for 'violation of due process', resigned the same month, rather than 'submit to the pressures to destroy López Ulaccio'. (IPYS)

Repeated and broadly scattered attacks on the media and 'media conspiracies' have become a regular feature of the four-hour radio programme *Alo Presidente,* a phone-in hosted by President Hugo Chavez. On 22 March, he denounced the existence of a 'media conspiracy'. On 4 April he launched a 20-minute diatribe against

Andrés Mato Osorio, editor of the daily *El Universal,* whom he accused of being a fraud and acting on behalf of 'international interests'. These may have been connected to José Maria Bellestas, a member of the rebel Colombian National Liberation Army (ELN) detained in March, and an assignment on his whereabouts undertaken by journalist **Adriana Cortés** of the newspaper *El Nacional.* Colombian TV station Noticias RCN reported on 4 April that Cortés was in fact a collaborator of Ballestas, a report repeated by Caracas TV stations. (IPYS)

The community radio programme *Responda,* broadcast daily on the state-run Radio YVKE Mundia, was suspended 18 May on 'orders from above', according to the official explanation. Journalist and programme host **Fernando Silva** said the ban was a response to his reports on alleged hiring irregularities by Caracas Mayor Alfredo Pena, a former minister. (IPYS)

VIETNAM

Nguyen Thin Thu set herself ablaze on 19 March to protest against the arrest of **Le Quang Liem**, leader of the Hoa Hao Buddhist sect who was arrested on 17 March and detained for 24 hours. The sect is persecuted because of its opposition to the Communist Party during the Vietnam War and its fight in support of human rights. Nguyen died of her burns. (Vatican.va)

ZAMBIA

The state-owned *Zambia Mail* and *Times of Zambia* published the first draft of the government's Freedom of Information Act in the last week in February. Attorney-General Bonaventure Mutale said its aims were to provide access to information, set out the scope of public information and promote transparency and accountability in public offices. However, ojections have been raised in response to Sections 5, 8 and 21 which deal with public officials' right to claim exemptions, presidential power to have sole responsibility for appointing a commissioner and the time delay for responding to requests for information. (MISA)

On 5 May freelance journalist **Obert Simwanza** was whipped by a policewoman and beaten by supporters of the ruling Movement for Multiparty Democracy (MMD). The supporters suspected him of being sympathetic to an MMD faction opposed to President Frederick Chiluba which had planned a rally but had been violently disrupted by police with tear gas and live ammunition. In the attack Simwanza suffered blows to the face. He was released without charge following a 20-minute detention. (MISA)

ZIMBABWE

President Robert Mugabe's Department of Information and Publicity castigated the *Daily News* for its alleged malicious reporting of the president's visit to Belgium. It claims that an article that appeared in the newspaper on 6 March sought to mislead readers into thinking that Mugabe was almost arrested by a 'gang of [gay] gangsters'. They threatened that the newspaper should no longer seek protection under freedom of expression, but under 'freedom of opposition'. (MISA)

On 8 March Eddison Zvogbo, MP for Masvingo South, heckled the Minister of Justice Patrick Chinamasa, claiming that the governmental decree that political parties could not own broadcasting stations was illegal and would limit the right to freedom of expression. He also criticised the regulation that requires 75% local content and the government's right to broadcast on every station whenever it wishes. (MISA)

On 9 March the state-owned *Herald* published an article which detailed that the forthcoming Freedom of Information Bill would require journalists to have professional qualifications before gaining a press card. In drawing up these new accreditation regulations the government plans to consult with unions, but not activist organisations. According to Minister of State for Information and Publicity Jonathan Moyo, the bill will facilitate the free flow of information, preserve standards of decency and deal with media ownership structures in order to prevent monopolies. (MISA)

Njabulo Ncube, a reporter with the *Financial Gazette*, received a death threat on 10 March from war veterans leader Abel Mahlungu. Mahlungu charged into the Bulawayo Press Club shouting that Ncube would 'not last up to 2002' because of his alleged links with the opposition Movement for Democratic Change (MDC). (MISA, AI)

On 2 April it was reported that **Pedzisai Ruhanya**, a journalist with the pro-MDC *Daily News*, had been barred from covering the ruling party's Harare provincial elections. Two war veterans confiscated Ruhanya's press card and made a death threat. He was then taken to a basement and subjected to questioning as to his political affiliation and his address. (MISA)

Minister for Justice Patrick Chinamasa and Attorney-General Andrew Chigovera dismissed the Parliamentary Legal Committee's report on the controversial Broadcasting Services Bill on the grounds that the committee had failed to follow the correct preparatory procedures, and had not kept minutes of their meetings. Chinamasa also alleged that the report had been produced by the MDC MP for Bulawayo North East, Welshman Ncube, rather than the chairman of the committee as it should have been. Ncube argued that the bill was riddled with unconstitutional sections and had been fast-tracked through parliament for this reason. **Mark Chavanduka** (*Index* 3/1999, 2/2000, 3/2000, 4/2000, 2/2001), editor of the *Standard*, called the bill 'a sinister piece of legislation'. It was passed into law on 3 April. (MISA)

On 4 April three journalists with the *Daily News* were charged with criminal defamation of President Robert Mugabe and Parliamentary Speaker Emmerson Mnangwa under the Law and Order Maintenance Act. The charges related to articles published last year, where it was alleged that Air HarborTechnologies had given bribes to senior politicians and business leaders in return for the the tender for Harare's new international airport. President Mugabe's nephew, Leo Mugabe, Palestinian Ambassador Ali Halimeh and the former editor of the *Herald* newspaper, Tony Sithole, are all implicated in the corruption allegation. Sithole has admitted receiving certain monies, but claims it was payment for an airport supplement that appeared in the newspaper. In a list publicised by Hani Yimani, owner of Air Harbor Technologies, Sithole received over Z$700,000 (US$13,000). *Daily News*'s editor **Geoff Nyarota** and reporters **Sandra Nyaira** and **Julius Zava** denied the charges. Three weeks later Sandra Nyaira threatened to sue Information Minister Jonathan Moyo and the *Herald* for defamation following an article in the *Herald in* which Moyo castigated Nyaira for reporting that Vice President Joseph Msika had begged veteran nationalist Edgar Tekere to rejoin ZANU-PF. Nyaira's lawyers claimed that article in was intended to demean and injure her. (MISA)

On 17 April a High Court judge upheld the right of the weekly *Zimbabwe Independent* to report the charges of embezzlement filed against Information Minister Jonathan Moyo. Moyo had initiated a court battle in an attempt to muzzle the newspaper. He is charged with embezzling US$100,000 from the Ford Foundation while employed in Kenya from 1993 to 1997. (MISA)

The investigation into the abduction and torture of **Mark Chivanduka** and **Ray Choto** is languishing in the face of political and bureaucratic obstacles. The two journalists with the weekly *Standard* were tortured while in army custody in January 1999. Former chief justice Antony Gubbay, who ordered an inquiry, has since been forced from office and, two years after the event, an identity parade has yet to take place, and Choto has not been approached for a statement. (MISA)

On 26 April three freelance photographers who requested anonymity were arrested while taking photographs of President Robert Mugabe's visit to the Zimbabwe International Trade Fair. The president's security personnel approached the men and handcuffed them, although they had official accreditation. They spent a night in prison cells and were only told upon their release the following morning that they had been arrested under the Law and Order Maintenance Act. They were required to pay Z$180 (US$3) in admission of guilt fines. **Grey Chitiga**, a photographer with the *Daily News*, was threatened by security at the same event. (MISA)

On 28 April **Samuel Mungadze**, a journalist with the *Standard,* was attacked by suspected ZANU-PF supporters in Ruwa Mandalay. The reporter was investigating claims that locals were being forced to attend independence celebrations at the Ruwa Rehabilitation Centre. The attackers had been urged to 'take on the enemy' in a speech given by the Marondera West MP, Brigadier Ambrose Mutinhiri. During the attack three passport-sized photographs of the victim were taken as well as notebooks, a watch and a bank card. (MISA)

For the second time in a month *Daily News* editor **Geoff Nyarota** has been charged with criminal defamation, it was reported on 10 May. The case concerns stories in which it was alleged that **Evelyn Masaiti**, opposition MP for Mutasahas, and three relatives of victims in the violence-hit June 2000 parliamentary elections, are suing President Mugabe in the USA for damages. (MISA)

Compiled by: Gbenga Oduntan, Shifa Rahman, Polly Rossdale (Africa); Ben Carrdus, Andrew Kendle, Anna Lloyd (Asia); Andrew Mingay, Victoria Sams (south and central America); James Badcock; Gill Newsham, Neil Sammonds (Middle East); Fabio Scarpello (north America and Pacific)

Ame

Estrella jail, Arizona: the world's first female chain gang.
Credit: Joan Klatchko / Camera Press Digital

rican gulag

The US prison system today has much in common with the old Soviet gulags set up by Stalin. An unprecedented 2 million prisoners provide plenty of forced labour to build the profits of corporations

Guest editor:
Mark Dow

PATRICIA J WILLIAMS

Payback time

Now that Timothy McVeigh has been executed, I suppose we're all supposed to stop talking about it – to 'enjoy closure', a bit like the election.

But McVeigh's execution was troubling on so many levels, it's hard to know where to begin. It was alarming to watch the procedural impatience, the official 'just get it over with' mentality, despite defence lawyers' not having had a chance to go through more than 4,000 pages of FBI documents that no one disputes ought to have been turned over before McVeigh's trial.

It was distressing to hear the semantic shiftiness of our president as he described the event. To us individualists at home, he said that it was McVeigh who 'chose' this method of reckoning; to a European audience it was 'the will of the people in the United States'. Like some libertarian Pontius Pilate, Bush washed his hands of any responsibility, skilfully uncoupling the role of the executive from execution. It's bad enough to have a death penalty; it is positively chilling when the chief Pooh-Bah shrugs it off as though helpless, assigning federally engineered death to forces beyond him.

It was incredible to see anti-death penalty commentators apologising constantly, always having to blither 'of course no one condones his actions' – as though arguing for life imprisonment made one the squishiest, most bleeding-heart of moral equivocators. As a *New York Times* commentary observed, 'Experts said it was the wrong case to debate – many people who do not approve of the death penalty wanted Mr McVeigh to die.'

Yet if one really wants to test the commitment of a civilisation to its expressed principles of justice, the McVeigh case is exactly the right case to debate. There was little question as to his guilt (even if the question of conspiracy remains an open one), his crime was inexpressibly reprehensible and he maintained a demeanour of controlled, remorseless calculation to the end. In other words, it is precisely the clarity of his wrongdoing that presses us to consider most seriously the limits of state force. The question is whether we want to license our government to kill, rather than restrain by imprisoning, the very worst among us.

Much recent debate about capital punishment has focused on probabilities: the repeated demonstration that 'beyond a reasonable doubt' is a matter of considerable uncertainty and outright error. I have recommended before, and do so again here, *Actual Innocence* by Jim Dwyer, Barry Scheck and Peter Neufeld. These lawyers' work with the Innocence Project has led to dozens of releases from death row and to calls for moratoriums in states where pro-death-penalty sentiment once ran high.

There is also the question of disparate impact, particularly upon minorities and the poor. 'There are no racial overtones in [McVeigh's] conviction,' wrote the *New York Times* in an editorial. Perhaps that's true if considered in a vacuum, but certainly not with regard to its procedural legacy. If the FBI couldn't get right the most important and supposedly most careful investigation in its history and still no stay was granted, then there is no hope in any other case. McVeigh's 'nonracial' fate, moreover, will surely be invoked high-handedly in all those more routine, less highly scrutinised cases. The fact that of the remaining federal death row inmates only two are white is, according to John Ashcroft, merely 'normal'. For more on this aspect of the debate, I recommend reading *Legal Lynching: The Death Penalty and America's Future*, by the Rev Jesse Jackson, Representative Jesse Jackson Jr and *The Nation*'s Bruce Shapiro. Forthcoming from The New Press, it is an eloquent argument against the inequity of the death penalty's administration and makes a compelling case against its violent irreversibility, its irredeemable finality as pursued by prosecutors, judges and juries who are, after all, far from all-knowing or divine.

As un-American a statement as this seems to be just now, I don't believe we should have a death penalty at all. In the annals of criminology, the passage of a little time has exonerated too many of the convicted for us to be engaging in the headlong rush towards Quick Death that seems so politically popular these days. And even in the absence of exoneration, the death penalty accomplishes nothing but the perpetuation of violent retribution.

One of the saddest parts of the McVeigh saga was listening to the
endlessly amplified testimonials of those survivors and family members
whose sentiments were premised on vengeance being 'mine' rather than
the Lord's. One woman wished the electric chair had been used, because
it would have been more painful. Another said, 'I think bombs should be
strapped on him, and then he can walk around the room for ever until
they went off and he wouldn't know when it would happen.'

Such traumatised expectations led to predictable disappointment. 'I
really wanted him to say something,' said one witness. 'I wanted him to
see me,' said another. 'I thought I would feel something more satisfying,
but I don't,' said a victim's son. 'For him just to have gone to sleep seems
unfair.' This sort of desire for 'more' leaves us poised on the edge of an
appetite for re-enacted violence and voyeurism. Given the horrific losses
McVeigh's crime inflicted, this primal hunger can be almost seductive –
a howl of mourning very hard to resist, never mind debate. But it is
dangerous if it allows us to lose sight of the fact that the debate we must
have is, again, about the limits of state force, not about devising the
perfect mirror of each victim's suffering.

Mourning the condemned as well as the innocent is something
we don't necessarily practise a lot in this era. But I think it is central to
the project of asking what it is that accounts for the enormous toll of
violence at this moment in American history. It is a task that requires us
not so much to turn to explanations of genetic inferiority and biological
disposition except in the most exceptional of instances, but rather
demands that we ask what it is that would make some lives so wildly
destructive. It involves seeing even killers as ruined human beings whose
potential has been lost to us, and whose loss means something to the
community, to the increasingly small world we all share. If we feel no
loss but only gain, I fear we are indeed on the wrong side of a thin line
whose logic leads to the worst kind of despotism.

I appreciate the extent to which my remarks will be interpreted as
an apology for nothing less than heinousness, which surely they are not.
Too many of us have seen friends murdered senselessly. I recognise the
need to confine murderers. But I do not believe in the death penalty.

I appreciate how hard my point will be to hear in an age when
television stations have sued to broadcast executions as part of our
constitutional freedom. How much we want to see but not hear death!
(Isn't it odd, when executions occur, that the newspapers always

print the last supper of the executed rather than his last thoughts? The organisation People for the Ethical Treatment of Animals even went so far as to suggest that Timothy McVeigh make his last meal a vegan one to advertise their cause – McVeigh declined politely, saying time was too short to debate the matter further. An altogether peculiar obsession – the advertisement of what he consumed, but not what he was thinking.)

I appreciate, in short, how unpopular it is to say that even the destructive life bears lessons whose social value we suppress at our own risk. But I think it is an integral part of never forgetting – to be reminded of how seductive murder is as a solution. How close the killer is to the executioner in the search for ultimate resolution. How like ourselves. How appealing it is to control life and death, and how implicated are those who 'assist' in death, in overcoming the body's resistance. Thus I think it is absolutely vital to allow prisoners to appeal as loud and long as they can. For as John Edgar Wideman observes, 'People are easier to kill if they come from nowhere. If they have no names, no fathers or mothers.' We should never be able to kill without that reminder of the body's resistance.

Let me try to press this difficult point again by posing the problem as a broad one about the limits of state force. What is, after all, the purpose in refraining from cruel and unusual punishment even for cruel and unusual crimes? Why didn't we just eviscerate Jeffrey Dahmer when we had the chance? Why don't we let the families of victims stone criminals, or slice off their tongues? Why don't we officially entomb prisoners alive, in soundproofed little boxes, a hole for air, a hole for drainage, and just wait for them to die like bugs in a jar?

Conventions on human rights and prisoners' rights remind us that casting criminals as subhumans, as animals, as non-citizens, is as much about us as it is 'them'. They remind us that demonising wholesale is a risky enterprise. We have not yet reached the point where we are completely unaware of this notion; few politicians could yet suggest that we stop pussyfooting around and execute everyone convicted of murder, period. O J Simpson and Susan Smith. Colin Ferguson and Gina Grant (the young woman admitted to Harvard before it was discovered she had bludgeoned her abusive mother to death with a candlestick). The Menendez brothers. Secretary of Defense Robert McNamara and Senator John Kerry, for all the war crimes they are now so willing to take responsibility for. We'd all sleep better afterwards. Better yet, we could execute them all at the same time. It could be the biggest, best execution in US history. If we want deterrence, what better way, right? The mothers of victims could step up and throw the first ball, so to speak, by plucking the eyes from the sockets of the condemned. And where once there were baskets into which heads would roll, we could have Jack Kevorkian – Dr Death himself – with a bucket for the hearts and lungs and livers. (Kevorkian has long been an advocate of 'harvesting' the innards of executed prisoners, although perhaps he has modified his views since being imprisoned himself. But, last anyone checked, he wants death row to *move*; shouldn't let all those healthy spare parts shrivel on the vine. What high-tech resurrection potential: death row as the ultimate recycling bin.)

Frankly, the current fashion in calling for what is effectively a public ritual of mockery and crucifixion of criminals is astounding in a nation as largely Christian as ours. It is quite pagan in form, the call for Death. Yet we have come close to the point, I fear, where all forms of punishment inflicted on criminals are deemed acceptable as crude but just payback. 'Slow bloodletting' is less than what the 'criminal slime' deserve, as a law student once put it so succinctly.

But it is democracy that dies when we become a nation of heartbroken vengeance-seekers. The seduction of the 'string-'em-up' mentality is not that it's 'frontier' justice in some cruel, cartoonish way. Its appeal is that it is a response of insatiable sorrow, immediate payback; it is heroically grief-stricken rather than reasoned. Moreover, the rage for retribution risks obscuring the possibility of innocence, the need for due process, the presence of mitigating circumstances and the dubiety of crooked informants. And in its most extreme forms, the bloodlust risks being used to justify the state practice of sadism upon all those guilty bodies so *needing* to be beaten, so *asking* to be broken. We despise murderers, we hate. But there is some point at which despising takes on a life of its own; when the death-dealing actually becomes satisfying and eventually pleasurable. That sense of relief, that rush of goodness, seems to be growing in this country, and we should resist it at all costs.

All this is why we have historically made the prosecutor's role that of representing The People of a state, rather than just the victim of a particular crime. The prosecutor, as surrogate for the interests of the state, is supposed to consider justice in an un-inflamed, long-term, social sense.

Arizona: Sheriff Joe Arpaio's female chain gang at work. Credit: Joan Klatchko / Camera Press Digital

But the risks of enjoying vengeance too much are troubling enough when we have spectacles like the barbecuing, sunbathing, rowdily celebratory crowds at serial killer Ted Bundy's execution. If one adds race to the brew, we must take history seriously enough to err on the side of extreme caution. The chain gang has made a comeback in several states. Domination fantasies have become disguised as lessons in work ethic. As long-time death row prisoner Mumia Abu-Jamal, still protesting his innocence in the face of dwindling hopes for further stays, wrote in *Live From Death Row* (Addison-Wesley, US 1995):

In the 1987 case McClesket vs Kemp, the famed Baldus study revealed acts that unequivocally proved the following: (1) defendants charged with killing white victims in Georgia are 4.3 times more likely to be sentenced to death as defendants charged with killing blacks; (2) six of every 11 defendants convicted of killing a white person would not have received the death penalty if their victim had been black; and (3) cases involving black defendants and white victims are more likely to result in a death sentence than cases featuring any other racial combination of defendant and victim . . .

Does this mean that African-Americans are somehow innocents, subjected to a set-up by state officials? Not especially. What it does suggest is that state actors, at all stages of the criminal justice system, including slating at the police stations, arraignment at the judicial office, pre-trial, trial and sentencing stage before a court, treat African-American defendants with a special vengeance not experienced by white defendants.

This is the dictionary definition of 'discrimination.'

One of racism's many manifestations is the collective wish that blacks were not alive – one can hear this expressed over and over again on talk-radio programmes around the country any day of the week. The wish that blacks would just go away and shut up and stop taking up so much time and food and air, and the world would return to its Norman Rockwell loveliness and the US could be employed and happy once more. Some times it's expressed as an actual death wish, but more often it comes out as a *disappearance* wish. But the sentiment is no less frightening to those of us on the receiving end of such euphemisms. Moreover, the killing wish takes on such public, even joyous legitimacy when blackness is paired with actual outlaw behaviour.

There is a relation, I think, between the restraint necessary in law enforcement and the First Amendment cliché about protecting most the speech one hates because it is a test for all the rest of our democratic principles. Should we not, through our government, practise and model the kind of restraint we wish killers would have had? We wish that before they had twisted that knife, pulled that trigger, they had considered the mind they were destroying, the family they were rending, the shattering, spinning loss – the shattered life so suddenly and eternally unrecoverable. Focusing on the crime they have committed reminds us of the need to make sure it never happens again, and we apply varying degrees of punishment, deterrence or rehabilitation. But focusing as well on *who* has committed the crime reminds us there is logic in each life. Not so much a logic to be endured or sanctioned, but sometimes a life course that sheds light on what should never have been.

We need to remember that there are prison guards who help prisoners in good and human ways, *and* that there are those who supply them with drugs. We need to know that there are guards who struggle thanklessly to do remarkable jobs under intolerable conditions, and those who, as Abu-Jamal describes, put lighted cigarettes in prisoners' ears. We need to know that the sides are not always as clear as night and day – that 'Harry Washington', demented on death row, was once a prison guard.

We need to consider these as possibilities, not just in the context of the death penalty or of life imprisonment, but in view of the very large numbers of Americans who are incarcerated generally. Some of those people who are in prison will be back among us – we have not yet decided to kill all of them – and if prison ends up spewing out people who are more dehumanised than when they went in, it will cost us dearly.

'9:03' reads the inscription on the Oklahoma City memorial. Would that we could undo that moment by some rite of sacrificial substitution: one life to bring back all the others. But that is magical thinking – the hubris of assumed divinity, the belief stucture of children and the utterly despairing. The difficult paradox of healing is having to live on and through that wilderness of grief, with no illusion of resurrection and no choice but not to kill again. ❏

Patricia J Williams is a professor at Columbia Law School and the author of The Alchemy of Race and Rights *(Harvard)*

Johnny Tremain, once of Camp Miller (see Photostory, p176). Credit: Jonathon Hexner

CHARLES KEIL

for the dean who shut down SUNY/Buffalo's degrees for prisoners

incarceration rates per 100,000
    in 1992
indonesia incarcerates 22
and other countries are very
    poor you see
mother india incarcerates 23
a real land of the brave and
home of the free
greece 60 and denmark 66
yes they have criminals
and they make their laws stick
japan incarcerates 36
industrial, rich and yet not so
    sick
158 jailbirds in the brand new
    czech republic
germany 80, france 84
civilised euro wrongdoers
    behind closed doors
australia 91 sweden 69
some pay a fine others serve
    time
when we get to the u.s. hold on
    to your hat
519
what do you think of that?

u.s. blacks 1,947
u.s. black men three thousand
    eight hundred and twenty two
(I'm spelling it out, kerry grant,
    just for you)
that's 3,800 more than
    indonesia puts the screws to
and if faculty at 'you be' reach
    out to these black males (and
    women too)
the dean turns pink, and then
    turns pale
what if the statistics should
    come alive
what if those inside survive
what if they should learn and
    strive
to understand the numbers and
    the plan
one of them might come look-
    ing for 'the man'
and one of the 3,822
might also come looking for
    you, or me
better we should just throw
    away the key? ❏

Charles Keil has recently retired as professor of cultural studies at the State University of New York, Buffalo. First published in the radical monthly First of the Month

RANDALL G SHELDEN

Inside the gulag

There are now about 1.5 million people in US prisons, with an imprisonment rate exceeding all other industrialised societies. Add another 600,000 in local jails and there are more than 2 million locked up on any given day. The largest jump in the US prison population began in the mid-1970s, just as the 'war on drugs' was beginning

Taking a long view of history, the incarceration rate in the US stood at 113 per 100,000 population in 1935; by 1975 it had remained largely unchanged, with a rate of 111, with some minor fluctuations during this 40-year period. By 1985, it had doubled to a rate of 202; by 1995 it had doubled again, reaching a rate of 411. At the end of 1999, it stood at 476. More recent figures are unavailable, but it is likely that the US rate of imprisonment is at or near 500. In other words, in just 25 years, the rate of imprisonment has increased more than fourfold.

The 'war on drugs' is obviously responsible for most of the increase, a war that has targeted racial minorities, especially African–Americans. Consider the following:

- Convictions for drug law violations accounted for almost one-half of the increase in state prison inmates during the 1980s and early 1990s.
- The rate of incarceration for African-Americans is around nine times the rate for whites; the odds of an African-American male going to prison are more than one in four (28.5%), compared with about one in 25 for white males.
- African-Americans constitute only around 12% of the population and 13% of all monthly drug users, yet they represent 35% of those arrested for drug possession and 74% of those sentenced to prison on drug charges. Drug-arrest rates for minorities went from under 600 per 100,000 in 1980 to over 1,500 in 1990. For whites they remained essentially the same.

From 1986 to 1991, in the middle of the biggest crackdown on drugs, the proportion of African-Americans incarcerated for drug offences went up an incredible 465%, compared with an increase of 110% for whites.

These figures are just a sampling of the human wreckage resulting from the punitive policies used in this country over the past 25 years. Part of it is the product of the 'war on drugs', which has mostly targeted the poor and the racial minorities, but it has been exacerbated by the emergence of a 'prison industrial complex'. A further result is the emergence of a 'new American apartheid' that stands alongside the already existing system of residential apartheid, since racial minorities constitute almost two-thirds of all prisoners.

Prisons seem to be everywhere you look, reaching into the most remote areas of the country. In fact, the overwhelming majority of the ones built during the past two decades are in rural areas, many in towns with populations of under 1,000. If one were to place a black dot for every prison on a map of the USA, you would probably not be able to see the map for the black.

Our first exposure to the term gulag came with the publication of Russian author Alexander Solzhenitsyn's *Gulag Archipelago* in 1970. The book exposed the existence of literally thousands of prison camps spread throughout the Soviet Union, mostly in remote such regions as Siberia. These 'forced labour' camps originally emerged in the 1920s under Joseph Stalin and were ostensibly set up to accelerate the growth of industrialisation after the 1917 revolution. One might assume that the gulag phenomenon was either an aberration or something restricted to Third World or totalitarian societies, but a close look at the modern US prison system suggests otherwise.

The US prison system today has many of the same characteristics as the Soviet gulags. There are numerous human rights abuses, such as cruel and unusual punishment (eg, long periods in solitary confinement); lack of educational opportunities (grants for college courses have been almost eliminated); lack of drug treatment (though the majority of prisoners need it); physical abuse by guards; and an overall 'culture of violence' tacitly condoned by officials. Moreover, there is a lot of forced – and cheap – labour, much of which produces profits for corporations. Most rural prisons, especially those in Texas and other parts of the

South, resemble the plantations from the days of slavery, where prisoners work in the fields and sing old-fashioned slave songs – not surprisingly, since at least half of all prisoners are African-Americans and, among the states with the highest incarceration rates, seven of the top ten are Southern states.

The modern prison system's description as a prison industrial complex is comparable to the 'military industrial complex', a term first introduced in President Dwight Eisenhower's farewell address in 1960, when he warned against the growth of a system generated by the use of fear tactics – in this case, the fear of communism. We now know how much this complex grew and how it was based on false fears. The rise of the prison industrial complex has been the result of similar scare tactics, only this time there is not an external enemy, but an internal enemy, namely 'crime'. As Cold War propaganda exaggerated the threat of communism, the more recent version exaggerates the amount of crime in the US. So, while the rate of imprisonment increased fourfold over the past 25 years, the overall rate of crime remained virtually unchanged, although there has been a slight increase in the rate of violent crime. The crimes that have increased the most, based upon arrest data, have been drug law violations, which increased by well over 1,000% during the last three decades.

But what also drive the increase in the prison population are noteworthy changes in the US labour market. Specifically, we have witnessed major declines in the manufacturing sector (with a corresponding rise in the service industry that accounts for roughly 90% of job growth in recent years); the 'downsizing' of much of the workforce; and – especially in rural areas – the closure of many military installations and factories. Literally thousands of rural communities have been begging states to build prisons in their communities.

To give an idea of the gulag look of the US prison system, consider Texas as a prime example. The state now boasts over 100 prisons (most have been built since 1980 and 80 were built in the 1990s), and the prison population of 163,190 ranks number one in the country, just ahead of California. Texas has so many prisoners that, in July 2000, it ran out of six-digit numbers to assign to inmates and created prisoner number 1,000,000.

The rural nature of most of these prisons can be gauged by sampling the towns where they are located (population according to the 1990 census): Iowa Park (6,072), Teague (3,268), Dilley (2,632), Brazoria (2,717), Kennedy (3,763), Dalhart (6,246), Marlin (6,386), Rusk (4,366), Richmond (9,801), Woodville (2,636), Navasota (6,296), Fort Stockton (8,524), Childress (5,055) and Cuero (6,700). A check of the 1998 *Rand McNally Road Atlas* reveals that several prisons are located in towns not even found on the map; places like Lovelady, Midway, Tennessee Colony (with three separate prisons each housing over 3,000 inmates), Rosharon (with no less than four prisons housing over 6,000 inmates) and a privately run prison in a town called Venus (with 1,000 inmates).

These institutions are found literally in every part of the state, from Woodville in the far east, to Lamesa in the Texas Panhandle to the south of Lubbock, and Fort Stockton south-west of Odessa. Then there's the town of Beeville, between Corpus Christi and San Antonio, along Route 181. With a population of just over 13,000, Beeville has two prisons with about 7,200 prisoners. Journalist Joseph Hallinan describes Beeville in his book, *Going up the River: Travels in a Prison Nation*, as a sort of 'prison hub', not unlike what Detroit was to cars. And they are trying to bring in more prisons.

The Texas prison system has more than 42,000 employees, operates its own health services system (with more than 8,000 personnel, including 200 doctors) and has 35 lawyers working for it. Farming is big business, with control of more than 134,000 acres (about 200 square miles), and among the largest horse and cattle herds in the entire state (1,500 horses and 10,000 head of cattle). The system also operates 42 factories within 32 prisons under its own 'Texas Correctional Industries'. The overall incarceration rate per 100,000 (local jails and prisons) in Texas ranks number two in the nation at 1,035, nearly double the national rate of 682 and Russia's rate of 685. During the 1990s, almost one in every five new prisoners in the US was incarcerated in Texas and the state's prison population tripled during the decade.

Employment within this 'prison industrial complex' is also about the fastest growing in the nation. Thousands of those employed as school teachers, police officers and a surprising variety of other occupations are seeking and getting relatively high-paid and secure jobs (with great benefits) in the prison industry. One supporter of prisons – and especially the building of private prisons – summed the industry up nicely, saying: 'It's like a hotel with a guaranteed occupancy.' Literally thousands of companies and investment firms are finding a lucrative market in the prison industry. A brochure from one firm advises investors: 'While arrests and convictions are steadily on the rise, profits are to be made – profits from crime. Get in on the ground floor of this booming industry now!' Profits are made in any number of areas, including long-distance telephone companies, food services, linen services, security firms, builders and architects among others. Wall Street giants like Merrill Lynch are 'bullish on prisons'.

How do we explain this recent growth in the prison population? The most obvious answer, as suggested already, is the 'war on drugs'.

Phoenix, Arizona, 1998: it's that man again (see pp124–31). Sheriff Joe Arpaio with his juvenile chain gang. Arpaio boasts that he is not only the first man to 'introduce female chain gangs' but that he makes his juvenile prisoners wear 'pink underwear' to humiliate them. Credit: Brad Armstrong / Rex / Sipa Press

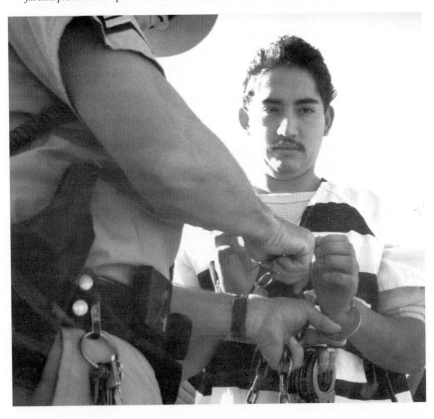

However, this explanation requires further explanation. The recent boom in incarceration can be seen as a method of class control; specifically, a method of controlling the 'surplus population'. Within a capitalist society there is a need, as Christian Parenti suggests in *Lockdown America*, to 'manage and contain its surplus populations and poorest classes with paramilitary forms of segregation, containment and repression'. This stems from the inevitable contradictions of capitalism, which needs and creates poverty, yet is threatened by the poor. In other words, capitalism needs the surplus population, 'yet faces the threat of political, aesthetic or cultural disruption from those populations'. The entire criminal justice system – but especially the prisons – functions to manage these contradictions.

One clue to the importance of the need to control the surplus population comes from estimates of how large this population actually is. As many critics have noted, the 'official' unemployment rate always underestimates the extent of the problem – perhaps intentionally – by ignoring those with part-time work but who want full-time work, and those who have given up looking. However, there is another large group that is excluded from these figures: those in prison or jail. With an estimated 2 million prisoners, this is a sizeable number. For African-American men, the unemployment rate becomes an astounding 40% if we include those in prison or jail. Thus, the surplus population in the middle of the so-called 'booming economy' is quite large and needs to be 'managed' or 'contained'.

Two methods of controlling the surplus population are legislation, which defines what is a 'crime', and sentencing structures, which define what crimes are 'serious'. Many sentencing structures have a built-in class and racial bias. A case in point is drug law, insofar as it relates to crack cocaine. The penalty for possession and/or sale of crack cocaine is far steeper than that for cocaine in powder form. It happens that crack is far more likely to be associated with African-Americans. When such legislation was passed in the mid-1980s, congressional leaders were told by experts that the laws would target racial minorities and fill the prisons. The advice was ignored.

Indeed, a most persuasive argument can be made suggesting a close correlation between the 'war on drugs', the growth of the prison industrial complex and the control of the minority population. The 'war' was declared on the poor and racial minorities. The police found drug buyers and sellers in minority communities because that is precisely where they looked for them, rather than, say, on college campuses. The results were immediate: the arrest rates for African-Americans on drug charges shot dramatically upwards in the late 1980s and well into the 1990s.

We live in times of great uncertainty as millions barely eke out a living while a small minority become richer and richer, despite proclamations by politicians and the media of 'economic recovery' and the booming stock market. More and more of our citizens are relegated to the ranks of the 'surplus population', a population rendered unneeded or 'superfluous' insofar as creating profits is concerned. Along with more and more corporate downsizing, there is the ominous disappearance of the semi-skilled and unskilled jobs once filled by urban minorities, especially African-American males. But this group is still very much with us and, from the point of view of those in power, they need to be 'managed' in some way. One way that has been used to control this population is to confine them to inner-city ghettos, but another way is to use the prison system as a mechanism of this form of 'management'. ❏

Randall G Shelden *is professor of criminal justice at the University of Nevada–Las Vegas, where he has taught for 25 years. He is the author of five books on crime and justice, the most recent of which is* Controlling the Dangerous Classes: A Critical Introduction to the History of Criminal Justice *(Allyn & Bacon, 2001). He is currently working on two books – a critique of the US criminal justice system and another on the prison industrial complex*

WILBERT RIDEAU

Madness and mercy

*In 1961, nineteen-year-old African-American Wilbert Rideau was sentenced to death
for the murder of Julia Ferguson, a white bank teller in Lake Charles, Louisiana. In
a succession of trials, three all-white juries sentenced him to death. The sentence was
commuted to life in 1972, after the US Supreme Court temporarily halted executions.
In December 2000, the Fifth Circuit Court of Appeals ruled that Rideau had
'established a prima facie case of racial discrimination in the process used to select the
grand jury that indicted him'. It ordered his conviction be 'reversed' and the 1961
indictment 'quashed'. He remains in prison.*

In prison, every day ends the same way – with a key being turned in a door,
locking me in for the night. Then we're counted, like things. And a little later
the lights are cut off and we're sent to bed, like children.

As the night creeps slowly by, it gets quieter and quieter. Apprehension
hangs heavily in the air, inmates dreading the minutes or hours of solitude
before the peace of sleep. This is the hardest time of the day. This is when the
walls seem to be closing in on you. During the day, there's work, intrigues and
a thousand little things that keep you moving, stirring, your mind occupied.
But at night, there's nothing but the silence . . . and your thoughts.

I lie there in my bunk a long time, the cold, frightening silence closing in
until a death-like stillness descends upon the entire dormitory. I'm not the only
one awake. There are always others like myself on any given night, lying there
watching the smoke from their cigarettes drift slowly up to the ceiling, trying
to ignore or hide the voice crying within them . . . but if you listen closely,
you can hear it, the voice of loneliness, the sounds of despair, of heartbreak –
muffled sobs, tears, the half-stifled scream of a man slowly going insane as a
result of the torment of emotional deprivation. Can even hear the sounds of
lovemaking between some of the men, men trying desperately to hang on to
the normality of life in an ocean of abnormality.

I watch the smoke of my cigarette, which so adequately symbolises my life,
as it drifts toward the ceiling, vanishing into nothingness. Questions assail me.
About life, my purpose in it, my goals. Then the cold realities: frustration, pain,
misery, guards, concrete walls and guns.

A silent cry tears through my veins, stealing the strength from my soul, as the haunting notion that I am destined to live and die here assumes a realness that threatens to engulf my being. Yesterday is lost to me forever and tomorrow seems too far away to be seen as anything other than a false dream.

I try to cling to the dreams that have kept me going all these years, but it's harder now. I can feel them slipping away like a tired woman and a creeping sense of hopelessness, of impending death, threatening entry. I've been locked up too long. Few men here have been locked up as long as I and I feel old with the knowledge of this.

I'm tired. I long to quit this ultra-masculine jungle, this barbaric dog-eat-dog world where men are deprived of every human need save hunger and thirst, this place where ruthlessness is the rule and mercy, the exception, this vacuum totally devoid of love, charity, brotherhood, beauty and all of the other things that others take for granted, but which are so important to us starved for them. I want to end this madness, to live again, but experience tells me that when hate and indifference control your destiny, to expect mercy or fairness is madness in itself . . .

It is becoming increasingly clear to me that being the much heralded 'model' prisoner is not the key to freedom . . . Now, I face the question of what to do. Where is the incentive in continuing the struggle when your efforts are ignored and your pleas fall upon deaf ears? Where is the sense in suffering for the sheer sake of suffering? This is a question that haunts each day of my existence, a question I've continuously refused to answer because I recognise the danger in it. I fear the answer. ❏

Wilbert Rideau *has co-edited two books and won the George Polk Award, the American Bar Association Silver Gavel Award and the Robert F Kennedy Journalism Award for his journalism. He wrote the film* Final Judgement: The Execution of Antonio James *and co-directed the Academy-Award nominated documentary* The Farm: Angola USA.

Originally published in the Baton Rouge News Leader; *reprinted in* the New Orleans States-Items *on 14 April 1976*

JUDITH GREENE

Nice little earner

Arrests and convictions are on the rise; profits from crime are there for the taking; Wall Street is bullish on prison stock. Get in on the ground floor of this booming industry now

At the end of the 2001 legislative session in Mississippi, legislators ignored the urgings of governor Ronnie Musgrove and corrections commissioner Robert Johnson to make improving education priority one in Mississippi. Instead, they tossed 6 million of scarce budget dollars into a pot for expanding the number of private beds for prisoners, despite the fact that more than 2,600 beds already stood empty in Mississippi's public prisons. They did this while cutting budgets in every other state agency.

The sponsors of the contract prison-funding measure made an end-run around vigorous opposition from their colleagues who head the legislature's corrections oversight and appropriation committees. Commissioner Johnson charged that they were funding beds for 'ghost prisoners'. Governor Musgrove vetoed their appropriations bills, arguing that they were creating a multi-year obligation with escalating costs for unneeded services, and investing in private prison corporations instead of teachers and students. Within two days, the sponsors mustered the necessary votes in both houses to override his veto.

What led to such an absurd outcome? The unprecedented rise in the US prison population since the late 1970s has helped spawn what many call a 'prison industrial complex'. Over the past two decades, new prisons – public and private - have come to be seen as the preferred economic development tool in rural US. As a result, policy decisions on prison expansion are now largely driven by economic concerns, and many rural areas have become almost completely dependent on prison construction and employment. Development authorities actively pursue prison sitings, offering land give-aways, infrastructure 'perks', tax breaks and bond funds as enticements. This is a national trend, and Mississippi –

one of the poorest states in the US – has proved itself no exception.

The racial aspects of what has come to be a policy of mass incarceration in the US are well known. With a prison population that is almost two-thirds non-white, the nation's prisons have become little more than rural warehouses for the containment of impoverished urban youth. The shameful history of racialised justice in Mississippi is rooted in the culture of plantation slavery, making the current drama particularly sordid. It pits the needs of poor, young students for a quality education against the likelihood that its denial may sweep them into the ever-widening net of a criminal justice system that ends with imprisonment or worse.

During the ante-bellum period, the vast majority of African-American slaves in Mississippi were excluded from the formal legal system, subjected instead to 'racial justice' by their white owners. After the Civil War, the passage of the Mississippi Black Codes brought freed slaves under the sway of the formal legal system, forcing huge numbers into the neo-slavery of the convict-leasing system. At the same time, white vigilantism perpetuated the systemic use of threats and violence to enforce a vicious system of US apartheid that remained unbroken until the middle of the 20th century.

Before a 1974 federal court order forced penal reform upon the Mississippi prison system, the state's infamous Parchman Prison Farm stood as a national symbol of brutal prison rule. With discipline enforced by cadres of armed inmate-overseers ('trusty shooters'), prisoners donned their notorious striped uniforms every day to labour as field hands under conditions that rivalled those on ante-bellum plantations.

The mid-1990s economic boom improved the fiscal outlook even in poor states such as Mississippi. Casino gambling produced both increased tax revenues and a powerful economic stimulus through increased jobs, tourism and retail sales. Feeling flush by 1994, the Mississippi legislature launched a massive prison expansion programme. After two decades of litigation that had forced Mississippi prisons into compliance with constitutional standards, the state was rocked by the national craze for 'get tough' sentencing and 'no frills' prisons. Meeting in 1994, legislators enacted a variety of 'get tough' measures to crack down on crime and youth violence. They voted to add prison capacity for more than 4,000 prisoners, including authorisation for two 1,000-bed private prisons.

The following year, they took up the fad for 'truth in sentencing', eliminating parole for all offenders sent to prison - violent and non-violent alike - and requiring that they serve 85% of their sentence before gaining release. Legislators expanded the prison budget by US$22 million, earmarked mainly for private prison contracts.

In 1997, legislators heeded demands to spread the prison boom across a wider span of local communities, authorising the Mississippi Department of Corrections (MDOC) to contract for beds in 'regional prisons' – a new type of county-level facility in which up to 250 state prisoners would be housed for a per diem fee. They also authorised counties to contract private prison firms to construct facilities to house federal prisoners. By March 1997, the Issaquena County Correctional Facility became the first regional prison to open its doors for business and the state promptly began paying US$24.90 per day for each state prisoner housed there.

In 1998, the legislature authorised construction of an additional private prison in Tallahatchie County, the first to import prisoners from other states. Tallahatchie is one of the poorest counties in the nation

Women's prison, California: working for the prison – industrial complex.
Credit: Armineh Johannes / Rex / Sipa Press

New York cemetery: paupers and prisoners. Credit: Rex / Sipa Press

and local officials, who hoped the prison would provide a permanent employment base, had pushed for contracting leeway in order to increase the likelihood of 'full occupancy'.

The prison's owner–operator, the Corrections Corporation of America (CCA), said it expected a mix of local, state and federal prisoners. But by the time the prison was ready to open in 2000, CCA had somehow failed to secure a contract with the MDOC to house state prisoners. They had offered its 1,104 beds 'for rent' on the 'national market', however, and were able to snag hundreds of prisoners shipped in from overcrowded prisons in Wisconsin.

In 1999, the legislature finally addressed the challenge of improving education. At US$31,913, the average pay for teachers in Mississippi is 30% below the national average. A plan to boost salaries by almost US$10,000 would be phased in over six years. Meanwhile, the massive prison expansion programme had not yet significantly reduced the crowding problem. Under a federal court order to restrict county jail population levels, the state was hit with a US$1.8 million fine for keeping too many state prisoners backed up in local lock-ups. Despite this problem, legislators rejected proposals to modify the 1995 'truth in sentencing' law.

Instead of sentencing reform, legislators appropriated an additional US$24.5 million to activate 1,500 new contract prison beds, including a 500-bed facility for prisoners with mental heath needs, operated by Wackenhut Corrections Corporation in Meridian, and four more 250-inmate regional prisons.

At the dawn of the 21st century, Mississippi's prison expansion programme had more than doubled the prison budget. Between June 1994 and June 2000, the state's prison population had grown from 10,699 to 18,379, but the prison expansion effort was finally beginning to spell relief for hundreds of prisoners stewing in overcrowded local jails. By the autumn, the number of state prisoners in the Lauderdale County jail dropped close to the level officially authorised. The handful of state prisoners who remained would be used for 'jail support' or work on county road crews, etc. Newly renovated cells at Parchman were nearly ready to receive prisoners, and 750 cells in three more regional prisons were slated for activation by January 2001.

At the start of this year's legislative session, prison issues seemed to slide to the back burner, while state legislators were consumed with heated battles over dwindling revenues and hot-button social issues. Commissioner Johnson announced that the budget for prison operations had run short. He warned that he might not be able to make payments after 1 April for contract beds in private prisons and 'regional jails'. Private prisons hold 3,188 of Mississippi's 18,247 prisoners, while 2,170 are in regional facilities.

Operators of the contract prisons, both private and regional, were pushing for more money. The MDOC contracts provided for a minimum occupancy level of 80%. With plenty of empty beds in the state's own prisons, and budget shortfalls for contract beds, Johnson's strategy had been to keep the count of prisoners in contract beds on the low side. In January, 13% of the regional beds reserved for state prisoners were empty, and the count in Wackenhut Corrections' 1,000-bed prison was averaging 910. But some contract facilities were barely filled to their guaranteed occupancy level. Contract prison managers, meanwhile, were angling for higher occupancy and, since this was not forthcoming from the executive branch, they hit the legislative trail at full force.

Wayne Calabrese, president of Wackenhut Corrections, was insistent that the MDOC fill more private prison beds. 'We want to make sure the price we give the state, which was based on full or nearly full occupancy, is in fact what we receive.' Legislators responded quickly to his demand, citing the critical need to retain local prison jobs. They approved funding to increase by 500 the number of prisoners guaranteed to a dozen different facilities. The annual price tag on the new population for the contract facilities totals US$6 million. Legislators also voted a US$16.4 million appropriation from the state's 'rainy day fund' to cover the deficit in funding the private and regional contract facilities. At the same time, they slashed the public school budget for textbooks and classroom supplies.

The chair and vice-chair of the Senate Corrections Committee opposed the increased prisoner-population guarantees, terming them a subsidy of contract facilities to the detriment of the department of corrections. When governor Musgrove vetoed the corrections spending bill he declared that 'education, not prisons, must be our state's priority'. That same day there were 2,616 prison beds standing empty in the state prison system. Within two more days, both houses of the legislature voted to override the governor's veto. ❏

Judith Greene is active with the US-based Prison Moratorium Project, the Coalition on Detention and Imprisonment and the Urban/Rural Coalition Against Prisons

DAVID R DOW

Volunteers for death

The conflicting purposes of religious counsellors and legal representatives can lead a prisoner on death row to forfeit his rights

Death row is a grim place: difficult to survive even with hope, and near impossible without. Yet death penalty law is such that a lawyer cannot in good conscience give her or his death row clients much cause to be hopeful. Death penalty appeals are increasingly pro forma: courts go through the motions but almost inevitably rule against the inmate. The law, in other words, cannot provide much in the way of hope.

Religious counsellors, unlike their legal counterparts, can sing messages of hope even as the walls are burning down. The courthouse door may be closed, but the door to heaven never is. That is a message that finds a congenial home on death row, but one the government – the state – should not be involved in spreading. The state is a secular institution and, on a secular front, hope is a lie.

George W Bush's proposed faith-based initiative has no place on death row. Inside prison, spiritual advisors and legal advisors are frequently at war with one another. Lawyers fight the state, while chaplains ordinarily urge inmates to submit to it. Given this conflict, it is immoral – and probably unconstitutional – for the state to funnel more chaplains into the prisons.

Death penalty lawyers use the term 'volunteer' to describe an inmate who chooses to give up his appeals and submit to execution without legal contest. For a death penalty lawyer, having a client choose to volunteer generates a dilemma that pits the lawyer's respect for the will of the client against the lawyer's reluctance to accede in the state's carrying out of such 'cruel and unusual' punishment.

Austin, Texas, 1998: anti-death penalty demonstration. Credit: Rex / Sipa Press

Yet this conflict arises routinely. Some inmates find the mere idea of imprisonment for life so intolerable that they would prefer death. Gary Gilmore and Timothy McVeigh, the two most famous volunteers in the history of the US death penalty, epitomise this basis for volunteering. Others volunteer not because they find prison life impossible, but because they come to believe that it is the right thing to do: that they deserve to die.

Nationally, somewhere between ten and 15% of the death row population volunteer. Since the death penalty was reinstated in 1976, approximately 70 execution victims have been volunteers. Some statistics suggest that most volunteerism is caused by the horror of prison life. Contrary to popular mythology, prison life is not a non-stop bacchanal of weightlifting, TV-watching and eating. On Texas's death row, for instance, inmates spend 23 hours a day alone in their 60-square-foot cells. The cells have solid doors, rather than bars, with a panel that allows food to be passed in and prisoners to be manacled before being removed. The cells have a thin strip of a window. Prisoners are not permitted to have television sets. Around a quarter of the death row population is allowed a radio. The men exercise privately during their one hour a day recreational release.

Oklahoma's death house is even worse. While the conditions are much as those in Texas, the entire prison unit is below ground. Fluorescent bulbs are the only source of light. Perhaps not surprisingly, more than one-third of Oklahoma's death row inmates have chosen to volunteer rather than contest their sentences; long though the odds may be, the inmate who appeals might win, and the winner would be rewarded with a life sentence in a subterranean tomb.

Inmates who volunteer because they want to escape from prison life are one thing; inmates who volunteer because they want to escape to somewhere else are quite another. Law and spirituality are not inherently in conflict, but they can be. When a death row inmate whose rights have been violated elects, for spiritual reasons, not to contest the legality of his incarceration or sentence but to surrender to God instead, then the lawyer's advice and the preacher's may well be at odds.

Lawyers who represent death row inmates have believed for some time that some spiritual advisors counsel convicted murderers to surrender their appeals. It has been difficult to gather the evidence to establish this claim in a courtroom for the obvious reason that the inmate who has been won over by the chaplain is unwilling to say that the decision to volunteer was anything but his own. Yet the influence of these spiritual advisors can be irresistible.

For an uneducated person, facing almost certain execution, to say no to the person offering salvation is hard. In prison, chaplains have captive audiences of men anxious to make Pascal's wager, because there is nothing else. Most of these men (and the occasional woman) were not religious when they arrived on death row, yet their final words are a prayer. Fear and priestly persistence are the cause.

Sister Helen Prejean.
Credit: Alan Wheller
/ Rex / Sipa Press

In the film *Dead Man Walking*, based on a book of the same name by Sister Helen Prejean, the central death row character, after proclaiming his innocence for nearly the entire period of his incarceration, suddenly confesses to the murder moments before the execution. The character in *Dead Man Walking* actually did commit the murder, and it is difficult to argue that honesty is a bad thing.

The problem is that these confessions occur because the ministration is offered in the suffocating confines of a death row. On death row, conversing gets you out of your cell. And that comfort may, in turn, lead to what is most insidious here: in stocking the nation's death rows with religious ministers, the state will be creating a mechanism that will inexorably motivate some, perhaps many, death row inmates to surrender their appeals – to surrender their legal rights.

There is no easy solution to this problem. The state is certainly not permitted to keep religious figures out of the prisons altogether and, as long as there are proselytisers in the prisons, there will be inmates who will trade their appeals for an earlier trip to the afterlife. If the state has condemned to death inmates whose constitutional rights have been violated, it should not encourage or subsidise more faith-based prison counsellors. It should be vacating their sentences, rather than deploying agents to persuade the inmates to turn the other cheek. ❏

David R Dow *is the George Butler research professor at the University of Houston Law Center. Since 1988, he has represented nearly 30 death row inmates in their habeas corpus appeals. He is co-editor, with Mark Dow, of* Machinery of Death: The Reality of America's Death Penalty Regime, *forthcoming from Routledge (2002)*

SPEEDY RICE

Sleeping sickness

Incompetent and cynical lawyers pave the way to death row

From outside, the US criminal justice system appears to be perfectly in order: we possess the finest system for the protection of those accused of crimes. But like a shiny apple that a worm has invaded, the inside of the criminal justice system has some very rotten parts. The blackest of these is its failure to ensure adequate representation of those accused of capital murder.

The starting point of inadequate representation is economics. If you are wealthy and can afford quality lawyers and mitigation specialists, it is unlikely you will get the death penalty. If you are not, then you have to be lucky. Lucky enough to get one of the few well-funded, well-trained and tireless public lawyers who treat capital defence as a calling, not a job. If you are neither, you have to hope you are a white person who has killed a black person and, therefore, are statistically unlikely to get a death sentence. If none of the above applies, welcome to death row.

In a country that claims a constitutional right to a lawyer in felony cases, how is it that you do not get a decent lawyer and why is it permitted? Because the courts of our land, charged with protecting those constitutional rights, have become corrupted with self-righteousness and vengeance towards the capital defendant. While attention is now starting to focus on the unfairness of the death penalty and its cousin, inadequate representation, the problem is not new.

In 1986, the US Court of Appeals for the Fifth Circuit said that the constitution does not require that the accused, even in a capital case, be represented by able or effective counsel (Riles v McCotter, 799 F.2d 947, 955). In a juxtaposition of decisions that could only make the Queen of Hearts proud, the Supreme Court held in the Roger Coleman case that because his attorneys had missed the filing deadline by one day and this was not excusable, Coleman must be executed. Conversely, the court held that a bankruptcy filing 20 days late was excusable and denial of the late filing by the lower court was reversible error. In our system of justice, life is worthless and money counts.

What does this mean in practice? In a trio of cases arising from the State of Texas and its former governor, George W Bush, a sleeping lawyer is no reason to believe that the capital defendant did not receive a fair trial. Yes, you read that correctly. George McFarland and Carl Johnson have both been executed even though it is undisputed that their lawyers slept through substantial portions of their trials. In McFarland's case, when his lawyer was asked if he truly had slept through most of the capital murder trial he replied: 'It's boring.' The Texas Court of Criminal Appeals agreed with the trial court ruling that our constitution guarantees you a lawyer, but doesn't guarantee you a lawyer who has to be awake. In Carl Johnson's case, his lawyer has had ten clients sentenced to death, but the trial judges in Houston liked his style. He was known for rushing through capital trials like greased lightning and sleeping through parts of them, but the Texas Court of Criminal Appeals found that this sleeping lawyer was not ineffective assistance of counsel.

Currently in the Court of Appeals for the Fifth Circuit is the case of Calvin Burdine. Burdine's lawyer slept through substantial portions of his trial. That was OK with the trial judge and OK with the Texas Court of Criminal Appeals. And why not? This is settled case law in Texas. When the issue was brought before the US District Court on habeas corpus, the judge was appalled. The court granted a stay of execution, finding that a sleeping lawyer is the equivalent of no lawyer at all (Burdine v Johnson, 66 F.Supp. 2d 854, 866). This thoroughly logical and sensible decision should have been the beginning of a new trial for Calvin Burdine but the Texas Attorney General appealed to that beacon of justice, the Fifth Circuit. There, in a 2 to 1 decision, the court reversed the trial court's grant of habeas corpus. The majority agreed that a sleeping lawyer was no worse then a drunk lawyer in a death penalty case. The single judge dissenting thought the decision 'shocks the conscience'. Fortunately, Burdine's case got a lot of publicity and Texas's favourite son was running for president, and the Fifth Circuit granted a review of the Burdine case. What this means is that all 14 judges on the Fifth Circuit will rehear the case and decide if it is constitutional to execute a human being whose legally mandated lawyer slept through most of his trial.

Sleeping is not the only way the capital lawyer can send his client to the gallows with the approval of the justice system. In case after case, courts have affirmed death sentences when the condemned had a lawyer who was drunk, on drugs or without any knowledge or preparation of the relevant case law. Proving that truth is stranger then fiction, John Young met his capital defence attorney for the first time a few weeks before his trial – Young was in a county jail and so was his lawyer, after pleading guilty to drugs charges. During Young's trial, it was clear the lawyer was unprepared and inept. Long afterwards, the lawyer admitted to being strung out on drugs, exhausted and severely distracted by personal and business problems. None the less, Young was executed.

Judy Haney faced her capital jury after her trial was suspended for a day because her court-appointed lawyer was too drunk to go forward. Neither the judge or jury, nor any court reviewing the subsequent death decision, seemed bothered that Judy and her lawyer were both brought to court the next day from jail. She was sentenced to death and her conviction and death sentence were affirmed all the way to the US Supreme Court.

Stories of lawyers being unprepared and with little or no knowledge of the necessary capital case law are legion. But if your lawyer can be asleep, drunk or drug-addicted, why should a lack of competence be a cause for concern? It is shocking to be told that the US has not executed an innocent person. How would we know with lawyers like these? ❑

Speedy Rice is director of the International Criminal Justice Law Clinic at Gonzaga University School of Law in Spokane, Washington

JENNIFER GONNERMAN

Seizing the spotlight

A stand-up comedian uses the media to fight the drug laws

One afternoon last February, Randy Credico leaned back in a chair in his Manhattan office, pressed a phone to his ear and worked himself into a lather. He was, as usual, performing his role as unofficial press agent for New York's drug prisoners. On the line was an Associated Press reporter. Credico had earlier introduced the journalist to Denise Smith, a prisoner serving a 10 to 20-year sentence for selling crack. According to Credico, Smith was an addict – not a dealer – and only guilty of passing along a couple of US$30 bags of crack.

'They should have put her in the hospital,' Credico shouted into the receiver. 'It's like having somebody with cancer out there. What was the point? It's a dirty thing for a cop to do. Just to pull that woman off the streets – a sick person off the street – and into prison? Now we're going to pay the tab and it's going to be up to US$700,000 for 20 years when we could have fixed her by putting her into a treatment center for US$12,000 a year.'

Several days later, the reporter faxed over his story and Credico tossed it into his plastic bin overflowing with newspaper articles. For Credico, the story was yet another tiny victory in his ongoing battle to publicise what he believes are the injustices of New York's drug laws. For three years, Credico, a 45-year-old comedian, has been project director of the William Moses Kunstler Fund for Racial Justice. With no full-time staff and an annual budget of only US$50,000, he has built a small movement of drug prisoners and their relatives and won exposure from virtually every major news outlet in New York.

An anti drug law rally Credico organised at the state capitol in March 1999 generated nearly 40 newspaper, television and radio stories in outlets. In 2000, Credico hooked up a *New York Times* reporter with Terrence Stevens, a first-time offender, nearly paralysed from muscular dystrophy and wheelchair-bound, who was serving 15 years to life for cocaine possession. After the reporter wrote two columns about Stevens, governor George Pataki granted him clemency and he was released. From 1998 to 2000, Credico organised semi-regular vigils at New York City's Rockefeller Center, generating dozens of news stories in a wide range of media outlets, including *Newsday*, the *Financial Times*, the *Daily News*, BBC Radio and the *Charles Grodin Show* on CNBC.

'He has been effective,' says *Newsday* columnist Jimmy Breslin who, like dozens of reporters around town, hears from Credico every few days. 'He's put it on people's minds.' But 'you can't write one [column] every day about the Rockefeller laws, which is what he wants'.

Governor Nelson Rockefeller enacted these laws, which require lengthy mandatory sentences for anyone convicted of a drug crime, in 1973. The Rockefeller drug laws helped fuel an explosion in New York's prison population from 12,500 to 70,000. This year, drug law opponents are optimistic that they may finally succeed in convincing state legislators to soften them. Governor Pataki unveiled a detailed reform proposal in January, and leaders of both the New York assembly and senate have said that they too favour reform.

As legislators who support drug law reform try to sway their more conservative colleagues, Credico's stories of prisoners' woes have become invaluable. 'They have been extremely effective in trying to personalise this battle, to show the human tragedies associated with the laws,' explains Queens assemblyman Jeffrion Aubry, a Democrat, who has led a fight to repeal the Rockefeller drug laws.

Fifty people and a handful of reporters came to Credico's first vigil, held at Rockefeller Center on 8 May 1998, the 25th anniversary of the Rockefeller laws. Back then, Credico had help from several other drug law reform groups. Most of his fellow organisers thought the vigil should be a one-off event. Credico disagreed. He spent weekend evenings in midtown Manhattan, handing out flyers to the hundreds of relatives boarding buses to visit prisoners across the state. As his literature circulated, Credico began to receive five to ten letters a day from inmates.

Credico set about searching for the most sympathetic cases. He weeded out those who had a history of violent crime or long rap sheets.

His system certainly was not foolproof, but he did find dozens of cases of prisoners with no prior convictions who had been sentenced to 15 or 20 years. And every now and then, Credico would hit the jackpot – like the day he received a letter from Terrence Stevens.

Credico phoned Terrence's mother Regina and invited her to come to the vigils he continued to hold every week or two at Rockefeller Center. Regina began to show up regularly. Sometimes, Credico's vigils attracted only five or six people. Other times, the crowd would grow to 20 or 30. The small numbers bothered Credico less than the absence of reporters. So Credico began to schedule events where he thought the media would be, holding demonstrations outside glitzy fund-raisers for George Pataki or George W Bush.

Florida, 1993: war on drugs. Credit: Rex / Sipa Press

A day or two before, he would send out hyperbolic press releases, usually riddled with typos. 'PATAKI, SUPPORTER OF ALLEGED COCAINE ABUSER GEORGE W BUSH, LETS ADDICTS ROT IN NY PRISONS,' shouted one. Another, from 1998, claimed that his three-month-old petition opposing the drug laws 'already boasts 100,000 signatures'. Asked if this figure was accurate, Credico says, 'It looked like 100,000 until I started counting.' What did it look like after he started counting? 'About 13,000 or 14,000.'

When they first meet him, most people find it tough to take Credico seriously. Maybe it is the coffee stains on his jeans, the half-open fly, the chewed-up cigar in his shirt pocket, the unlaced sneakers or the badge showing Mayor Rudy Giuliani sporting a Hitleresque moustache. 'I think he's a nut, but he's true to what he's doing,' Regina Stevens says of Credico. 'He puts his all into it. It really touched me because he doesn't have anyone in prison, and he works just as hard, if not harder, than people who do. You just don't find that devotion.'

Terrence Stevens showed up at his first anti-drug law rally on 28 February, four weeks after he left prison. Credico had decided to hold the event in front of the office of Queens district attorney Richard A Brown, who, like all his fellow prosecutors, opposes overhauling the state's drug laws. Credico sent invitations to 200 prisoners' relatives, then hired Terrence to make follow-up calls.

'Terrence is now a huge weapon because he's smart,' says Credico. 'He's an MX missile. When you see him on TV, people are going to say, "What the fuck are we doing? We spent US$300,000 to keep that guy in a prison?" You do that to Hannibal Lecter. But a kid in a wheelchair? The guy did four more years than Sammy Gravano.'

Sixty prisoners' relatives and other supporters showed up at the noon rally. Many had worked double shifts, skipped classes, or scraped together cash for babysitters so they could stand in 30-degree weather and hold posters. Most of the protesters were rally regulars, including Regina Stevens and Al Lewis, the perennial Green Party candidate who played Grandpa in the 1960s TV comedy *The Munsters*.

'We are going to show the skeletons in the closet,' Credico hollered towards Brown's office. 'You are a fraud and this is a fraudulent prosecution of the laws. Come out here and face your accusers!' The audience for this show was a dozen police officers, plus whoever wandered by. There were also seven journalists and eight photographers.

After several prisoners' relatives had taken turns at the microphone, Terrence rolled forward in his wheelchair. Suddenly, all the photographers edged closer.

'There is so much suffering going on with the families that something needs to be done,' Terrence said. 'I have to be put on and off the toilet. I have to be bathed . . . What kind of threat to society am I, to be warehoused in an upstate maximum-security state prison for 15 years to life?' The next day, Credico would declare the event a success. Stories about the rally appeared in the *Daily News*, *Newsday* and *El Diario*. *Newsday* also published a photo of Terrence. Ninety minutes after the rally began, nearly all the journalists had left. Credico seized the microphone.

'You guys who are assistant DAs, get a real job,' he hollered. 'Quit destroying lives!' Turning back to his ralliers, he paused for a moment. 'OK, now I need US$500 to pay for this sound system,' he said, shoving a hand in his pants pocket. 'Does anyone have US$20?' ❏

Jennifer Gonnerman is a staff writer specialising in criminal justice issues for New York's Village Voice *where a version of this article first appeared*

STEPHEN K HARPER

Juvenile injustice

In the last decade, the US has executed more juvenile offenders than all the nations of the world combined. The only other countries that still execute offenders under 18 are Nigeria, the Democratic Republic of Congo, Saudi Arabia and Iran

In the early 1990s, sociologist – now presidential advisor – John DiIulio coined the term 'superpredator' and predicted a new and different wave of 'remorseless and impoverished youth' who might pose a great danger to public safety. Then congressman Bill McCollum of Florida and many other politicians threw gasoline on this inflammatory term. In 1996, McCollum stated that a growing number of 'fatherless superpredators' would trigger a 'coming storm of unprecedented violence'. Such a storm never materialised. While there was a sharp upward spike in juvenile crime – particularly, violent crime – in the early 1990s, overall juvenile crime, including violent crime, is down to levels of the mid-1980s. Juvenile homicides are down to levels of the mid-1960s. But the idea that there is a different kind of dangerous kid that society just can't handle is very much alive, malignantly so.

In response to that temporary spike in juvenile crime, as well as concern for victims and public safety, over 40 states changed their laws to facilitate or require the transfer of children into the adult criminal justice system. A recent example of this trend towards 'adultification' is the Lionel Tate case in Florida.

On 25 January this year, 12-year-old offender Lionel was convicted of first-degree murder in a criminal court for having beaten a six-year-old girl to death. The decision to transfer Lionel to a criminal court was not made by a neutral, well-informed juvenile court judge after a full adversarial hearing, but by a prosecutor and a secret grand jury.

Lionel was legally presumed to have the capacity to formulate the intent necessary to be found guilty of first-degree murder. (Two hundred years ago, children under 14 were legally presumed to lack the capacity to formulate evil intent.) He was forced to make a decision about whether to take a plea or go to trial, thereby risking a life sentence if he were found guilty. No one ever considered or raised – until it was too late – the issue of whether a 12-year-old boy had the cognitive competency necessary to make that life decision. The jury that convicted him was not legally permitted to consider his youth or his possible sentence. The judge had no discretion with respect to sentencing. He was required by law to send Lionel to prison for the rest of his natural life with no possibility of parole. The judge's sentencing order stated that Lionel's acts were not those of a child even though, in fact, they were.

These days, we hear slogans like 'adult crime – adult time'. When Palm Beach, Florida, prosecutor Barry Krischer prosecuted 14-year-old special education student Anthony Laester as an adult for allegedly hitting another boy in school and taking US$2, Krischer stated that there must be 'zero tolerance' for violence in school and 'the victim doesn't care how old the offender is or whether he has a disability'. To decision-makers like Krischer, it is irrelevant that the offender is a disabled adolescent.

This kind of rhetoric and decision-making is being furthered by legislation. For example, in 1994, Florida gave prosecutors – not juvenile judges – the power to transfer children into the adult criminal system. It also changed the primary purpose of the juvenile justice system from balancing the best interests of the child with the protection of the public to simply protecting public safety. Last year, California passed Proposition 21: this increased the number of kids to be transferred to adult court even though juvenile crime there was significantly down. In Florida, 10% of those who now enter the adult prison system do so for offences committed while they were under 18. All of this is being done even though research has repeatedly found that those who are transferred to the adult system reoffend more seriously, more quickly and more often than kids who remain in the juvenile system. Black and Hispanic children are disproportionately affected at every point along the way: in numbers arrested, charged, convicted, transferred to adult court, imprisoned and, ultimately, sentenced to death.

This single-minded pursuit of public safety has even gripped the psychological sciences. Popping up everywhere now are actuarial risk instruments which will supposedly assist authorities in profiling and identifying potentially dangerous youths. Canadian psychologist Adele

Forth is developing a 'youth version' of the Hare Psychopathology Checklist Revised – an instrument that purports to be able to 'identify' adolescent psychopaths. Risk instruments flip the traditional values of the justice system on their heads. Risk instruments don't presume innocence or protect liberty; they don't view the individual as an individual but simply look to how he or she comes out on an actuarial table of danger.

Perhaps the best illustration of the devolving treatment of children in the US can be found in the practice of executing 16- and 17-year-old offenders. Approximately 73 juvenile offenders are awaiting execution: 51% are black, 18% Latino, 31% white. All are male. In the last decade, the US has executed more juvenile offenders than all the nations of the world combined. The only other countries that still execute offenders under 18 are Nigeria, the Democratic Republic of Congo, Saudi Arabia and Iran. In executing juveniles, we ignore international treaties such as the International Covenant on Civil and Political Rights and the United Nations Convention of the Rights of the Child, both of which outlaw the death penalty for juvenile offenders.

Just this past March, the state of Missouri came within two hours of executing 16-year-old offender Antonio Richardson when the Supreme Court entered a temporary stay, not because he was a juvenile but because he was also retarded. The governor of Missouri was quoted as saying that he saw no reason to grant clemency because Antonio 'was convicted as an adult'. Ironically, the Missouri legislature is considering abolishing the death penalty for retarded offenders because, in the words of one legislator, 'it would be wrong to execute someone with the mind of a child'.

Historically, children have always been viewed by our culture as 'sacred actors' who are developmentally different and more malleable than adults. However, if the ways in which the US treats its most vulnerable and troubled children reveal its vision of childhood, we are experiencing a dramatic cultural shift. Notwithstanding President Bush's oft-repeated slogan, 'leave no child behind', the US seems more willing to treat increasing numbers of children as simply disposable. Less and less do we acknowledge that they are less culpable and more capable of rehabilitation. Inevitably, if some children are disposable, then all are simply less valued by the culture. ❏

Stephen K Harper is an attorney and an adjunct professor at the University of Miami School of Law where he teaches juvenile justice

TIM WISE

The price of white denial

Yet one more school shooting and suburban white America continues to bury its head in the sand, blind to the violence that is destroying their children

Two more children are dead and 13 injured; another 'nice' community is scratching its blond scalp, utterly perplexed as to how a school shooting the likes of the one in Santee, California, could happen. After all, as the mayor of the town said in an interview with CNN: 'We're a solid town, a good town, with good kids, a good church-going town . . . an all-American town.' Maybe that's the problem.

I said this after Columbine and no one listened. I'll say it again: most white folk live in a state of self-delusion. We think danger is black, brown and poor and, if we can just move far enough away from 'those people' we'll be safe. If we can just find an 'all-American' town, life will be better, because 'things like this just don't happen here'.

In truth, 'here' is about the only place these things do happen. Mass murder, wholesale slaughter, take-a-gun-and-see-how-many-you-can-kill craziness seems made for these safe places: the white suburbs or rural communities.

And yet the FBI still insists there is no 'profile' of a school shooter. In the last two years, 32 young men have either carried out or planned to carry out (and been foiled at the last minute) mass murder against classmates and teachers – 30 of these have been white. And yet there is no profile? Imagine if these killers and would-be killers had nearly all been black: would we still hesitate to put a racial face on the perpetrators? Indeed, if any black child – especially in the mostly white suburbs of Littleton or Santee – were openly to discuss his plans to murder fellow students, as happened at Columbine and Santana High, someone would have turned him in and the cops would have beat a path to his door. But when whites discuss their murderous intentions, our racial stereotypes of danger too often lead us to ignore it – they're just 'talking' and won't really do anything, we tell ourselves. How many kids have to die before we rethink that nonsense? How many dazed parents, mayors and sheriffs do we have to listen to, describing how 'normal' and safe their community is, and how they can't understand what went wrong?

I'll tell you what went wrong and it's not TV, rap music, video games or a lack of prayer in school. What went wrong is that white America decided to ignore dysfunction and violence when it only seemed to affect other communities, and thereby blinded themselves to the chaos that never remains isolated for long. What affects the urban 'ghetto' today will be coming to a Wal-Mart near you tomorrow; was probably

Fort Worth, 19 September 1999: Columbine High School students lead the mourning for victims at Wedgewood Baptist Church. Credit: Camera Press

there already. Unless you address the emptiness, pain, isolation and lack of hope felt by too many poor, Latino and black children, don't be shocked when the support systems aren't there for your kids either.

What went wrong is that we allowed ourselves to be lulled into a false sense of security by media representations of crime and violence that portray both as the province of those who are anything but white like us. We ignore the warning signs, because in our minds the warning signs don't live in our neighbourhood, but across town, in that place where we lock our car doors on the rare occasion we have to drive there. That false sense of security – the result of race and class stereotypes – then gets people killed. And still we are amazed.

But listen my fellow white Americans: your children are no better, no nicer, no more moral and no more decent than anyone else. Dysfunction is all around you, whether you choose to recognise it or not. And it's not just school shootings that are at issue here.

According to the Center for Disease Control's Youth Risk Behaviour Survey, and the *Monitoring the Future* report from the National Institutes on Drug Abuse, it is your children, and not those of the urban ghetto, who are most likely to use drugs. White high school students are seven times more likely than blacks to have used cocaine; eight times more likely to have smoked crack; ten times more likely to have used LSD and seven times more likely to have used heroin. In fact, in raw numbers there are more white high school students who have used crystal methamphetamine (the most addictive drug on the streets) than there are black students who smoke cigarettes.

What's more, it is white youth, in the 12–17 age group, who are more likely to sell drugs: 34% more likely than their black counterparts. And it is white youth who are twice as likely to binge drink and nearly twice as likely as blacks to drive drunk. And white males are twice as likely to bring a weapon to school as are black males.

And yet I would bet there aren't 100 white people in Santee, California, or almost any other 'nice' community, who have ever heard a single one of the statistics above. The media doesn't report on white dysfunction.

A few years ago, *US News* ran a story entitled 'A shocking look at blacks and crime'. Yet neither they nor any other news outlet discussed the 'shocking' whiteness of the school shoot-'em-ups. Indeed, every time media commentators discuss the similarities in these crimes they mention that the shooters were boys who got picked on, but never seem to notice a certain highly visible melanin deficiency. Colour-blind.

White-blind: these folks would spot colour very fast indeed were it to stroll into their community. Santee's whiteness is so taken for granted by its residents that the mayor, in that CNN interview, thought nothing of saying on the one hand that the town was 82% white, but on the other hand that 'this is America'. Well, it isn't America, and it certainly isn't California, where whites are only half the population. This is a town removed from America, even though its mayor thinks they are the normal ones – so much so that, when asked about racial diversity, he replied that there weren't many different 'ethni-tis-tities'. Not a word. Not even close.

I'd like to think that after Santee people will wake up. Take note. Rethink their stereotypes of who the dangerous people are. But deep down, I know better. The folks hitting the snooze button on this none-too-subtle alarm are my own people, after all, and I know their blindness like the back of my hand. ❏

Tim Wise *is a writer and activist based in Nashville, Tennessee*

MARK DOW

Outpost of the gulag

Outside the gulag proper, the US Immigration and Naturalization Service holds 23,000 deportees, thousands of whom have no home to be returned to and little prospect of release

Kim Ho Ma is no angel. That's why we need to listen to him. At the age of two, Ma fled Cambodia with his family; aged seven, he entered the USA legally as a refugee. As a teenager, Ma endured taunts of 'gook' and 'chink' on the way to the corner store because his family ate rice and spoke differently. Fellow 'foreigners' banded together and eventually Ma was part of an Asian gang. At 17, Ma was convicted of manslaughter for his participation in a gang-related shooting and, after completing his two-year criminal sentence, was taken into custody by the US Immigration & Naturalization Service (INS) to be deported 'back' to Cambodia, as if that were somehow where he belongs.

Kestutis Zadvydas was born to Lithuanian parents in a displaced persons camp in occupied Germany after World War II. His parents came to the US legally and he has been here for 44 years. After a string of drug-related convictions, Zadvydas, too, having served his time, was taken into INS custody. Immigration legislation passed in 1996 and signed into law by Bill Clinton severely limits the judicial review available to legal residents such as Ma and Zadvydas. Before the 1996 laws, according to INS figures, half of such cases would have been granted reprieve from deportation based on work and family ties established in this country. Now such people are being deported, even when they do not speak the language of 'their' home country.

But neither Zadvydas nor Ma can be deported. Zadvydas is stateless; there is nowhere to send him. The US cannot return Ma to Cambodia because the two countries do not have a repatriation agreement. Ma was detained for about a year before a district court ordered his release. The INS appealed against that decision, and the case reached the US Supreme Court, which heard oral arguments last February for the two cases together (Reno v Ma and Zadvydas v Underdown).

Of its total prisoner population of about 23,000, the INS holds 4,000–5,000 detainees who cannot be deported because their 'home' countries will not accept them. The largest groups are from Cuba, Cambodia, Vietnam and Laos, as well as Libya, Iraq and republics of the former USSR. Journalists often call them 'lifers' or 'unremoveables,' but the agency prefers the term 'post-order detainees'.

Cases of 'resident aliens' such as Ma and Zadvydas confront us with the ultimately arbitrary nature of who belongs here and who 'we' are. In Zadvydas's case, the INS has gone so far as to ask the Dominican Republic to accept him purely on the grounds that his wife, who lives in the US, was born there. It's as if the government were saying, 'We don't care where he's from, just ship him out of here.' Colorado attorney Carol Lehman told me in 1999 that when she asks people what they think is most important about being a US citizen, their answer is pragmatic, not patriotic: 'They can't make you leave.'

These cases also highlight the unbridled authority the INS claims as its prerogative in applying law enforcement tactics to our geographical and psychological borders. The INS is always arguing for more and more unchecked authority. Whatever the issue, it reminds justices that courts traditionally grant wide discretion in matters of immigration and foreign policy. The name of the attorney-general may change; executive attitudes remains the same.

The attorney-general – who heads the justice department of which the INS is an agency – must 'remove' aliens within 90 days of their deportation order. Criminal aliens, however, may be held beyond that period if found to pose a 'risk to the community' or to be an escape risk. But since the INS is only authorised to detain someone for the purpose of deportation, not as a punishment, how long can the agency hold a person when there is no reasonable chance of ever removing him?

The court will decide 'whether there is statutory authority for the INS to indefinitely detain individuals it cannot deport, and whether such indefinite detention violates the individual's right to substantive due process,' writes Ma's attorney Jay Stansell. While much hinges on the interpretation of the word 'reasonable', the government made the case to the Supreme Court that there is no limit on how long the INS can hold someone like Ma or Zadvydas. Deputy solicitor-general Edwin Kneedler told the court, 'I do not believe there is any reasonable time limitation within the statute.'

Attorney Laurie Joyce of the Catholic Legal Immigration Network notes that the quality of 'custody reviews' for the release of indefinite detainees has improved slightly since December last year as Washington INS officials have played a larger role. But she worries that an adverse ruling in the cases against Ma and Zadvydas would give local INS officers 'license to be even more abusive and arrogant' towards the prisoners whom she calls 'eternally condemned'.

Secrecy and intimidation are natural corollaries to excessive policing power, and the INS uses both. Dan Malone, staff writer for the *Dallas Morning News*, says he was naive when he started looking into the circumstances of long-term INS prisoners back in 1997. He spoke with Russell Bergeron, head of INS public affairs, who referred to a document that listed the agency's detained population under headings such as nationality, length of detention, etc. Bergeron told Malone that, according to the document, 53 detainees had been in custody for more than three years because their countries would not accept them. Intrigued, Malone decided to find out who they were.

He filed a Freedom Of Information Act (FOIA) request to obtain the names and 'alien numbers' of those 53 detainees. The department of justice/INS FOIA unit replied that 'no records' on this subject had been found 'in a search of our headquarters, including our public affairs office'. The FOIA specialist said that public affairs chief Bergeron had denied to her the existence of the document he had mentioned to Malone. When Malone tried to help out by telling the INS FOIA specialist that Bergeron had identified one Kristine Marcy as an INS field officer who was knowledgeable on the subject, the specialist responded that she was unable to locate any such INS employee. Malone then called the INS switchboard, which gave him Marcy's number.

The INS continued its refusal to provide the information on the grounds that it was protecting the privacy of the detainees; it claimed, moreover, that such a policy was consistent with Federal Bureau of Prisons guidelines. Malone pointed out that his own 'request to the

Somewhere in the gulag: Iraqi INS detainee awaits justice. Credit: Steven Rubin

bureau of prisons for the names of all persons incarcerated under a federal death sentence was promptly answered by fax with the information requested'.

After further denials, Malone and the *Dallas Morning News* sued in federal district court to compel the INS to release the requested information. In a settlement, the agency provided the list of those who had been held for more than three years. It ranged from criminal aliens to asylum seekers. And there were not 53, but 852. Under the terms of the settlement, the INS withheld the detainees' last names and identifying alien numbers, but did agree to deliver letters to all of them from the *Morning News*. The paper had the letter seeking further information about the individual cases translated into a dozen languages, and reporter Malone is finally getting to learn about them as hundreds of responses come in from around the country.

The INS restricts media access to detainees who are the 'centre of attention'. A New York-area attorney reports that detained clients have 'felt alarmed and intimidated' by INS pressure over contacts with the press. Last year, when I arranged to talk to Olu Balogun, a Nigerian detained in Houston, the local INS told me that an interview was 'not in [his] best interest'. They told Balogun himself that signing the media-interview authorisation form might affect his case. 'There is nothing else I have to be afraid of,' Balogun said. 'They couldn't do more than they have done already.'

Mohammed Bachir has been a legal resident of the US for 20 years. After he served two years for contempt charges related to a parental kidnapping conviction, the INS detained him for almost three years. Born in a Palestinian refugee camp in south Lebanon after his parents fled Haifa in 1948, Bachir is stateless and has never been deported. In his years of detention, the INS held him in 17 jails and detention centres in nine states. The problem? He rallied other prisoners and the local media wherever he went, generating stories from southern California, where he was beaten badly for organising a large-scale hunger strike, to upstate New York. 'We had a problem keeping him in different facilities,' Boston INS official Bruce Chadbourne said. 'He would kind of get some of the other detainees going . . . [He was] sort of an instigator.' Bachir was finally released in April on condition that he did not create 'a media circus'. He reportedly also agreed to keep that condition secret.

Two years ago, in Aurora, Colorado, a group of young Asian detainees, who had already done more time in the Wackenhut-run INS detention centre than they had served on their felony convictions, told me they had decided against a peaceful sit-down protest, knowing that it could prejudice the lone INS bureaucrat with the power to decide their fate. They were not being paranoid. Kim Ho Ma's participation in a hunger strike while detained in Seattle was still being used against him by the government in its Supreme Court brief. 'Indefinite detention,' mused Ma as we discussed the terminology, 'in other words, for ever. They [used to] tell us every day, you're not getting out. I'm nobody to argue with them.' He added, 'I'm from a different country, but I'm as American as anybody. I didn't even know I was from Cambodia till I went in there.' ❏

Mark Dow *is a poet and freelancer in New York. He is working on a book about the US Immigration Service and co-editing, with David R Dow, the forthcoming* Machinery of Death: The reality of America's death penalty regime *(Routledge 2002)*

Voices from within and without

S treet Poets United are all veterans of Camp Fred Miller, a juvenile detention centre run by the Los Angeles County probation department. Founders and veterans, too, of the weekly poetry workshops started in Camp Miller in 1995 by Chris Henrikson, a volunteer teacher who subsequently started DreamYard/LA, a charitable organisation dedicated to creativity as a force for personal transformation.

Behind chain-link and barbed wire they took up pens to begin a long, redemptive journey. After being released from Camp Miller, they continued to write on their own; in 1998, the group performed their first – intended as their only – show at the Los Angeles Theater Center.

Despite the increasingly popular belief in California that minority gang-related violence is raging out of control, here was a demonstration to back the overwhelming statistics to the contrary. Nevertheless, the passage of Proposition 21 on the California state ballot last year demonstrated the culture of fear that now drives white America, by drastically increasing penalties for young offenders and giving prosecutors, politically motivated to be 'tough on crime', the power to put juveniles through the adult criminal system (see p163).

Three of the Street Poets, who were given a second chance in Camp Miller where they radically transformed their lives, would, most likely, have been shipped off to the adult system. All the evidence indicates that they would still be inside.

When a campaign against Prop 21 picked up steam, Street Poets joined in, performing in front of large rallies, leading teach-ins for local high schools and church groups, appearing on local and national news programmes to educate people on the dangers of this legislation.

They lost the battle: Prop 21 passed with over 60% of the vote. Since then, however, they have become key players in the fight to reverse the trend that puts retribution rather than rehabilitation at the centre of laws dealing with young offenders, in particular those from the black and Latino minorities.

Street Poets: voices from inside and outside the LA juvenile detention system, a collaboration between Street Poets, DreamYard and the photographer Jonathon Hexner, is currently looking for a publisher in the US.
JVH

*All photographs are by Jonathon Hexner, a young artist and photographer who
has been working with Chris Hendrikson and Street Poets for five years*

Who am I?

The son of a smoker
Another black offspring with no role
    model
Used as collateral for crack
More comfortable with the dopeman
The babysitter Mama never met
At least he had my back
I grew confused
Tired of seeing my bedroom in local
    pawn shops
I wanted answers but none came
Just deranged looks and strong vibes

Like 'Mind your own'
Losing respect rapidly for you
The man who hotboxed my
    emotions
Wishing Mama 'Happy Father's Day'
But she can't teach me to be the man
    you weren't
No one plans to fail
But you failed to plan
Giving birth to your replacement
Now watch your back
Who am I?

Keith Jones

Introducing . . .

Cursed with criminalistic characteristics
Symptoms of insanity and plenty rage
I reside in the 'ghetto star' tradition
In existence with strong addictions and deadly plagues

I fiend for the materialistic wealth
That my closet people would kill me to get
But I still love them unconditionally
Even the bastards who inflicted
Seven gunshots to my flesh

My prayers are like American Express
I never leave home without them
And I'd sacrifice my life to be blessed
'Cause my sins were pretty astounding

Ever since my focus was abducted
From the truest values of myself
I spent my adolescence lost
Roaming through oblivion into death

Chasing memories away with liquor
Blowing nightmares up in smoke
But I'm still haunted by the miserable recollection
Of my past character Doobie-Loc

So at times I still find myself hiding
From this corrupt and wayward soul
Though the spirit of Johnny Tremain
Has now taken complete control

(ADDITIONAL STANZA TO COME . . .)

Johnny Tremain

Runaway Temper

The chill that is truth
In this stone cold world
Pushed me to the brink of insanity
Causing me to abandon
All that seemed real in my wildest dreams
Then to have fallen short
Proven not to be the master of my emotions
But still they question me
No electrodes or candy for the nose
Will handicap this soul fighter
Last to be loved with every reason to die
But I'm unbreakable nevertheless
Beat–downs told the story that lies could not hide
Wrapped up in that fear that makes a man a killer
I dance for them all
Call me a fool with a fistful of misplaced anger
Raised on force-fed broken promises
That I fuse together with poetry and prayer
My fist open like a rose

Ezel Careuthers

Johnny Tremain, Jorge Nuñez, Keith Jones and Ezel Careuthers

Eye & I

Look into my eyes
And you'll see round objects
Shining in disguise
Cause you can't see what I can
You can't see what my eyes have
Look into my eyes
And I'll tell you what you see
Look deep inside
And it won't be a mystery
Look closely and you'll see fear
Look closer – no, not that near
Cause the rage will hurt you for
    a lifetime
No escape from the reality in my
    eyes
You see death mad-dogging you
You see a 13-year-old boy
Going down from gunshot wounds
You see a woman giving her body
For a blast of crack
And worse you see her own son
Selling her that
You see kids having kids
Then a girl getting raped
Homies call her 'hood rat'
Just to escape their mistake
This is just a preview of what's inside
So next time think twice
Before looking in my eyes

Jorge Nuñez

Dead End

I remember my dream of an ever-lasting high
An abnormal kid just trying to get by
Fighting agony and pain
As I watch the sunrise
A 12-year-old dope fiend
Running out of time
Rolling emoes, smoking primos
Feeling I know nothing
But what my father passed on
How to jack
Smoke crack and
Turn your car on
Rolled with the crowd that was me
That was it
That was all
That was how
But no one knows me now
I shout inside for help
As my soul drips and melts
Blaming others for all my troubles
As my heart beats double
A disgrace to my mother
Bad vibes in her eyes
Another chase, another case
And she's not even surprised
I hear a whisper in my ear
'Dumb-ass get out of here'
But I've got no place to go
Besides these streets that I fear

Ivan Nuñez

Spanky (left) with Ivan Nuñez, holding a picture of his brother Jorge on the day of his high school graduation for which he studied in Camp Miller

Eleven Years Old

I just graduated the 5th grade
    The Junior HIGH

Time to get paid
Get laid?
Fool, I've done that before
Pussy? It's everywhere, like the sky

Ain't no sitting on the floor
    Playing marbles in the dirt
        Now I'm doing the dirt

I got this chrome .38 Special with hollow points
Shit hurts
This is my best friend
Every day I wonder is this the end?

Eleven years old and dead?

Still I serve candy to the local heads
and BUZZZZ of this grass I just mowed
I'm hot tonight, baby
One touch and like a land mine I explode

Four feet ten inches
The downest youngster around
So I always get first pick on the hales
First in the house, first in the car
My room is like Sears
My closet's a garage
From Daytons to the latest fashion
It's a three-dimensional collage
And I ain't even twelve yet!

Then one day I said
Fuck this, it's time for me to change
Walked outside to breathe the air
And got shot by a rival gang

Chris Corona, aka Plekz

Boo!

Why you looking at me?
Cuz I'm skin bald khakis sagging to my knees?
In and out of court sipping whiskey
Puffin' Newports with police chasing me?
You never knew this thug had a heart
I'm quick to say thank you, please and hi
I have manners when I see old folks riding by
It's just too bad you don't see it in me
All you do is trip off the clothes I'm wearing
Quit staring
I thought life was supposed to be about loving
     & caring
You can call me hardheaded
You can call me trash
But don't judge me cuz I got khakis
Hanging from my ass

Narit Keobunta

Redemption

Picture my vital signs all replenished
After being crucified and diminished
To continue questing for my destiny
With new hopes of peaceful living
Evading prisons and controversy
Keeping a positive state of mind
Elevating above adversity
Maintaining my focus all the time
Evaluating observations
Contemplating plans to prosper
Evacuating from my nature
Anything that brings a bother
Perfecting flaws with assistance
Unresistant to reality
Absorbing wisdom on my mission

Which upgrades my mentality
Creating a legacy with the best of me
While the rest remains in hell
Backstabbing plots and seven shots
     couldn't defeat
What my prophecy's here to tell
Legendary and immortal
Characteristics fill my genes
Bestowed 'pon me bleeding prayers
In final stages of the breed
Between me and what I reaped
Down my past path of self-
     destruction
Picture my second life redeemed
By written rituals and instructions ❑

Johnny Tremain

INDEX EVENT: VOICES FROM BEYOND THE DARK

Rufus Sewell

With this issue of *Index on Censorship* subscribers will receive a copy of Ariel Dorfman's powerful new play *Speak Truth to Power: Voices from Beyond the Dark*, given its London premiere by *Index* on 3 June at the Playhouse Theatre. Ten years ago, *Index* published the first English translation of Dorfman's *Death and the Maiden*, which was subsequently made into the award-winning film starring Sigourney Weaver and Ben Kingsley.

Based on Kerry Kennedy Cuomo's book of the same name, *Speak Truth to Power* brings to life interviews with 50 of the world's leading human rights defenders around the world; from as far apart as China and Guatamala. Thanks to an all-star cast – and despite the sobering subject – the audience had an excellent evening.

In particular, we would like to thank Amita Dhiri, Rupert Graves, Saeed Jaffrey, Andrew Lincoln, Louise Lombard, Bill Nighy, Rufus Sewell, Janet Suzman and Harriet Walter for giving so generously of their time and talent. Similar thanks go to the director Gari Jones, who has been involved with the project from the beginning, assistant director Adam Speers and the technical team led by Pendabede Stally. Thanks also to the management of the Playhouse for allowing us use of the theatre; to The Economist Group for their support; FMCM Associates; Kerry Kennedy Cuomo; Nan Richardson and, of course, Ariel Dorfman, for allowing us the privilege of bringing *Speak Truth to Power* to London.

Janet Suzman

And, finally and most important, our thanks to all our friends and subscribers, whose continuing loyalty makes our work possible.

The cast. All photographs credit: Sarah Weal

GRIGORY PASKO

Singing to the deaf

On 20 June, the Russian environmental journalist Grigory Pasko stood up again before the military court in Vladivostok, charged for the second time with treason. If convicted, he faces a prison sentence of 12–20 years. Pursued by the Russian authorities for almost four years, Pasko was an investigative journalist with the Russian Pacific Fleet paper Boyevaya Vakhta. *He was initially arrested on 20 November 1997 and accused of passing classified documents to the Japanese television network* NHK; *he claims he was prosecuted for blowing the whistle to Japanese media on Russian nuclear waste-dumping in the Sea of Japan (*Index *3/1999, 1/2001, 2/2001). After 20 months in prison awaiting trial, he was acquitted of treason, found guilty of 'abusing his authority as an officer' and sentenced to three years' imprisonment. He was released under an amnesty but recharged after the Military Collegium of the Russian Supreme Court overturned the verdict of the lower court and called for new hearings on 21 November 2000.* Index *presents the first English translation of excerpts from his prison diary.* **JVH**

In the evenings they turf you out for a walk. I amble past the interrogation rooms which are empty now. All that's left of the day is a smell – a mixture of perfume (from the women barristers) and good cigarettes (from the men). I go up to the roof of the prison block, and find myself in a dirty, grey, dark little pocket of a yard. It's so grey and squalid it seems almost embarrassed about it. The sun is going down but you can't see it. Only its last, slanting rays – cold and unfriendly – light up the top of a wall just where the grille begins. The yard has a barred ceiling and the sky is literally, not metaphorically, chequered.

I start to walk and think. It's good to walk and to think. I catch myself remembering a line of poetry: 'we roam a circle of anticipation'. I've turned it over in my head before because there's been more than enough anticipation and waiting in my life. And here it is again: round and round a circle of anticipation. . . . But the courtyard is a rectangle. Almost a square. A square of anticipation? No. I cut corners when I want. Squaring the circle. I know. I've read about it, I've heard it before.

anya! The bathhouse! The word's enough to make any prisoner quiver in anticipation, frantically collect his soap, loofah and towel, smooth the hair stuck to his scalp and grin from ear to ear.

I remember when I first arrived in the common cell in prison, I waited to hear the word for more than 30 days. I got there in the end but it was too late, my body was already covered in scabs. And the memory of the bathhouse (over 30 people under 4 showers in 10 square metres of space) still makes me flinch.

And now it's *banya*-time again! The first shower in 17 days of isolation in the penal wing. They say that it was announced 10 days ago but the water was ice-cold so they didn't bother me. Luckily I managed to heat water in my tiny kettle (big ones were forbidden) and wash in the lavatory pan in my cell. This time, they said, everything was fine.

I was the only one left in solitary in the penal isolation wing; Zhora had been moved a few days before. The bathhouse attendants in penal isolation aren't the same as in the common bathhouses – here you get your own *banya* – so once again my wash began with the usual interjections: 'Take a look at that! He's on his own! Must be dangerous!' There's nothing you can do. Not everyone reads the papers and if you're in prison it stands to reason you're a criminal. But being alone proved a privilege. I washed on my own, longer than the others. But 'wash' is an overstatement. After soaping myself I'd leap under a stream of boiling water for a few seconds and risk scalding my privates. Perhaps 'longer' is an exaggeration, too: everyone else got ten minutes to wash, I got 15.

But it was fine. I was red as a lobster and seemed to have managed to wash off not just the dust but the dirt as well. 'You're the cleanest inmate in the seventh sector,' the bathhouse sergeant said as he opened the door. The lock rattled and stuck, and the sergeant swore. Then he started opening the second, barred door and cursed even louder and more viciously: it wasn't giving. 'Do you ever get out of here?' he asked. 'Yes,' I said. 'Once a day for a walk and once a fortnight for a shower.' The sergeant swore to his heart's content and went off pleased that he'd got all ten penal isolation cells washed quickly – a total of about 40 people.

But the walk never happened. They announced it immediately after the bath but it had already snowed and the wind was howling. Nobody wanted to risk it. Particularly as the guy with the hot fish soup appeared just then. We usually get back from our walk to find the supper's been taken round the cells and has gone cold.

They knocked from the TB floor in the night and shouted out my cell number. I called back. Who? Where from? Been in long? Me, from such and such, been in so long. 'Need to get a letter out?' 'Not really.' That's it. End of conversation. I really don't need the clandestine post. It's not that I haven't got anyone to write to, I just don't feel like it. As a rule it's a wasted effort which ends up with a plea for what really matters: flog us a bit of tea or tobacco, paper, envelopes, newspapers, matches, the criminal code, or write my parting message for me. After a year I've had enough. Another thing is I'm on my own in the cell and physically can't drag myself up every time. The third thing is that I already have a dependant from the next-door cell. The hole between the cells remained unblocked even after they did the overhaul. Every 2–3 days, Kolek Portnoy comes by for a pay-off. He's got so cheeky he's talked me into giving him a tin of food, even though you don't do that in prison. And then there's the discourse: who's been round (he can hear my door opening), what did they bring and so on. Then a paragraph about his past as an orphan, his bachelor life now, and his future as a down-and-out. The conversation always ends with a request: give us a couple of matches, a sheet of paper . . . and I always do: packets of cigarettes (Prima), tea in handfuls, boxes of matches, newspapers in armfuls.

Kolek is being held under two articles, he says: 'keeping my mouth shut' and 'so much crap'. Most probably 158 [infringement of authors' rights Ed] and 146 [theft Ed]. I sometimes think that in this country people are plain inept at stealing and swindling. Here you are with no money to pay for a barrister or persuade your friends to send you parcels. It's a very Russian, slovenly form of crime: stole, drank it away, off to prison. No future, just the present. Kolek has been on his own too, recently. He remembers what a gasbag his cell-mate was. So do I: he promised to return my magazines, beating his breast as though he was about to crack. Then he left the prison with them. Kolek was there so he doesn't ask me for magazines.

As we walked Kolek asked: 'What are you reading?' 'Dostoevsky.' 'He's hard going.' I've often heard this said here about Dostoevsky's work. I'd love to know where they picked it up. Perhaps they've read him, but I doubt it. Next time I'll say I'm reading Alexander Klizovsky's 'Living Ethic' and await Kolek's reaction.

'Officer, there's a law that says . . .'
'Why aren't your hands behind your back? Hands behind your back!'

'. . . a prisoner has the right . . .'

'Why are you wearing that cap?'

'It's cold!'

'Take it off right away! It's forbidden!'

'Officer?! They haven't given us . . .'

'Show what you've got in your bag! That's enough talking!'

. . . The inspection proceeds down to my cell. The lock turns and the first iron door opens with a clang and metallic yowl. The second which is barred hasn't been touched yet. The entire inspection team looks through it at my wretched abode. 'He's alone,' they say in a friendly sort of way, 'what does he need to come out for?' So I don't go out into the corridor, and my bag and mattress stay in the cell. A woman with a sheet of paper in her hands asks:

'Mattress and a pillow?'

'Yes,' I say. 'No thanks to the prison.'

'Doesn't matter,' the woman says,' the main thing is they're here . . .'

An inspector with a young guard come into the cell. The first knocks on the bars with a wooden hammer, the second examines the pictures on the walls: three photographs from the magazine *Ogonyok* and, under the battleship *Peresvet,* a big cutting with the heading 'Do we need freedom?'

'These will have to come down,' the inspector says. 'Commander, you know I don't deal in trivia.'

'I know,' he mutters, 'but it's not allowed . . .'

Having turned over the mattress, leafed through the exercise books on the table, the inspector suddenly fixes his gaze on the huge metal box with the big key. And a thought stirs. 'Why don't we look through your safe,' he suggests in a friendly sort of way, as though he anticipated fishing out something unusual and spectacularly forbidden – secret documents, for example. He knows that according to the law 'On keeping prisoners under guard . . .' you're forbidden to keep secret documents in cells. He also knows I should have been given an official indictment stamped 'top secret'.

I take the newspapers off the box and open it. The inspector's sandy head dives in. It emerges and, with undisguised disappointment and annoyance, he says to his colleague: 'It's empty.' I find it hard not to laugh. The box is so empty there's not a spider's web in sight. . . . After that, interest in my cell and my things waned. With a sigh, the inspection team cast a parting glance over my miserable home decorated with photos from *Ogonek,* and departed.

Soon after, there was a disturbance in the neighbouring cell as the prisoners left.

'Look lively, step on it . . .'

'We are . . .'

'What's that? Talking? Clothes off. Down to your underpants!'

Sounds like the inspector's mate. He picks on anything he can.

'Perishable food is forbidden!' he shouts, mindless of the fact that prisoners are fed survival rations and any grub is worth its weight in gold.

'We only got our parcels yesterday,' objects one of the prisoners timidly.

'Silence!' the guard interrupts sharply. 'What's in your bags?'

. . . The inspection goes on.

I suppose I must be beginning to understand something about life. After the murder of state deputy Galina Starovoitova [in 1998 *Ed*] I was expecting them to announce an increase in the powers of the interior ministry and the FSB [former KGB *Ed*]. They did: by presidential decree. Now the murderers can be caught. Or rather handed over. The murder was necessary so that the authorities could have carte blanche for the implementation of repressive measures. In my (not necessarily biased) view, the FSB plays a role that cements crime rather than controls it. With KGB/FSB help, Russia became – and now definitively is – a criminal state. With FSB help, a government and parliament will be established ('elected' for the benefit of the West) which will assist in the revival of the former power of the interior ministry and KGB. A totalitarian police-informer state with a thin stratum of private business, a few millionaires at the top and a mass of grey, silent people working like dogs for a few kopeks. The number of prisons, prison camps and internal troops will grow, as will the number of police schools and institutes. There will even be competition to get in. Police privileges will be increased. The first to be armed and fed will be the militia, the FSB, internal troops, tax office employees, customs, public prosecutor's offices and the law courts. Then the army, or rather what's left of it.

People who are clear-headed, despite their nefarious ways, have stayed on in the KGB/FSB. When the scandal broke about the KGB officers who had dared to tell journalists that there were criminals working in the FSB, the FSB organised Starovoitova's shooting. The silent majority's attention was diverted. The killers are unlikely to be found this time; they seldom are. Somebody will be made the fall guy. The FSB will have to prove how professional they are and how necessary; they'll have to deliver on the powers they've been given.

People are downtrodden and fearful. They are afraid of everybody: the authorities, deputies, militia and particularly the FSB. As soon as someone outstandingly able, with independent judgement, appears on the scene – he or she immediately comes to the FSB's attention. After that there are four options: become an informer, be killed, be imprisoned or be put away in a psychiatric hospital. All are time-honoured methods, approved by silent public acquiescence. Gorbachev's thaw is long over. The next, if it happens, will not come for 30 years.

Now, just before the parliamentary elections [December 1999 Ed], there will be several very public murders, a few dozen less public ones and hundreds which won't even be noticed by journalists.

But the FSB will notice journalists. They will all be bought, bribed, terrorised and made to sing along with the FSB. There will be scarcely any opposition – anyone who opposes will be killed.

The gap between us and the West will grow. They need our raw materials, but not our criminal ways which are also spreading west. Financial aid, like any other, will only help to strengthen the personal position of the criminals in power.

The arrogance and cynicism, the shabby insidiousness of the generation taking over from the KGB dinosaurs and the party nomenklatura will astonish everyone: the people who will be silent, the oldest dinosaurs who will have their privileges taken away, and the entire western world whose affluence will be threatened.

And I can see no force that can halt the onset of the KGB's and the interior ministry's criminal and chaotic rule. ❑

Grigory Pasko's prison memoirs My poem glukhim (We Sing to the Deaf) *published by Russko-Baltiiskii Informatsionnyi Tsentr BLITZ (St Petersburg, 2000, edition of 3,000 copies). First English translation by Irena Maryniak*

Culture

Watching plays can seriously damage your health p192

London, 1704: anti-theatre pamphlet. Credit: The British Library

Massacre in Chechnya. Credit: Eddie Opp / Kommersant

Index publishes the first English-language translation of Russian poets on the Chechen war p198

SARAH A SMITH

An ignoble history

**Theatre censorship is almost as old as the dramas it prohibits.
Even today, particularly in the UK, archaic attitudes continue
to influence what we may and may not see on the stage**

The title *Politics, Prudery and Perversions* neatly summarises the
motivation behind British theatre censorship. The twin engines
which have driven the control of the theatre have always been the
protection of private men and public morals. As theatre critic Nicholas
de Jongh's new book on the final 67 years of stage censorship illustrates,
censorship results from political self-interest and puritanical ignorance.

De Jongh was the first journalist to access the records of theatre
censorship after they were made available at the British Library in 1990.
And his book is the first clear account of both the collapse of censorship
in 1968 and its absurdities in the 20th century. It is an impassioned
work, horrified by the roll-call of world drama judged morally dubious
by the British censor (including August Strindberg's *Miss Julie*, Luigi
Pirandello's *Six Characters in Search of an Author* and Tennessee Williams's
A Streetcar Named Desire). It is also the first to argue that past censorship
isn't just something to laugh over, a hiccup in history which saw
Noël Coward's *The Vortex* as an omen of class war and prompted long
discussions over the use of the word 'crumpet', but an insidious attack
on theatre. According to de Jongh, censorship has had a long-lasting
effect on both how we respond to drama (see the outraged response
to 1990s plays on violence and homosexuality such as Mark Ravenhill's
Shopping and Fucking and Tony Kushner's *Angels in America*) and how it is
written and performed – de Jongh cites the scarcity of plays on modern
atrocities.

Theatre censorship in the 20th century forms part of an ignominious
strand of British political history which stretches back to the 10th
century. The earliest records of theatrical performance are also records
of its prohibition: theatre history relies on details of the ecclesiastical

injunctions and legal depositions against performers as much as on details of actual performances. The first record of theatrical activity is a complaint: in 960, reference was made to 'mocking entertainers' in public squares and marketplaces. Attempts were soon made to place limits on performance. The cycles of medieval Mystery plays, the first extant examples of vernacular drama in Britain, came under Church control. Medieval theatre troupes needed a patron's livery and letter to tour. After 1557, they also needed the permission of the local mayor to perform in public. Quite where they would perform is a problem for historians – in 1559, a proclamation banned performances in hostels and taverns, though it is hard to tell how widely this was enforced.

The first edict censoring material came with the Reformation, when the 1543 Act for the Advancement of the True Religion banned plays likely to challenge the new religious doctrine. Sixteen years later, local authorities were empowered to prohibit plays 'wherein either matters of religion or governance of the estate of the common weale shall be handled or treated'. Shortly after this comes evidence of more stringent censorship: a patent granted to the Earl of Leicester's troupe in 1574 stipulated that they could perform only plays 'seen and allowed' by the Master of the Revels, an officer of the court under the control of the Lord Chamberlain. With the advent of permanent playhouses in London in 1576, the Master of the Revels' powers were more fully defined in a series of edicts. The great period of English drama – the Elizabethan and Jacobean age – took place as censorship was getting an official hold.

Initial prohibitions focused on politically sensitive topics. The deposition scene from Shakespeare's *Richard II* was prohibited during a time of political instability. Ben Jonson and George Chapman were briefly imprisoned for 'seditious matter' (irreverent treatment of Scottish courtiers, a risky subject with a Scottish king on the throne) in *Eastward Ho!* (1605). Thomas Middleton's allegorical attack on Catholicism and the Spanish crown, *A Game at Chess*, ran for only nine days in 1624 before a warrant was issued for Middleton's arrest and the play withdrawn. That these last two works survived is unusual; most banned works disappeared or exist only in fragmented form.

The theatre also faced attack from religious sources. Puritan pamphlets such as Philip Stubbes's *Anatomy of Abuses* (1583) make plain the dangers inherent in theatre attendance. John Northbrook's 1577 *Treatise* suggests that attending 'interludes' provides an education in 'how to deceive your husbands, how to allure to whoredom, how to murder, how to disobey and rebel against princes'. This disapproval of the stage triumphed during the English Commonwealth with the ultimate censorship – the closing of the theatres at the outbreak of the Civil War in 1642 and their destruction in 1648.

The restoration of the public theatre under Charles II in 1660 is thought of as a time of theatrical liberty. One type of censorship – the popular prohibition on women's appearance on the public stage – was overturned when the king issued a royal patent in 1662 stating that only women were to appear in women's roles. Yet limitations continued: the granting of patents to build and manage theatres was in the king's hands. Only two were initially given, to William Davenant and Thomas Killigrew. The Master of the Revels was still censor-in-chief, although Davenant and Killigrew were also required to 'peruse all plays that have been formerly written and to expunge all profanesses and scurrility from the same'. Political and religious censorship still took place, affecting plays as seemingly innocuous as Shakespeare's *The Tempest* (John Dryden and Davenant replaced Prospero's Arcadian idealism with a more pragmatic approach).

Censorship took modern form in 1737. Robert Walpole's unpopular premiership had provoked so much theatrical criticism (including John Gay's *The Beggar's Opera* of 1728 and Henry Fielding's *The Historical Register for the Year 1736*) that he took legal measures to stifle dissent. The Stage Licensing Act was the first systematic attempt at censorship, giving the Lord Chamberlain powers to censor as he chose. All new plays were to be submitted for licensing 14 days in advance of performance. This remained in force until 1968, with no explanation of the reasons for prohibition required, no appeal possible and fines for those who defied the rulings. To add insult to injury, theatre managements were required to pay for the privilege of censorship.

Walpole's innovation wasn't watertight, but the act had an impact. By 1742, political satire on stage had disappeared. Meanwhile, public controversies which might once have excited theatrical comment (the Irish problem, Catholic emancipation, demands for reform) never reached the stage. Playwrights no longer wrote about such topics: self-censorship had begun.

Criticism of the aristocracy was prohibited. Even Lady Eglantine Wallace's mildly satirical *The Whim*, a play about a Saturnalian feast in which masters and servants swap roles, was affected. Private individuals occasionally intervened to protect themselves and their families. Different topics became sensitive at different times. Plays on marriage were awkward at the close of the 18th century because of the Prince of Wales's marital circumstances; productions of Shakespeare's *King Lear* were discouraged during George III's mental illness.

Few playwrights argued against censorship during this period, and increasing moral propriety meant that the censor wasn't troubled by theatrical ribaldry. The Victorian censor focused his attention on social issues. One particular source of anxiety was Newgate drama, which became so popular and led to such horrifying tales of copycat crimes that parents and teachers demanded the Lord Chamberlain's office crack down on it. Plays based on Harrison Ainsworth's novel *Jack Sheppard* and Charles Dickens's *Oliver Twist* were duly banned. Meanwhile, plays on trade unionism, industrial relations and the workhouse were restricted, and references to the royal family, government ministers and other public figures strictly prohibited. Political comment was limited to *burlettas*, pantomime and the music hall, which were outside the censor's jurisdiction.

It was not until the last quarter of the 19th century that agitation against censorship really began. W S Gilbert challenged the Lord Chamberlain with his political burlesque *The Happy Land* (1873). The producers of M Felix's season of French plays publicised the cuts demanded by the censor in a letter to *The Times* and attacked him in advertisements. A more effective strike against the censor was the use of private theatre clubs, which were not covered by legislation. Shelley's *The Cenci* (1819) was performed privately in 1886 and marked the way for prohibited drama for the next 80 years. The history of 20th-century dramatic innovation is really the history of the private theatre clubs, where everything from Shaw's *Mrs Warren's Profession* (1894) to Genet's *The Maids* (1956) to Edward Bond's *Saved* (1965) was forced to premiere.

With the establishment of a two-tier system of theatre and increasing demands from writers and directors to end censorship, it seemed that the Lord Chamberlain's office would collapse. But it was a slow process. The censor continued to act to protect British relations with foreign powers, most ignobly in the case of Terence Rattigan's mild anti-Nazi farce, *Follow My Leader* (1938). He continued to guard against the discussion

SARAH A SMITH

From The Sphere, *3 October 1925: 31 years after it was written,* Mrs Warren's Profession *was still thought to be 'very frank in its outlook'. Credit: © The Board of Trustees of the Victoria & Albert Museum*

of sexuality, keeping Lillian Hellman's *The Children's Hour* (1934) from the stage for 26 years. And he continued to protect the memory of the revered dead, as in the case of Queen Victoria and Florence Nightingale in Bond's *Early Morning* (1967).

The row over the Royal Court's productions of *Saved* and John Osborne's *A Patriot for Me* (1965) triggered the passing of the 1968 Theatres Act. This ended official censorship, putting dramatic performance on a par with books, magazines and periodicals (covered by the criminal laws of libel, slander, race relations, public order and obscenity). But some plays were slow to reach the stage. Noël Coward's *Semi-Monde* (1926), which he never dared submit, is only now receiving its West End premiere. And the idea that there should be some control over what we can see lingers. At root we are afraid of theatre, of what truths it might tell us, what thoughts and feelings it might provoke. The idea of sympathetic magic — that by enacting something one makes it so — still casts a spell over otherwise sane people. It was there in the self-censorship that led Max Stafford-Clark to drop Jim Allen's purportedly anti-Zionist play *Perdition* (1989) and Edward Kemp to rewrite the Mysteries for the Royal Shakespeare Company in 1997, removing all references to the Jews. It was there in Mary Whitehouse's private prosecution under the Sexual Offences Act of Michael Bogdanov, director of Howard Brenton's *The Romans in Britain* in 1982. And it was there in the hysterical critical reaction to Sarah Kane's grand guignol *Blasted* in 1995. Have we really come very far from the Puritan view that the theatre is set on 'the exaltation of vice and the mockery of virtue'? ❏

Sarah A Smith is a UK-based writer and critic
Politics, Prudery and Perversions *by Nicholas de Jongh was published in 2000 by Methuen*

The time of 'Ch'

This book, illustrated by Chechen schoolchildren (which, as far as I can see, is the only formal Chechen participation), is the work of over 100 poets writing in Russian across the expanse of Russia reacting in poetry to the events in Chechnya. One-quarter of them are women, remarkable in a 'war book'. I know no equivalent Russian poetry book arising out of the war in Afghanistan.

The oldest poet, Semyon Lipkin, is 89, the youngest 18. Nikolay Vinnik, the compiler, is at pains to assert that the book should not be taken as a 'political gesture' but rather gives the opportunity to many poets to express themselves on the tragic events in Chechnya: 'it is our deep conviction that opinions are not the most important thing that the poet can share with the reader. Much more important is how the poet sees what is happening and what the poet feels.'

Although all the poems are inspired by Chechnya and some are direct, almost journalistic descriptions of the highest order though always with the sting of poetry, there is room for poems in a more allegorical vein, even for 'pure poetry' such as Viktor Krivulin's 'War in the Old Capital'. Viktor (whose cycle 'The Gallery', translated by Michael Molnar, is due out in Ten Russian Poets, ed. Richard McKane, Anvil Press, summer 2001) died recently of lung cancer at the age of 56. His cycle of poems and Mikhail Sukhotin's long 'Poem on the First Chechen Campaign' are the best in the book. No amount of TV journalism and media coverage, vital, shocking and essential as it is, could have produced this book. As such, it echoes Osip Mandelstam's words to Anna Akhmatova in the mid-1930s, that poetry should tackle 'civil themes'.

The tiny, by Russian standards, print run of this book (1,500 copies) means that it will not be mainstream reading and there may be attempts at censorship – indeed, by any standards it is an uncomfortable read, as it should be. The Chechen war continues, a joint venture with millions at stake, prosecuted by retrogressive elements with vested interests in the military, FSB (former KGB) inside the Kremlin and in Chechnya: they could and should read this book. It is the real intelligence.

Richard McKane

The poems below are from *The time of 'Ch'*, compiled by N Vinnik and published by Novoe Literaturnoe Obozrenie (Moscow 2001). First English translation by Richard McKane

VLADIMIR GUBAYLOVSKY

b. 1960. Poet, lives in Moscow

The Leader's Death

The round sky is overturned over Chechnya.
Like a scratch on a pale blue ceiling
the rocket slides down the beam
of the mobile telephone.
Fractions of seconds remain –
no time to blink or groan.
Time is numbered for the lynch law
and holds tight to your elbow.
The trees, leafless and gaunt,
crown your body with posthumous fame,
where there'll be ten minutes' walk
from your left arm to your right.

1996

NATALYA OSIPOVA
b. 1958, Moscow. Poet, psychologist and translator

What's this? Smoke?
That's the villages burning, the Daghestan villages.
What's this? Is the earth shaking?
That's the rockets flying into town, the Chechen town.
That's the last generations of October
blown up by an anti-personnel mine,
made in a factory in the Urals,
where with frozen hands . . .
in a Krupps factory
dismantled happily one spring
fifty years ago
by a mate.
Who threw himself under the tanks?
Under the tanks?
That's a few drunks lost in a tunnel.
That was in Prague, in Prague . . .
What's this? The police are at the stops?
That's someone blew up the houses in another
workers' area . . .
How much rubbish and trash there was in them . . .
Sleep, my child, sleep.
In our broad expanses
from the wonderful Caucasus mountains
to the wondrous tundra
killing is the best business.
The only way to victory
is to do that which under no circumstances
and for nothing in the world should be done.

SERGEI STRATANOVSKY

b. 1945, Leningrad. Poet, bibliographer at National Library
of St Petersburg, samizdat editor and author in 1970s and 80s,
Brodsky Prize-winner 2000

Clean out the people
        from the surrounding villages,
the peasants and peasant women
        the filthy kids,
the firing squad for the weak,
        drive out the rest,
so that there'd be no trace of them
        only the wolves, the wolves
and flocks of evil crows.

   . . .

Grozny is destroyed . . .
        vacuum bombs . . .
Who believes in God there?
        But they say there are
no atheists in the trenches
        and the bullet of the hated enemy
will not get you if you
        pray to Allah
or the God of the Russians.

   From *Poems* (1994)

SERGEI TRUNEV

b. 1973. Lives in Saratov, teaches philosophy at Saratov University

You remember how he lay on the snow,
his legs splayed wide. Have they no shame?
His mouth was open and instead of his stomach
there was a gaping pit
and white flies swarmed round his lips.
The words were frozen in his gullet
and did not express what the corpse thought
as it flew to Nirvana.
Completely alone among the Asiatic mountains,
he felt the breathing of the wind on his cheek,
slender fingering of crystal strings . . .
Warm him, earth, in your bloody bowels.

    20 December 1995

IVAN AKHMETEV

b. 1950. Lives in Moscow. Poet, writer, critic, compiler for www *of Russian poetry and prose 1950s–80s, two books of poetry*

and lead us not into Ingushetia . . .

    1994

        Holidays to the cannonade's thunder . . .

        January 1995

disarmament
at the price of total
embitterment . . .

    1995   hysterical attempts
                to preserve this
                territorial integrity
                that is needed by no one . . .

                2000

ALEXANDER LEONTIEV

b. 1970, Volgograd. Poet, four books of poetry including Cicada *(1996),
read at Rotterdam Poetry International*

9 May 1995 (Victory Day)

*The angry Chechen crawls on to the bank
and sharpens his dagger . . .*
Lermontov

The huge country is ready for the fiftieth anniversary:
the border is under lock, the hands bolted.
Remembering the fallen, these days I mourn
the living who meet these times of our imperial shame.
Throw your medal into the captured spirits, like an acid solution,
you yourself will see: your bravery will melt
without trace and your animal terror
and there are none left alive who burn with shame.
But here's one of them who was *there*
fifty years ago. This is how he finished his story:
'Put all the f—ing non-Russians up against the wall
(judge them as vile,
there's the rhyme Dzhugashvili)
and if Stalin was here now . . .'

The huge country is preparing for a drinking bout,
the hospital is crammed, the troops are brought in.
My fallen, don't let God give you
a second life: the same ravings, horror, anguish.
Tell me, Tsar Boris, at night in your steady eyes
do you see the images of bloodsoaked boys?
The huge country is not sleeping in its Health Ministry beds:
artificial limbs in sleeves, cemeteries blossoming.
Fathers are bringing their children to be sacrificed again,
the shadow of Grozny, the terrible,★ lay on the ruling house . . .
The rulers of the country are ready to put in order
their bloody needs, so difficult to manage.

★ Grozny means 'terrible' (as in Ivan the Terrible), or 'threatening',
as well as being the Russian name for the capital of Chechnya

VIKTOR KRIVULIN

1944–2001. Lived most of his life in Leningrad / St Petersburg. Poet, essayist, samizdat editor, activist, vice-chair St Petersburg section of Russian PEN, author of 14 books of poems, unpublished in USSR until 1986

War in the Old Capital

I'm freezing at the centre of the former empire
soon I'll be totally crested and go over to birds' chatter
I'll talk in the Khan language
with Bo Tzyu the drunkard

here, respected, in this old capital
among the Chzhurchzhens and Northern Shu
we live as in a frontier garrison
I've not been writing poems for a long time

so, notes to the commanders about the moral situation
with a white brush on blue paper
too heavy and thick
for full-mooned conversations

all about the same thing – about the moral situation
about eastern winds, they're always at hand
behind the collar and in the dressing-gown sleeve
and in the hieroglyph for night

the coals in the iron brazier
go cold like blue under the nails
of a boy soldier from the new recruits –
where did they get that lot from?

Many troops disperse in the area
the more dense the fighters the more dark the night
the days are shorter and the noodle soup
is more transparent

the barbarians love silk and eat off slender plates
my terracotta teapot does not attract them
rough red earthenware of the Tsins' era –
who's here to recognise its worth now?

SEMYON LIPKIN

b. 1911 in Odessa. Now lives in Moscow. His first work as a poet was published in the censored Metropolis. *He has been published in Russia since 1989*

The River of Death

I'm writing to you by accident, it's true!
Lermontov

I remember a dense mountain forest.
The village of Akhchoy hid there.
I remember the sharp cries of the eagles
over the mountain river Valerik:
the people of Ichkeriya
call it the River of Death.
A certain lieutenant described the cruel
battle in the ravines among the cliffs.
That battle died down one hundred
                                       years ago.
Then there came another detachment,
then another detachment came
and the faithful sons of the fatherland
were awarded decorations,
but were not participants in the war
but more participants in atrocities:
two fighters for five families.

Let's sum up one family:
a grey-haired old man, a blind rhapsode,
a Dzhigit with a heavy crutch,
a legless invalid from Dnestra,
an old woman in mourning dress
gripping her bundle with a gaunt hand,
a mother breast-feeding her baby,
no need to know if the road is long,
daughter-in-law stands with a harmonica,
the she-goat is in a bad way,
it is drawn to the hearth ash –
it's so good to be in the warmth!

Forget the goat – there are six in the
                                       family –
but how many miles is any one's guess.
Many die in the cattle wagons,

they transport the half-dead,
not only the people's flesh but their spirit
for forced labour in Kazakhstan.

It's almost half a century
since I was in those alien parts.
The words the Vainakh composed
I repeated in Russian poems.
I am not stirring up the past,
I am not writing this to you by accident.

1994 ❏

GEORGE JONES

Down the Welsh road

Should the linguistic rights of the Welsh-speaking minority dictate the educational syllabus of the English-speaking majority?

The United Kingdom is still not used to thinking of itself in anything other than monolingual terms. Those native minority languages existing within its boundaries are tolerated to a greater extent than their analogues in some other states within Europe and they benefit from the occasional governmental concession. But the notion of speakers of these languages – Welsh, Scottish Gaelic, Irish or Cornish – enjoying rights purely as members of a linguistic group is fairly underdeveloped.

There are exceptions to this rule. Since 1967, Welsh speakers have had the right to speak their language in court and have access to the services of an interpreter if necessary. And 1993 legislation acknowledges that they have a right to expect some level of access to services and to communication with officialdom through the medium of Welsh, stipulating that public bodies (but not private or charitable ones) must draw up language plans to be approved by a statutory language board. It omits any specifics about exactly what place is to be given to the language, referring vaguely to what is 'reasonable and practical'.

But this is a far more substantial legal status than is enjoyed by the other native British minority languages. Scottish Gaelic has a very circumscribed legal existence. The current provision is more or less that one member of the Scottish Land Court and one member of the Crofters' Commission must be a Gaelic speaker; that knowledge of Gaelic satisfies the language conditions for naturalisation; that local authorities have a duty to provide the teaching of Gaelic in Gaelic-speaking areas; that Gaelic broadcasting is due a certain amount of governmental funding; that financial support may be given to Gaelic education and to the promotion of the language and culture; that bilingual road signs are permissible and that local authorities may take a Gaelic name.

Welsh is spoken by half a million people in Wales and Scottish Gaelic by around 65,000 people in Scotland. Irish is spoken in the six counties of the north of Ireland by a substantial number of people who have learned it as a second language. Cornish, which died out as a community language a couple of centuries ago, is now spoken only by the few hundred people involved in its revival. The positions of these languages are, then, quite diverse. However, they have certain elements in common in their history, which might be summed up as an exclusion in modern times from many fields of public life. The Acts of Union of Wales with England, for instance, a series of laws passed between 1536 and 1543, explicitly stated that the only language of public office in Wales was thenceforth to be English. The place that these languages have managed to gain in various public fields in recent times has been due to piecemeal concessions, often gained after heavy lobbying and campaigning.

Those concerned with the promotion of minority languages do not necessarily all sing from the same ideological hymn book. It is common to hear the rhetoric of heritage preservation rather than that of human rights when steps are being discussed to shore up the position of a minoritised language. This is the tone taken in much of the European discourse on the subject, European institutions being generally more or less the sum of the nation states represented within them and unwilling to rock the boat by over-politicising the issue. That said, the 1990s saw the drafting of a Council of Europe charter on minority or regional languages whereby the signatories will (usually, for it is a complicated charter containing a variety of options) grant a measure of concrete support to the languages concerned. Even then, it states:

> The charter's overriding purpose is cultural. It is designed to protect and promote regional or minority languages as a threatened aspect of Europe's cultural heritage.

> The charter sets out to protect and promote regional or minority languages, not linguistic minorities. For this reason emphasis is placed on the cultural dimension . . . The charter does not establish any individual or collective rights for the speakers of regional or minority languages.

The purely 'heritage preservation' approach is vulnerable to utilitarian interrogation by those demanding to know what the 'use' of certain languages is, and why everyone does not dedicate him/herself to the streamlining of communication by using as few languages as possible. This is often answered by appealing to the importance of the different *Weltanschauung* inextricably bound up with each different language, rather than by dismissing the demand that speakers of a language should be obliged to justify it, and treating the issue from the perspective of a basic human right: the use of one's own language in one's own country.

Since language is a phenomenon that occurs primarily in interaction between people, however, the concept of language rights sometimes leads people to think in terms of collective rights as well as individual ones. For people, individually, to have the right to use Welsh or Gaelic – say with the local authority or the police – is one thing, and doubtless very useful as far as it goes, but the possibility of using the language in practice is severely limited unless it remains spoken by a hefty percentage of the inhabitants of a given area. Ensuring that that remains the case may require action based on notions of collective rights.

The numerical swamping by English monoglot migrants of Welsh speakers in the parts of Wales which have had, until recently, a great majority of Welsh speakers is therefore the cause of not a little tension and controversy. Such migrants are often fairly ignorant even of the existence of Welsh and it is not uncommon for them to be hostile, particularly when faced with any demands that they or their children learn it. Calls have come in recent years for legislative action to limit the degree to which people can move into these areas, prompting accusations of racism.

Such accusations are also made from time to time when knowledge of the Welsh language is stipulated as a necessary condition of an employment contract. Race relations and anti-discrimination legislation have, on occasion, been invoked in opposition to the language being made a qualification for certain posts. In 1998, a youth worker in Anglesey, backed by his trade union, brought a discrimination case against the county council on the grounds that he was not shortlisted for a vacancy because he did not speak fluent Welsh. On that occasion the case failed, but others have succeeded.

The clash between the notion of a collective right to maintain a Welsh-speaking community and that of individual rights is well

First among equals: Welsh/English signposts in Cardiff. Credit: Keith Morris

illustrated in the context of education. Precise policy on the use of Welsh in schools varies from one local education authority to another, but more or less all state schools in Wales, at least, teach the language as a subject. In many schools, it is also used as a medium of instruction. It is claimed by some English-speaking in-migrants that their children's education is compromised by the requirement that they be brought up to speed in Welsh so as to follow lessons through the medium of that language.

Those opposed to compulsory schooling in Welsh did, for a period, form a vocal organisation known as Education First, which consisted, it is fair to point out, not only of English-speaking in-comers. This group may have made little practical impact, but the fact that education in

Britain's minority languages is still seen as precarious, depending as
it does chiefly on the say-so of individual local authorities, is well
illustrated by the case of Gaelic-medium education in Perth and Kinross
in Scotland. At the time of writing, the local authority had just agreed
to maintain a Gaelic unit after much lobbying, having given serious
consideration to doing away with it entirely. This situation is less likely
to occur in the most strongly Gaelic or Welsh-speaking regions, but does
indicate the vulnerable nature of provisions which cannot rely on a firm
legal base.

The UK is, of course, a stranger to the notion of inalienable,
constitutionally guaranteed rights in any field. Parliament giveth and
Parliament taketh away. That said, if we look at the position of Breton,
the sister language of Welsh, we see that in France the constitution is
itself a problem from a minority-language perspective. French is the
language of the republic and Breton has no official existence whatsoever;
the state refuses even to count the number of speakers; and state
provision in the fields of broadcasting and education is tokenistic
to the point where private ventures have stepped in to fill the gap.

It is sometimes asked why, if one is to accept that a full range
of public functions ought to be carried out in Welsh or Gaelic, the
same should not be true for the myriad other languages belonging to
immigrant groups. The notion of autochthony, closely analysed, may
indeed be something of a fiction, and a distinction, in principle, between
the status of 'autochthonous' and 'non-autochthonous' languages
difficult to justify. It is hard to see any objection to the use of as many
languages as possible, and for as many functions as possible, if that is to
what the speakers of the languages aspire. The issues are somewhat
different, however, where a language is not identified with a certain
territory.

Many of those involved with the minorised 'aboriginal' languages in
the UK believe that their languages must have a territorial base in which
they are used for a full range of functions, both public and private, if
their speakers are to have access to them as fully functional modes of
communication. It is precisely this linguistic territorial base that has
been denied to speakers of all present-day Celtic languages. The speakers
of many of the more recent immigrant languages, on the other hand,
even if they have no direct physical access to their language's primary
territorial base, may enjoy many of the benefits brought about by its

existence. A language used somewhere on the planet as a fully-fledged state language will not, for example, have had its terminological integrity compromised and will probably be the medium of some form of publishing and broadcasting activity, the fruits of which are ever easier to enjoy wherever on the planet a speaker happens to find him/herself. Admittedly, where migration took place some time ago, media provision emanating from the 'homeland' is not always of great interest or relevance.

Will the recent devolution in Scotland, Wales and the north of Ireland bring about an improvement in the rights accorded to the speakers of Welsh, Scottish Gaelic and Irish? It is still too early to say, but the abandonment by the Scottish Labour government of its commitment to what was known as 'Secure Status' for Gaelic last autumn does not give grounds for optimism. In an interview, the then first minister, the late Donald Dewar, said Scotland would not 'go down the Welsh road' whereby public bodies would be obliged to provide services in Gaelic. It is also noteworthy that the Scottish parliament has already passed an education act in which Gaelic is not mentioned at all.

Another indicator that increased autonomy will not necessarily protect the speakers of these languages is the post-independence history of the Irish language in the Republic of Ireland. On paper Irish is the first language of the republic but, in practice, opportunities to use the language outside the designated Gaeltacht areas are severely limited. If the rights of speakers of Welsh, Scottish Gaelic, Irish or any language in a similar minorised position are to be safeguarded, then not only must there be very specific legislation guaranteeing this, but also close monitoring of implementation and strong bodies charged with the adjudication of complaints. Otherwise, it will be left to individuals to bear the cost in financial and other terms of bringing cases of infringement to the courts. ❏

George Jones is research officer with the Mercator Media Centre at the University of Wales Aberystwyth. He also edits Mercator Media Forum, *an annual journal concerned with the use of minority languages in the media*

LORI BERENSON

No singing, no laughing, no sound

In 1995, Lori Berenson, a US citizen, was arrested and sentenced to life imprisonment by a 'hooded' court for allegedly conspiring with the Tupac Amaru Revolutionary Movement to take over the Peruvian Congress. In May this year, US pressure resulted in a retrial on the lesser charge of 'terrorist collaboration'. Here, for the first time since her imprisonment, and through the voices of women who shared it with her, she writes of the conditions in which thousands of detainees convicted under Peru's anti-terrorist laws continue to be held

Peru, like many other Latin American countries, has a rich, pre-Hispanic cultural history, largely rejected or ignored since the Spanish conquest. For centuries, Peru's native majority have suffered inequality and ingrained injustice. Even during colonial times, as well as post-independence, there were rebel movements, two of which have become prominent over the past three decades or so: the Maoist Peruvian Communist Party (Shining Path) and the smaller Tupac Amaru Revolutionary Movement (MRTA).

In 1992, then president Alberto Fujimori disbanded all branches of government, rewrote the constitution and took over control of the state in an internal coup. Having destroyed all opposition and neutralised the rebel groups in a 'dirty war' that included arbitrary detention, torture, disappearances and extra-judicial executions, he imposed his neo-liberal economic policies. The Supreme Presidential Decrees 'legalised' the violation of fundamental rights, as did anti-terrorist laws which abolished due process and prescribed long prison sentences with no access to parole or other legal benefits. Judges were given carte blanche to convict even when there was insufficient evidence through the use of 'criteria of conscience', in other words, the personal and arbitrary decision of a judge.

Hooded military and civilian judges condemned thousands in summary trials. The anti-terrorist laws were applied retroactively to those detained before the coup. People were arrested on the hearsay of other detainees. These were called 'repentants' and, in return for their testimony, were promised privileges. Six of the nine women whose testimony appears here were arrested as a result of 'repentant' hearsay. Seven of them were condemned by 'criteria of conscience' in either civilian or military courts.

With the exception of the six leaders held in military jails, political prisoners were put in maximum security prisons where a repressive 'closed prison regime' was enforced. With only half an hour's respite, prisoners were locked up all day in small cells with no light. Visits by adult family members were allowed once a month and children only once every three months. Visits were for half an hour through metal grilles. Visits and yard time could be arbitrarily suspended. All newspapers, magazines, radio and TV were prohibited. Letters, books, work materials, even pens and paper, were limited and randomly prohibited. As prosecutor Navas said in my recent trial: 'Prisoners have no rights.'

Although Fujimori's dictatorship has ended and a new government was elected in June, prisoners' futures remain uncertain. They are still subject to the anti-terrorism laws and carry the stigma of being labelled 'terrorist' by a government that blamed the rebel groups for all the country's ills.

The following testimonies come from political prisoners I've been held with in maximum security prisons. They take us to Yanamayo in the high plains, Socabaya in the southern province of Arequipa, Chorrillos women's prison and Castro Castro men's prison in Lima, and the prison at the naval base in Callao, also near the capital. The women who speak below are all accused – as am I – of being members of the MRTA.

'I was detained in the provinces and brought to the local army base for interrogation. In addition to the beatings, they put my head in filthy water (*la tina*, or the tub) until I lost consciousness. They brought me to Lima and, before being taken to DINCOTE (anti-terrorist police headquarters), I was tortured in the underground cells of the National Intelligence Service (SIN). I had wounds from where they cut me.' **CCH**

'I was first detained in June 1986, right after the MRTA took over a radio station to denounce Alan Garcia's government's massacre of Shining Path prisoners. They beat me, took me to the beach, threatened to drown me. They were known to tie up detainees and throw them into the ocean. Later in DINCOTE they hung me by my wrists, hands tied together behind my back (*la colgada*) and put me through *la tina*.

'The 1992 closed regime was brutal and relentless. Unlike when they tried to institute it in 1986, in 1992 not all prisoners fought against it. The Shining Path's imprisoned leadership signed a "peace agreement" with Fujimori in 1993 that made them change the tone of their demands. It was basically the MRTA and "non-peace accord Shining Path" prisoners who struggled to change the prison regime from inside the jails. In the MRTA, we looked for moral strength in the example of our suffering country, of our heroes. We held on to our convictions, ideals and morale to beat the situation and change it. It had to change. Today, despite the difficulties prison entails, we have the satisfaction of knowing we had the strength to overcome obstacles. They weren't able to break us. We overcame bars, chains and tomb-like jails . . .' **YCS**

'I was detained in Puno, six months pregnant. They beat me anyway and constantly threatened to make me abort. They pointed to my belly exclaiming: "That larva won't see the light of day."' **PHT**

'I was found by the police lying in the yard of the house they attacked. I was wounded trying to escape with five bullet wounds and several fractures. Pressured by the police, the doctors in the hospital patched me up without really examining me. More than a week passed before the hospital director himself, alerted by strange particles of excrement in my urine, found that the bullet that entered my groin had passed through my bladder and uterus and lodged in my colon. Ten days after being shot, I had surgery to extract the bullet and to open my colon. From then on, I have used a colostomy bag. Two days after the operation, the police interrogated me. I don't even remember what they asked. I was unable to speak. A day or so later I was taken to DINCOTE in spite of the hospital director's objections. They left me alone on a filthy mattress in a dirty cell. I was too weak to lift my head or yell for help, much less eat on my own.

'When the three of us were brought to Chorrillos in 1996, we were punished, held for two years in the Shining Path pavilion. We weren't allowed to read or write. Only knitting materials were permitted after three months. One young woman with me became anaemic, the other contracted tuberculosis. Officials refused to take me to the hospital to repair my colon, so I had to use colostomy bags for nearly two years. To harass me the prison personnel would "lose" the bags the Red Cross brought.' **LRL**

'I lost my three-month-old foetus because of the beatings and attempted rape.' **MPG**

'I was tortured in front of my husband. They beat me on the street in the police car. In DINCOTE they stripped me naked and gave me *la colgada*. While blindfolded, I heard them say: "Unless you talk, we'll keep torturing her." They made my husband watch the whole time . . .' **MCG**

'I was detained in 1991 when all political prisoners were in Castro Castro. After the April 1992 coup it became a closed regime. There was a state of emergency throughout Peru, including jails, which meant that the constitution and all laws were violated. They suspended all constitutional guarantees including habeas corpus. Nobody, not lawyers, families, or human rights groups had access to us. We were in grave danger. In May 1992, the government massacred about 100 Shining Path prisoners . . .

'The worst part of my detention wasn't *la colgada* that left my arms unusable for months; it wasn't the beatings that left me bruised, my eyes filled with blood and my lips cut. It was the sexual abuse, constant since the day I was detained. At DINCOTE the police stripped me naked, blindfolded and handcuffed me, and tossed me around in a vulgar, perverse way. They touched and pulled at me, climbed all over me. It was sickening, especially because it apparently sexually excited them to see me suffer. This was repeated several times and also combined with other forms of torment, the worst being thrown on the floor, face down, naked and blindfolded. They took the handcuffs off and one of the torturers sat on my thighs and buttocks and pulled my arms up. They questioned and insulted me, made me scream with pain as they dislocated my arms meanwhile getting sexually excited and ejaculating on my back. It wasn't one or two policemen, it was several at each session. It was obscene, much worse than the pain in my arms or the beatings.' **HFB**

'I had photos of my two sons in my wallet. The police claimed they were already looking for them, that they would bring them into DINCOTE to torture them to make me talk.

'MRTA prisoners were victims of more repression and reprisals after my husband Nestor Cerpa Cartolini led the capture of the Japanese ambassador's residence in December 1996, calling attention to the situation of political prisoners in Peru. I received the brunt of Fujimori's revenge against Nestor. Many of my relatives were detained that year. My children, forced into exile after my arrest in 1995, have never been able to visit me. In August 1999, I was isolated briefly at Socabaya and later at Castro Castro Men's Prison for over a year. I was constantly mistreated physically and psychologically. It was more of Fujimori's revenge against the MRTA. Because even though they riddled Nestor's body with bullets, they still feared him and his example.' **NGC**

'I was taken to Chorrillos in June 1992. For several months there was a 24-hour lock-up in cells (2m by 2.5m) built for two, but occupied by five or six. We could not speak between cells. Everything was prohibited: books, paper, pens, work materials, toiletries, food other than our meagre unhygienic rations. The diet consisted of tea and bread in the morning, rice and potatoes in the afternoon, tea at night. Malnourishment took its toll. I was pregnant and had lost my amniotic fluid twice during detention in DINCOTE. Luckily, my son Camilo survived and was born by Caesarean section. I was taken from the hospital before the doctors discharged me. In Chorrillos, my stitches were removed and the wound became infected. Antibiotics and malnutrition diminished my ability to lactate.' **PHT**

We had rights under the constitution, even if the jail regime prohibited them. We made them respect our rights with little things like saying "good morning" (which was prohibited), or singing revolutionary songs and co-ordinating hunger strikes and protests in various prisons. We would protest until things were tacitly permitted. We got punished, even beaten, moved, isolated, but we kept fighting. That's how we gained the right to radios, contact visits, workshops.' **AAS**

Prisoners in all jails have managed to maintain their dignity through continued protest. I know from government sources and prisoners' relatives that in the jail in the naval base where Miguel Rincon (arrested in the same case as I) is currently held, prisoners have also struggled for their rights and to be moved to civilian prisons. The regime there is extraordinarily harsh, especially for the MRTA prisoners who are isolated from the outside world and from each other. The cells are narrow and high (about 4.5m) with no windows, only a hole in the roof about 30cm square to let in air. Prisoners are under the constant surveillance of armed, masked guards.

Three or five or eight years of these conditions takes its toll. It was visible when I saw Rincon in court. He is now nearly blind. All political prisoners in Peru agree that the naval base prison must be closed. ❏

Lori Berenson *was found innocent of being a member of MRTA on 21 June, but guilty of collaboration and sentenced to 20 years in prison. She continues to protest her innocence*

SIMON KUPER

Albania diary

Socialist heads and Albanian SurRealizmi

Bulevardi Deshmoret e Kombit, Sunday 11 March
In Tirana, surely the fastest-growing city in Europe, nobody uses street names. Too many streets have appeared unacknowledged in the decade since the revolution, and many others have changed their names. In any case, Albanians were never very good with maps, which were forbidden under communism. But it is easy to find this boulevard, the only one worthy of the name in Tirana. It has the broad fascist grandeur that you would expect of a creation of Mussolini's Italians.

The Italians were better architects than the Stalinists who followed them. Their boulevard culminates just before Skanderbeg Square with two marvellous Italianate ministries, restored last year. The guards outside point their guns at the pedestrians.

The groups promenading down the boulevard in their finest clothes this Sunday evening in early spring could easily be Italian too. ('What is an Italian?' goes the joke. 'An Albanian in a nice suit.')

Even more eye-catching than the Albanians (in Tirana, men are men and women are women) is the traffic. The boulevard is an endless procession of Mercedes. This city, where private ownership of cars was forbidden under communism, may now have the most Mercs per capita in Europe. They aren't all come by legally.

Crossing the boulevard is a local sport. Tirana now has cars, but still almost no traffic lights or road signs and only the vaguest rules of the road. It is pointed out to me that some cars are driven by women. This, apparently, was unthinkable only two years ago.

Hotel Rogner, Monday 12 March
The hotel, about halfway down the boulevard, was built by the Austrians. Rooms start at US$210, and a group of foreigners, obviously from an NGO, is huddling over a laptop in the lobby. 'Maybe we *need* to

be political to gain support . . . If they want ownership, they'll have to
. . . The idea of doing it over dinner: why don't we think about that?'

In a natty suit in the hotel bar sits Gramoz Pashko. Son of a
communist minister and deputy minister, Pashko managed to become
a leader of the student rebellion of 1991. He founded the Democratic
Party with Sali Berisha but, after falling out with Berisha (a common
fate in Albanian politics), left the country to teach economics in
Glasgow and Washington, D.C. Now he is back home advising
32-year-old Ilir Meta, the youngest prime minister in Europe.

In the hour we spend in the bar, Meta and his entourage walk in,
prompting frantic waves from Pashko; Edi Rama, once a basketball star,
later a painter in Paris, now mayor of Tirana, takes the next table; the
editor of the Kosovar newspaper *Koha* joins us for a drink; and Pashko's
mobile rings non-stop. In between, Pashko argues that legality is
breaking out in Albania. 'Now you don't see people shooting guns
on the street. Three years ago here, it was hell.'

Six-hundred-and-seventy-thousand weapons were looted from state
armouries in the Pyramid Revolution of 1997. When communism fell,
most Albanians thought of capitalism as a simple get-rich-quick scheme.
So when some Albanian entrepreneurs began touting pyramid schemes
as a way to make a million fast, about half the population jumped.

The schemes had an obvious appeal. Investors were offered giant
interest rates for their cash – 40% a year, say – and as long as their money
kept pouring in, these rates were actually paid. President Sali Berisha's
government thought the schemes a wonderful thing. Until, in 1997, the
cash stopped coming. Inevitably the pyramid schemes collapsed and half
the population had lost all its money. In the ensuing riots – against the
government, the entrepreneurs, the neighbours, everybody – much of
the country was destroyed and more than 1,500 people killed. Today,
many of the looted weapons have been returned. However, there are still
apparently great stashes in the mountains around Tirana. For now, the
city feels, as Pashko claims, much safer than Washington, D.C. The main
streets are full after dark – again, not the case two years ago.

Skanderbeg Square, Tuesday 13 March
If only it were possible to cross the road, Skanderbeg Square would
be a wonderful place. Not because of its Stalinist museum and opera
buildings, but because of the southern Albanian climate (the country's

one undeniable blessing) and the small fun fair in the middle of the square. Children go round on the roller coaster and adults sit in the sun chatting. It is possible to imagine that one day tourists might start coming to Albania. No one hassles the foreigner – in fact, no one recognises foreigners as foreigners any more.

Inside the opera house is the MBA Sport bar. Men in leather jackets sit around drinking Italian coffee – very good in Tirana – and filling in betting slips with the concentration of students sitting an exam. Most of the betting is on Italian football, and you can bet legally or illegally. One advantage of the latter method is that you get paid immediately after the match. Kiosks all over town sell the betting forms.

Upstairs from MBA Sport is a hall where men play 'telebingo'. Prizes include a Volkswagen, a Tirana apartment and US$3,000 in cash. These more honest forms of gambling seem to have replaced the pyramid 'investment schemes'.

One day at Rinas Airport, Tirana

A western diplomat drove to the airport to return one of his country's stolen passports to its rightful owner. At the airport, he was ushered into a room where he was greeted by men with guns. 'You know how things work in Albania,' they told him. 'We paid US$5,000 for that passport, so it's ours. You are not leaving the room with it.' He handed it over.

That is only the most expensive way of emigrating. Other Albanians pay for a spot in a speedboat to Italy, or simply sneak across the Greek border at night. Educated people are sometimes allowed to work in Canada, a country that is brain-draining much of the third world. Some Albanians get asylum in the West by claiming to be Kosovars: the UK government now estimates (quietly, so as not to upset the *Daily Mail*) that 90% of the 'Kosovars' it has taken in are in fact Albanians from Albania.

Altogether, over half a million Albanians – about 15% of the population – have emigrated in a decade. Children as young as 13 go alone. The money they send home accounts for about one-third of Albanian national income.

Tirana National Gallery, Friday 16 March

On the first floor are the two most reviled exhibitions in Albania. In one room, packed in tight rows, are 'Socialist Heads' taken from statues of the communist era. In the next, under the title 'SurRealizmi Socialist', are Socialist Realist paintings.

There are no visitors in either room, but the Socialist Heads in particular are fascinating. There is Mao Tse Tung (depicted before he disappointed the Albanians by going soft on Richard Nixon), Karl Marx, Enver Hoxha in tie and jacket, a few World War II partisans (a largely mythical species in Albania) and an aviator (again, never much in evidence in real life). By the window is a collection of little gargoyles, most of them villains of the Albanian past. Here are pashas, elderly husbands buying young wives, and frog-faced, big-eared men with moustaches and ties and curling chins like Popeye – capitalists, or even imperialists, one of whom is being crushed in a worker's fist.

The paintings next door, with their bright colours, strong lines and huge canvases, have an undeniable appeal. Happy families around the dinner table; partisans reading a little red book or trekking through the snow or liberating Skanderbeg Square; prisoners waving a red flag out of a cell window as a man is about to be hanged. There is some very good art here, says Gëzim Qëndro, the gallery's curator. These painters trained in great centres like Moscow.

Qëndro has taken much abuse for these exhibitions. Only ten years after communism, the public is not yet able to view Hoxha or Marx with irony. He was accused of 'nostalgia for the dictator'. The artists

Tirana National Gallery: head cases. Credit: Gëzim Qëndro

Tirana National Gallery: SurRealizmi, intellectual, soldier, worker, poet, hero. Credit: Gëzim Qëndro

were angry, too. 'They said, rightly, that I had made an installation of their works,' Qëndro explains. 'I think the only man who understood it was the leader of the Albanian Communist Party, a very small party now. He wrote in the guestbook, "Despite the irony that the curator puts in the show, everyone can see the grandiosity and the value of Socialist art."'

Foreigners love it, too. The US ambassador is particularly fond of the heads. He sends all his visitors to see them.

Kaneta, outside Durres, Friday 16 March

In 1991, Tirana had about 250,000 inhabitants. Now it has almost three times that number; nobody knows exactly how many, as people simply arrive from the countryside, build a house and start living.

On the road out of Tirana are some marvellous villas. The favoured architectural style is Costa del Sol kitsch: pastel colours, and wrought-iron balconies in heart shapes. In a field in the middle of nowhere are some pink rococo mansions. Families build these things on weekends, with money sent by relatives working abroad. Even in Kaneta, a new shanty town with several thousand inhabitants outside Durres, there are some nice houses and the odd Mercedes. But there is no running water, no school and not much electricity.

When the subsidies from the communist regime ended, people in isolated villages in the north began to starve and came south. Kaneta arose on a reclaimed swamp in 1994. Then in 1997 the pyramid schemes collapsed. People who had sold their houses to buy stakes were left with nothing. Many came to places like Kaneta. Others fled here from 'blood feuds', an ancient north Albanian tradition which has revived in the last decade. Often the 'feuds' are just a struggle for resources: a field, a flock of sheep, a small farm. Altogether about 350,000 Albanians – 10% of the population – are now estimated to be internal migrants.

In summer, children in Kaneta swim in the raw sewage in the ditches. There is not much else to do. Two little boys have made themselves drums out of USAID vegetable oil tins. More than 80% of children in Kaneta are thought to be wholly illiterate. This is as poor as Europe gets.

An old woman virtually drags me into her one-room shack and forces me to eat. She lays out sweets, dried fruits and, from a fridge covered with Arnold Schwarzenegger stickers, lemonade and raki. 'We are Albanians from the north,' she explains. Hospitality, like blood feuds, is prescribed by traditional law. The woman says she sold her house in Bajram Curri, in the northern badlands of Albania, to invest in the pyramid schemes. Even this one-room shack in Kaneta is not hers. She is looking after it for the owner, and must leave any day now.

She is sharing the shack with two of her daughters. Her three other children have been farmed out elsewhere. What can she do? With five children, she can hardly emigrate illegally. Anyway, even for that you need money. And she is ill, so she cannot work. 'I feel sorry for my children,' she says, 'because we hoped that with democracy things would get better. I don't feel sorry for myself, because my time is already past.' How old is she? Forty-two, she says. She looks 60. Western charities are keeping her alive. It is still better to be poor in Albania than in Africa.

That night, in bed in Tirana, I hear the only gunfire of my visit. Two years ago, people say, the Kalashnikov serenades were a nightly event.

Murphy's Irish Pub, Tirana, Saturday 17 March

Tonight, Tirana is celebrating St Patrick's Day. Murphy's opened about a year ago as a haven for westerners, but by now most of the clientele are young Albanians. Many of them work as translators, secretaries or drivers in the NGOs.

As the evening livens up, a few Albanian women (customers, not professional dancers) start dancing on tables. When Randy Newman's 'You Can Leave Your Hat On' strikes up, one woman feigns a mock striptease on the bar. Again, I am told that two years before this had never happened in the history of Albania. Albanians and westerners alike sing along to The Beatles, The Clash and Serbian pop songs. Apparently, the favourite song in Murphy's – the one that gets the whole joint bouncing – is a Serbian number called 'Kalashnikov'.

Tirana is something of an aid worker's paradise. Poor enough to need aid, but with a nightlife, a Mediterranean climate, good food, safe streets and lots of other aid workers for friends. 'What are we doing here?' asks Nina, who works for a medical charity called Merlin and has recently arrived from Sierra Leone. 'This is by far the nicest country we work in.' And it's only an hour by plane to Italy (one woman has gone to London for the weekend for a wedding).

That proximity is why the West is stuffing money into Albania. This is the nearest the third world encroaches on the European Union. Illegal emigration, car crime, Aids and Islamic fundamentalism are more frightening here than, say, in Mali (although the Albanians have not yet shown much interest in Islamic fundamentalism). About 9% of national income is foreign aid.

After midnight, a buzz of excitement passes through the aid workers in Murphy's. People are saying that a few hundred refugees from the fighting along the Kosovar–Macedonian border have fled into Albania. Few Albanians seem very interested in this conflict: there is no apparent sentiment in Tirana for a Greater Albania, partly, perhaps, because more Albanians would mean more people with whom to share the foreign aid. But for the aid workers, the refugees represent a new job, another reason to stay in Tirana. ❏

Simon Kuper *is a columnist with the London* Observer